Making the GRADE

rader

Everything ds to Know

Elena R. Arrigo

BARRON'S

About the Author

Elena R. Arrigo began her career as an elementary school teacher in Illinois, where she created a varied and engaging curriculum to meet the needs of her diverse student population. She has completed independent research in alternative education practices and has interviewed homeschooling families. Elena holds a B.A. in English and a B.A. in Spanish from Cornell College.

All inquiries should be addressed to:
Barron's Educational Series, Inc.
250 Wireless Boulevard
Hauppauge, New York 11788
http://www.barronseduc.com

Library of Congress Catalog Card No. 2003056297

International Standard Book No. 0-7641-2477-3

Library of Congress Cataloging-in-Publication Data
Arrigo, Elena R.
    Everything your 2nd grader needs to know / Elena R. Arrigo.
      p. cm. — (Making the grade)
    Includes bibliographical references and index.
    ISBN 0-7641-2477-3
    1. Second grade (Education)—Curricula—United States. 2. Home schooling—Curricula—United States. 3. Curriculum planning—United States. I. Title: Everything your second grader needs to know. II. Title. III. Making the grade (Hauppauge, N.Y.)

    LB15712nd .A77 2004
    372.24'1—dc21   2003056297

Printed in China
9 8 7 6 5 4 3 2

Table of Contents

How to Use This Book vii

For Homeschoolers xi

Communicating Between Home and School xvii

Meet Your Second Grader xix

ing PROMOTING LITERACY

Lesson 1.1 Investigating Fiction 3

Lesson 1.2 Understanding Creative Writing 11

Lesson 1.3 Exploring Fantasy 15

Lesson 1.4 Comprehending Verbs 25

Lesson 1.5 Using Articles 31

Lesson 1.6 Understanding Nouns 35

Lesson 1.7 Working with Compound Words 39

Lesson 1.8 Reading Folktales 43

Lesson 1.9 Examining Poetry and Writing in a Journal 49

Lesson 1.10 Exploring Biographies 53

Lesson 1.11 Reading Nonfiction 59

Lesson 1.12 Using Conjunctions 65

Lesson 1.13 Exploring Prepositions 69

Lesson 1.14 Understanding Suffixes and Prefixes 73

Lesson 1.15 Investigating Antonyms and Synonyms 79

Lesson 1.16 Comprehending Homophones 85

In Your Community 89

We Have Learned Checklist 90

MATH 91

Lesson 2.1   Generating Number Sense 93

Lesson 2.2   Exploring Patterns and Numbers to 100 99

Lesson 2.3   Adding Two-Digit Numbers 105

Lesson 2.4   Subtracting Two-Digit Numbers 109

Lesson 2.5   Investigating Patterns and Numbers
to 1,000 113

Lesson 2.6   Adding and Subtracting Three-Digit
Numbers 119

Lesson 2.7   Understanding Money 125

Lesson 2.8   Using Fractions 129

Lesson 2.9   Exploring Multiplication and Division 135

Lesson 2.10   Investigating Algebraic Methods 141

Lesson 2.11   Understanding Geometry 145

Lesson 2.12   Learning to Measure Up 151

Lesson 2.13   Telling Time and Reading Calendars 157

Lesson 2.14   Collecting and Using Data 161

In Your Community 165

We Have Learned Checklist 166

SCIENCE 167

Lesson 3.1   Investigating Animal Life Cycles 169

Lesson 3.2   Discovering Plant Life Cycles 173

Lesson 3.3   Exploring Plants and Animals 177

Lesson 3.4   Understanding Your Senses 183

Lesson 3.5   Maintaining a Healthy Diet 189

Lesson 3.6   Caring for Your Teeth 193

Lesson 3.7   Learning About Earth's Natural Resources . . . 197

Lesson 3.8   Understanding Changes on
Earth's Surface 203

Lesson 3.9   Exploring Earth and the Moon 207

Lesson 3.10   Getting into Motion 213

Lesson 3.11   Learning About Sound 217

Lesson 3.12   Investigating Light and Heat 221

Lesson 3.13   Researching a Science Topic 225

In Your Community 229

We Have Learned Checklist 230

SOCIAL STUDIES 231

Lesson 4.1   Discovering Maps and Charts 233

Lesson 4.2   Understanding and Comparing
Communities 237

Lesson 4.3   Exploring Communities in the World 243

Lesson 4.4   Caring for Earth 249

Lesson 4.5   Discovering How We Work Together 255

Lesson 4.6   Understanding Our Local and
State Governments 261

Lesson 4.7   Celebrating Freedom 265

Lesson 4.8   Meeting the Native Americans 269

Lesson 4.9 Exploring the Early History of
the United States 275

Lesson 4.10 Learning About Our Growing Country 281

Lesson 4.11 Recognizing America's Diversity 285

Lesson 4.12 Investigating Landmarks 289

Lesson 4.13 Connecting Our World 293

Lesson 4.14 Researching a Social Studies Topic 297

In Your Community 301

We Have Learned Checklist 302

Assessment 303

Assessment Answers 341

Answers 345

Glossary 351

Venn Diagram 353

Comparison Chart 353

Web 354

Sequence Chain 354

Writing Lines 355

Index 356

Credits 362

How to Use This Book

Welcome to the *Making the Grade* series! These seven books offer tools and strategies for hands-on, active learning at the kindergarten through sixth-grade levels. Each book presents real-world, engaging learning experiences in the core areas of language arts, math, science, and social studies at age-appropriate levels.

Who should use this book?

Whether you're a stay-at-home or working parent with children in school, a homeschooler who's guiding your children's education, or a teacher who's looking for additional ideas to supplement classroom learning experiences, this book is for you.

- If you have children in school, *Making the Grade* can be used in conjunction with your child's curriculum because it offers real-world, hands-on activities that exercise the concepts and topics he or she is being taught in school.
- If you're a homeschooler who's guiding your children's education, this series presents you with easy-to-access, engaging ways to interact with your child.
- If you're a teacher, this book also can be a source for additional activities.

This book is your passport to a whole new world, one that gives you enough support to be a successful educator while encouraging independent learning with one child or shared learning among your children. *Making the Grade* offers enriching educational opportunities and encourages a student-directed, relaxed learning environment that optimizes children's interests.

What is *Making the Grade*?

We're glad you asked! First, we'd like to tell you what it's not. It's not a textbook series. Rather, each book in the series delivers age-appropriate content in language arts, math, science, and social studies in an open-ended, flexible manner that incorporates the "real" world. You can use this book as a supplement to your core learning instruction or use it to get a jump start on the fundamentals.

Each subject section presents lessons comprised of both "teaching" pages and "student" pages. And each book in the *Making the Grade* series is perforated for flexible learning so that both you and your child can tear out the pages that you're working on and use one book together.

How do the lessons work?

The teaching and student pages work together. The lesson instruction and teaching ideas for each specific lesson appear first. Activities that offer opportunities for your child to practice the specific skills and review the concepts being taught follow. Throughout each lesson, hands-on activities are incorporated using concepts that are meaningful and relevant to kids' daily lives. Each lesson also reveals how to enrich the learning experience through field trips, online research, excursions to the library, and more. Creativity and imagination abound! The activities account for all kinds of learners—that is, visual, auditory, and kinesthetic. (For more information on learning styles, see the Glossary on page 351.) Be encouraged to allow ample time for discovery of the concepts in each lesson— whether that be a few hours or a few days—and ample time for unstructured independent exploration. Your student can help guide the pace. Follow your child's interests, as it will make learning fun and valuable.

Objective and Background

Each lesson opens with an objective that tells you exactly what the lesson is about. The background of the lesson follows, giving you the rationale behind the importance of the material being addressed. Each lesson is broken down for you so that you and your student can see how the skills and concepts taught are useful in everyday situations.

Materials and Vocabulary

Have you ever done a project and found out you're missing something when you get to the end? A list of materials is given up front so you'll know what you need before you begin. The lessons take into account that you have access to your local library, a computer and the Internet, writing instruments, a calculator, and a notebook and loose paper, so you won't find these listed. The materials are household items when possible so that even the most technical of science experiments can be done easily. The *Making the Grade* series paves the way for your learning experience whether you and your student are sitting side by side on the couch or in a classroom, at the library, or even on vacation!

Following the materials list, vocabulary words may be given offering clear, easy-to-understand definitions.

Let's Begin

Let's Begin is just that, "Let's Begin!" The instructional portion of the lesson opens with easy, user-friendly, numbered steps that guide you through the teaching of a particular lesson. Here you'll find opportunities to interact with your student and engage in discussions about what he or she is learning. There also are opportunities for your student to practice his or her critical-thinking skills to make the learning experience richer.

In the margins are interesting facts about what you're studying, time-savers, or helpful ideas.

Ways to Extend the Lesson

Every lesson concludes with ways to extend the lesson—teaching tips, such as hints, suggestions, or ideas, for you to use in teaching the lesson or a section of the lesson. Each lesson also ends with an opportunity for you to "check in" and assess how well your student has mastered the skill or grasped the concepts being taught in the lesson. The For Further Reading section lists books that you can use as additional references and support in teaching the lesson. It also offers your student more opportunities to practice a skill or a chance to look deeper into the content.

Student Learning Pages

Student Learning Pages immediately follow the teaching pages in each lesson. These pages offer fun opportunities to practice the skills and concepts being taught. And there are places where your student gets to choose what to do next and take ownership of his or her learning.

Visual Aids

Throughout the book you'll see references to the Venn Diagram, Comparison Chart, Web, Sequence Chain, and Writing Lines found in the back of the book. Many lessons incorporate these graphic organizers, or visual methods of organizing information, into the learning. If one is used in a lesson, it will be listed in the materials so that prior to the lesson you or your student can make a photocopy of it from the back of the book or you can have your student copy it into his or her notebook. See the Glossary for more information on graphic organizers.

What about field trips or learning outside the classroom?

One very unique feature of the *Making the Grade* series is the In Your Community activities at the end of each subject section. These activities describe ways to explore your community, taking advantage of your local or regional culture, industry, and environment while incorporating the skills learned in the lessons. For example, you can have your student help out at a farmer's market or with a local environmental group. These unique activities can supplement your ability to provide support for subjects. The activities give your student life experiences upon which he or she can build and expand the canvas upon which he or she learns.

These pages are identified in the Table of Contents so that you can read them first as a way to frame your student's learning.

How do I know if my student is learning the necessary skills?

Although each lesson offers an opportunity for on-the-spot assessment, a formalized assessment section is located in the back of this book. You'll find a combination of multiple-choice and open-ended questions testing your student on the skills, concepts, and topics covered.

Also, at the end of every subject section is a We Have Learned checklist. This checklist provides a way for you and your student to summarize what you've accomplished. It lists specific concepts, and there is additional space for you and your student to write in other topics you've covered.

Does this book come with answers?

Yes. Answers are provided in the back of the book for both the lessons and assessment.

What if this book uses a homeschooling or educational term I'm not familiar with?

In addition to the vocabulary words listed in the lessons, a two-page Glossary is provided in the back of the book. Occasionally terms will surface that may need further explanation in order for the learning experience to flourish. In the Glossary, you'll find terms explained simply to help you give your student a rewarding learning experience free from confusion.

Will this book help me find resources within the schools for homeschoolers?

In Communicating Between Home and School, there are suggestions for how to take advantage of the opportunities and resources offered by your local schools and how these benefits can enhance your homeschooling learning experiences.

I'm new to homeschooling. How can I find out about state regulations, curriculum, and other resources?

In For Homeschoolers at the beginning of the book, you'll find information about national and state legislation, resources for curriculum and materials, and other references. Also included is a comprehensive list of online resources for everything from homeschooling organizations to military homeschooling to homeschooling supplies. You can also contact your local school or school board.

How can I use this book if my student attends a public or private school?

Making the Grade fits into any child's educational experience—whether he or she is being taught at home or in a traditional school setting. Student-selected activities can be found in nearly all lessons, which can enhance and build upon his or her existing school learning experiences. At the end of each subject section, you'll find In Your Community activities that provide ways to discover your local region while incorporating information from the lessons. Let your student be the guide!

For Homeschoolers

Teaching children at home isn't a new phenomenon. But it's gaining in popularity as caregivers decide to take a more active role in the education of their children. More people are learning what homeschoolers have already known, that children who are homeschooled succeed in college, the workplace, and society.

Whether you're new to homeschooling or have been educating your children at home for quite some time, you may have found the homeschooling path to have occasional detours in finding resources. Families choose homeschooling for different reasons. This book hopes to minimize those detours by offering information on state regulations, homeschooling approaches and curriculum, and other resources to keep you on the path toward a rewarding learning experience.

Regulations

There never has been a federal law prohibiting parents from homeschooling their children. A homeschooler isn't required to have a teaching degree, nor is he or she required to teach children in a specific location. Each state has its own compulsory attendance laws for educational programs as well as its own set of regulations, educational requirements, and guidelines for those who homeschool.

Some states and areas of the United States have stricter regulations than others. Alabama; Alaska; Arizona; California; Delaware; Guam; Idaho; Illinois; Indiana; Kansas; Kentucky; Michigan; Mississippi; Missouri; Montana; Nebraska; New Jersey; New Mexico; Oklahoma; Puerto Rico; Texas; Virgin Islands; Washington, D.C; Wisconsin; and Wyoming are considered to have a low level of regulation. Maine, Massachusetts, Minnesota, Nevada, New York, North Dakota, Pennsylvania, Rhode Island, Utah, Vermont, Washington, and West Virginia are considered to have a high level of regulation. The remaining states and areas not mentioned are considered to have a moderate level of homeschooling regulation.

But what do low, moderate, and high regulation mean? These classifications indicate the level of regulation that a particular state can enforce upon someone who has chosen to teach a child at home. Within each of these levels, there also are varying rules and laws.

These regulations begin with how to enter into the world of homeschooling. Some states, such as New Jersey, don't require parents to notify the school of their intent to teach their children at home, yet a letter of intent often is submitted out of courtesy. New Jersey's regulations require that all children of compulsory school age must be in an instructional program equivalent to that provided in the public schools. Similarly, in Texas, another state that's considered to have a low level of regulation, parents don't have to notify anyone of their intent to homeschool their children. Texas homeschools are considered private schools and aren't subject to state regulation.

States with moderate levels of regulation often require that letters of intent to homeschool be submitted, as well as regular logs of instruction be kept, and other guidelines be followed. Florida, for example, requires that parents send a letter of intent to their local superintendent. Florida homeschoolers also have to log schoolwork and have their child annually evaluated using one of the methods of evaluation.

Other "moderate" states have different requirements for their homeschoolers. In South Carolina, parents who intend to homeschool their children must have either a high school diploma or have passed the GED (general educational development) test. Parents have three choices for homeschooling in this state: (1) they can maintain instruction under the supervision of their local school district, which would vary by district, (2) they can home-school under the direction of the South Carolina Association of Independent Home Schools (SCAIHS), which would require them to pay annual dues, have their child tested annually, and have their curriculum reviewed, or (3) they must be accountable to one of the state homeschooling associations.

States that are considered to have a high level of homeschooling regulation often require parents who teach their children at home to follow guidelines throughout the school year. Pennsylvania has a strict policy for homeschoolers, and requires parents to submit a notarized affidavit of intent to homeschool, along with medical records and learning objectives for certain subjects. Note that the school only has the authority to say whether the required documentation was submitted, not to determine whether the homeschooling plan of instruction is acceptable or unacceptable. The parents also must keep records of instruction and of attendance during the year. At the end of the school year, the child must be evaluated by either a certified teacher or a licensed psychologist, a portfolio of schoolwork needs to be submitted, and in certain grades the child must take a standardized test. Also, the parents who plan to teach their children at home must have a high school education. Pennsylvania, however, does offer another homeschooling option. Parents can have children homeschooled by a tutor who is a certified teacher, in which case the parents only need to submit the tutor's credentials and criminal record.

Parents intending to homeschool their children in New York, another state considered to have a high level of regulation, must file a letter indicating their intention and submit an IHIP (Individualized Home Instruction Plan). As in Pennsylvania, the school doesn't have the authority to determine the acceptability of the IHIP, only whether information was submitted as outlined by the state. The parents also must submit quarterly reports during the year and engage the child in at least 900 hours of instruction per year for grades K–6. At the end of each school year, the homeschooled child must be assessed, which can mean taking a standardized assessment test in some years and having the parents provide a narrative of assessment in others. In Minnesota, another state that has a high level of regulation, parents must submit the names and birth dates of the children they plan to homeschool annually. Parents also must have a bachelor's degree, or else they will have to submit quarterly report cards to the school. Parents also must provide supporting documentation about the subject matter that is being taught; although, what information is needed may vary from school district to school district. In addition, homeschooled children in this state must be tested annually, but the school doesn't need to see the test results.

Regardless of the level of regulation your state has, there are ways to operate your homeschool with success. Here are a few tips as you negotiate the homeschooling waters:

- Be aware of your district's and state's requirements.
- Don't let these laws, rules, and regulations deter you. The National Home Education Network (NHEN) may be able to help. Go to the association's Web site at *http://www.nhen.org*. For more information on your state's laws and related references, see Homeschooling Online Resources that follow. They can help you find information on your specific state and may be able to direct you to local homeschooling groups.
- Veteran homeschoolers in your area can be a fountain of practical knowledge about the laws. Consult a variety of homeschoolers for a clear perspective, as each family has an educational philosophy and approach that best suits it.

Homeschooling Military Families

Frequently moving from location to location can be exhausting for families with one or more parent in the military. If you have school-age children, it can be even more complicated. Schools across states and U.S. schools in other countries often don't follow the same curriculum, and states often can have varying curriculum requirements for each grade.

The Department of Defense Dependent Schools (DoDDS) is responsible for the military educational system. There are three options for military families in which they can educate their children:

1. attend school with other military children
2. if in a foreign country, attend the local school in which the native language is spoken, although this option may require approval
3. homeschool

Homeschooling can provide consistency for families that have to relocate often. The move itself, along with the new culture your family will be exposed to, is a learning experience that can be incorporated into the curriculum. Note that military families that homeschool must abide by the laws of the area in which they reside, which may be different from where they claim residency for tax purposes. If your relocation takes your family abroad, one downside is the lack of curriculum resources available on short notice. Nonetheless, military homeschoolers may be able to use resources offered at base schools.

Approaches and Curriculum

If you're reading this book you've probably already heard of many different approaches to and methods of homeschooling, which some homeschoolers sometimes refer to as *unschooling* (see the Glossary for more information). Unschooling is not synonymous with homeschooling; it's a philosophy and style of education followed by some homeschoolers. It's important that you choose one approach or method that works best for you—there's no right or wrong way to homeschool!

The curriculum and materials that are used vary from person to person, but there are organizations that offer books, support, and materials to homeschoolers. Many homeschoolers find that a combination of methods works best. That's why *Making the Grade* was created!

Support Groups and Organizations

Homeschooling has become more popular, and the United States boasts a number of nationally recognized homeschooling organizations. Also, nearly every state has its own homeschooling organization to provide information on regulations in addition to other support. Many religious and ethnic affiliations also have their own homeschooling organizations too, in addition to counties and other groups.

Famous Homeschoolers

Many famous people were once homeschooled, including Ansel Adams, Louisa May Alcott, Alexander Graham Bell, Pearl S. Buck, Charlie Chaplin, Agatha Christie, Charles Dickens, Thomas Edison, Benjamin Franklin, Wolfgang Amadeus Mozart, George Patton, and Mark Twain. A number of U.S. presidents also have been homeschooled, including George Washington, Thomas Jefferson, Abraham Lincoln, Woodrow Wilson, and Franklin Delano Roosevelt.

Homeschooling Online Resources

These are some of the online resources available for homeschoolers. You also can check your phone book for local organizations and resources.

National Organizations

Alliance for Parental Involvement in Education
http://www.croton.com/allpie/

Alternative Education Resource Organization (AERO)
http://www.edrev.org/links.htm

American Homeschool Association (AHA)
http://www.americanhomeschoolassociation.org/

Home School Foundation
http://www.homeschoolfoundation.org

National Coalition of Alternative Community Schools
http://www.ncacs.org/

National Home Education Network (NHEN)
http://www.nhen.org/

National Home Education Research Institute (NHERI)
http://www.nheri.org

National Homeschooling Association (NHA)
http://www.n-h-a.org

Homeschooling and the Law

Advocates for the Rights of Homeschoolers (ARH)
http://www.geocities.com/arhfriends/

American Bar Association
http://www.abanet.org

Children with Special Needs

Children with Disabilities
http://www.childrenwithdisabilities.ncjrs.org/

Institutes for the Achievement of Human Potential (IAHP)
http://www.iahp.org/

National Challenged Homeschoolers Associated Network (NATHHAN)
http://www.nathhan.com/

Military Homeschooling

Department of Defense Dependent Schools/Education Activity (DoDDS)
http://www.odedodea.edu/

Books, Supplies, Curriculum

Federal Resources for Educational Excellence
http://www.ed.gov/free/

Home Schooling Homework
http://www.dailyhomework.org/

Home School Products
http://www.homeschooldiscount.com/

Homeschooler's Curriculum Swap
http://theswap.com/

HomeSchoolingSupply.com
http://www.homeschoolingsupply.com/

General Homeschooling Resources

A to Z Home's Cool
http://www.gomilpitas.com/

Family Unschoolers Network
http://www.unschooling.org

Home Education Magazine
http://www.home-ed-magazine.com/

Home School Legal Defense Association (HSLDA)
http://www.hslda.org

Homeschool Central
http://www.homeschoolcentral.com

Homeschool Internet Yellow Pages
http://www.homeschoolyellowpages.com/

Homeschool Social Registry at Homeschool Media Network
http://www.homeschoolmedia.net

Homeschool World
http://www.home-school.com/

Homeschool.com
http://www.homeschool.com/

HSAdvisor.com
http://www.hsadvisor.com/

Unschooling.com
http://www.unschooling.com/

Waldorf Without Walls
http://www.waldorfwithoutwalls.com/

Communicating Between Home and School

For homeschoolers, often there is limited contact with the schools beyond that which is required by the state. Yet a quick glance at your local schools may reveal opportunities, resources, and benefits that can offer you flexibility and that can supplement your child's total learning experience.

Special Needs

If you have a child with special needs, such as dyslexia or ADHD (attention deficit hyperactivity disorder), taking advantage of the programs and services your public school provides can expand your support system and give you some relief in working with your child. In many instances, the easy access and little or no cost of these services makes this a viable option for homeschoolers.

Depending on your child's diagnosed needs, some school districts may offer full services and programs, while some may only provide consultations. Some school districts' special education departments have established parent support networks that you may be able to participate in as a homeschooler. States and school districts vary in terms of what homeschoolers are allowed to participate in so check with your local school administrator and then check with your state's regulations to verify your eligibility.

Two organizations, the Home School Legal Defense Association (HSLDA) and the National Challenged Homeschoolers Association Network (NATHHAN), offer a wide range of information and assistance on services and programs available for special needs children. Check them out on the Internet at *http://www.hslda.org* and *http://www.nathhan.com.* Your local homeschooling group—especially veteran homeschoolers—will have practical information you can use.

Additionally, some homeschooling parents combine the resources of a school with those offered by a private organization to maximize support.

Gifted Children

If your child is considered gifted, your local public school may have programs available for students who require additional intellectual attention. Check with your local school administrator and your state's regulations first. In addition to providing information on special needs children, HSLDA and NATHHAN offer resources for parents of gifted children.

Don't be afraid to check out the colleges in your area, too. Many times colleges, especially community colleges, offer classes or onetime workshops that might be of interest to your child. Check with your local schools to see how you can take advantage of these opportunities.

Extracurricular Activities

Opportunities abound for homeschoolers to get involved with extracurricular activities. Clubs and interest groups allow children and parents to interact and share ideas with other homeschoolers. Extracurricular activities not only enrich the learning experience, they can also provide opportunities for friendship.

You might want to meet regularly for planned activities focusing on a particular subject matter, such as math. You could meet at someone's home or perhaps at a community or religious center. A parent can lead the discussions on a particular topic, but sometimes other knowledgeable individuals can be invited to teach, either for a fee or on a volunteer basis. Another enriching idea is to form a theme group, such as a science-experiment club, an adventure book club, or a nature club. Or just get together to simply share ideas or plan group activities, such as a craft project or a book discussion. Parents and children can work together to plan activities and events.

If you can't find a meeting on a particular subject area or theme in your region, don't hesitate to form one in your community. One way to begin might be to check out the Homeschool Social Register at *http://www.homeschoolmedia.net*. Here you can find other homeschoolers in your area and homeschoolers who share your educational philosophy and interests.

Other extracurricular activities, such as 4-H, Girl Scouts, Boy Scouts, religious youth groups, arts and crafts, athletics, music, and language or debate clubs, may be offered in your community. They can provide additional opportunities for your homeschooler to interact with his or her peers and have a valuable learning experience at the same time. Extracurricular activities offered at local schools also may prove worthwhile to investigate.

Returning to School

If you plan on having your child return to school, taking advantage of the programs and opportunities offered can help ease the transition back into the classroom. Your child will already experience a sense of familiarity with his or her surroundings and peers, which can help smooth the transition to a different structure of learning.

Meet Your Second Grader

Second graders are hardworking, serious, and thoughtful, which can be quite a change from the silly and boundless demeanor of first graders. You may notice that your child is moving inward and feeling things more deeply at this age. Of course, all children are influenced by unique personal and environmental circumstances and develop at different rates. Even so, children of the same age tend to show surprisingly similar characteristics. As you nurture and support your second grader, understanding the common behavior patterns that characterize his or her age will help you make decisions that are beneficial for both of you.

Recognize Developing Intellect

Second graders tend to be heady and live in a world of thought. They are aware of their brains and relate thinking to the head and the mind. At this age, there is a great love of learning. A second grader attempts to analyze and understand just about anything that he or she finds interesting. A natural mental organizer, second graders are apt to arrange things into categories in order to understand and study them.

Much of a second grader's mental life is spent reflecting and finding logical conclusions about how things work. A second-grade child who appears to be daydreaming is more likely pondering a thought. Children at this age are taking large developmental steps in language and in spatial perception. A second grader strives to speak correctly and precisely. His or her vocabulary is expanding and often includes more adjectives and adverbs. A second grader's descriptions are more precise and include location and positioning details such as upside down, left, and right.

Accept Emotional Struggles

Emotionally, second graders can be rather serious. They have probably withdrawn, calmed down, and become more mature. Children at this age tend to approach issues and tasks thoughtfully and with perseverance. Woven into this newfound seriousness is a tendency to emphasize and dwell on the negative. You may regularly hear your second grader verbally express feelings of defeat and inadequacy. He or she may often cry over small things and insist that a situation is horrible. Silliness and humor won't work, as your second grader's new sensitivities won't tolerate teasing or making light of a seemingly grave situation. Second graders may even revel in doom and gloom, using morbid or morose thoughts as a safe haven or retreat. Although your child may seem to enjoy this behavior and create it intentionally, he or she isn't consciously trying to be disagreeable. Moodiness, fear, and worry are natural behaviors that accompany the growth process for seven- to eight-and-a-half-year-olds.

In an unconscious effort to release tension, second graders are usually very fidgety. Your child may pick or chew on nails or clothing or play with his or her hair. Playing with objects, as well as picking up objects that don't belong to him or her and carrying them around, are also common. Collecting things and holding on to them or keeping them close by seems to be a method of comfort for second graders.

Allowing time for free play is critical to the emotional and intellectual development of a second grader and may serve as a way to work through emotional anxiety. Free play is any type of unsupervised, spontaneous play. Leaving your child uninterrupted, minimizing television, and allowing him or her enough unplanned time to do something new will encourage free play. Make available imagination-inspiring play items such as treasure boxes, costume jewelry, funny hats and other interesting clothing, cardboard boxes, and so on.

Acknowledge Worries and Confront Fears

Fear and worry may be a daily issue for your child at this age. In fact, some people claim that the term *worrywart* was first used to describe a second grader. Your child may be worried that he or she will make a mistake or not be liked by other children. Your second grader may also claim that you favor a brother or sister or that he or she has no friends. Second graders also often express a fear of disaster, financial instability, and death, especially the death of parents. Hypochondriac behavior may also be present.

Don't buy into your child's worries, but do acknowledge them as real and valid. You can break the worry cycle in your child's head by helping him or her address the fears. For example, ask, "What could you do if you were at play group and you felt left out?" or "What would happen if you made a bad kick during the soccer game?" Similarly, if your child expresses a fear of your death, let him or her know that you plan on staying alive for a very long time, but that if you ever are away there will be someone familiar ready to take care of him or her.

Second graders also point their fear antennae toward world problems. Your second grader may worry about deforestation after seeing a television show or obsess about the possibility of war after hearing the radio news. Creating supposed solutions to these fears probably won't work as it did when your child was younger, although going through the motions of scaring away spooks from behind the door may still be necessary. If your second grader is concerned about the possibility of war, help him or her write a letter to the White House or your congressional representative. If your child fears that all Earth's trees will be cut down or otherwise worries about the environment, help him or her contact an environmental group to find out what is being done to protect habitats and how he or she can contribute.

Provide Privacy and Be Objective

As your child works through this more inward stage, he or she is likely to be less emotionally giving with others. Your second grader may show a need and appreciation for personal space and for possessions that are his or hers alone. Second graders can be loners and prefer to work or play alone or with one other friend. This desire may inspire your second grader to seek out private spaces in the house to read or play. He or she may even build makeshift "rooms" of his or her own out of blankets or cushions.

Second graders also tend to be very family oriented. Your child may be concerned about his or her place in the family and relationship with other family members. Your second grader may even want to take on certain household chores if he or she sees other members of the family doing their parts and creating a sense of teamwork and appreciation.

Although very sensitive, a second-grade child will most likely lack social maturity and have a tendency to make excuses, blame problems on others, or tattle. You may hear horror stories of maltreatment by friends or of the unfairness of adult authority figures. These perceptions are probably another manifestation of the victim syndrome so common at this age. Remain calm and sympathetic, and don't allow yourself to get pulled into the conflict. Your best chance of creating change and establishing harmony is by staying free of emotional entanglement while letting your child know you are on his or her side. Except for abusive situations that require adult intervention, most of these conflicts are best left for your child to clear up on his or her own with only the help of your guidance.

Note Intense Focus and Perfectionism

Second graders need their work and actions to be correct and are often perfectionists. A child as this age is very self-critical and is intensely aware of his or her mistakes. The demands a second grader places on himself or herself when trying to accomplish a task are often unrealistic.

A second grader's vigilance and concern with mistakes make him or her a notorious eraser. Your child may even write and erase holes right through the paper. You may also notice that your second grader has a very tight visual focus and tends to bring his or her face very close to the page when reading or writing. Your child may show signs of eye fatigue or nearsightedness. Don't panic. This behavior is normal and will most likely pass before long. Of course, true signs of vision difficulty, such as problems reading street markers or recognizing familiar people from a distance, should be checked with a doctor.

Monitor Time and Share Schedules

Second graders generally have difficulty ending an activity once it has begun. Without intervention, a child at this age will continue with a task or an activity indefinitely or until he or she has become exhausted. Absorbed in a world of thought, the second grader can become disconnected from his or her sense of time and physical needs. Designating alternating periods of close work and physical activity can be helpful. You can also help your second grader by identifying a closing point for his or her activities. For instance, offer guidance such as "When the CD ends you can get your pajamas on" or "We'll finish one more lesson activity and then we'll go to the park."

The second grader who is prone to worry or anxiety may find comfort in knowing the plan for his or her day ahead of time. Verbally walking your child through each step in the day's schedule in the morning, especially on busy days or days involving new experiences, can create a sense of emotional comfort even if the day doesn't go exactly as planned. Maintaining predictable morning and evening routines may also put your second grader at ease. At bedtime you might keep a consistent ritual of changing into pajamas before snuggling up with a short story. In the morning, perhaps designate a regular time to have a family breakfast.

Encourage Learning

In academics, second graders are usually hardworking and good at following directions. Second graders want to feel a sense of accomplishment and will struggle with their work to get it right. Aware of mistakes, a second-grade child needs your encouragement more than ever. The superficial praise that satisfied your child as a first grader will fall flat with your more mature and intellectual second grader. Let your second grader know that you're paying attention to his or her achievements. Observant statements such as "Your science research seems well thought out" or "I appreciate the way the title on your poster is so clear and easy to read" will provide your second grader with the encouragement needed to sustain his or her confidence.

Commonly, second grade is the time when children begin to overcome characteristic first-grade habits, such as forming letters and numbers backward or with awkward strokes. Some children take longer to develop accurate writing skills, and the continuation of these habits may simply mean that your child needs a little more time to mature in this area. However, if your second-grade child is also having trouble with reading or other academic skills, this is the time to investigate whether he or she has a learning difficulty that can be identified and addressed. *Making the Grade* provides ample opportunities for reading, as well as on-the-spot assessment of new skills, to help pinpoint potentially troublesome areas.

Accept and Enjoy

Accompanying your second grader through his or her worrisome journey may be easier if you're willing to accept your child's increased sensitivity, sulking, and moodiness along with the other, more positive characteristics of this age. Enjoy the calm internal demeanor of your second grader. Before you know it, an unbounded, energetic, loud, and talkative third grader will appear.

Promoting Literacy

Promoting Literacy

Key Topics

Fiction
Pages 3–10

Creative Writing and Fantasy
Pages 11–24

Verbs and Articles
Pages 25–34

Nouns and Compound Words
Pages 35–42

Folktales, Poetry, and Journal Writing
Pages 43–52

Biographies and Nonfiction
Pages 53–64

Conjunctions and Prepositions
Pages 65–72

Prefixes and Suffixes
Pages 73–78

Antonyms, Synonyms, and Homophones
Pages 79–88

Investigating Fiction

Through fiction we encounter new people, places, and things.

OBJECTIVE	BACKGROUND	MATERIALS
To have your student read a fictional story and understand the elements of fiction	Fictional literature is popular among both children and adults because it allows readers to explore different settings and times. In this lesson, your student will read a fictional story and identify the elements of fiction. He or she will also use this lesson to practice reading strategies.	■ Student Learning Pages 1.A–1.C ■ 1 copy Web, page 354

VOCABULARY

PORTABLE able to be moved easily

ANNOUNCER a person who describes things on the radio or television

SUDDENLY unexpectedly or sooner than expected

Let's Begin

1 **INTRODUCE** Tell your student that fictional stories are made up by the author. Explain that there are different types of fiction. For example, realistic fictional stories have characters who act like people in real life. The plot, or events, of a realistic fictional story could happen in real life. Tell your student that some fictional stories are fantasy. A fantasy story includes events that could never happen in real life. Invite your student to think of an event that might happen in a realistic fictional story and one that might happen in a fantasy story.

2 **DISTRIBUTE AND READ** Distribute Student Learning Page 1.A. Ask your student to read the story aloud. Guide him or her as necessary.

3 **DISCOVER** Point out that stories don't always explain everything completely. Sometimes the reader has to use story clues along with his or her own knowledge to figure out what happened. Ask, *Why was the phone line busy when Dan's mother and father tried to call the power company?* [a lot of people from the neighborhood were calling] *Why did it take so long for the power company to send a truck to fix the broken line?* [because the weather was bad; a lot of other lines were broken, too]

4 **EXAMINE** Distribute Student Learning Page 1.B. Remind your student that most stories have characters, a setting (a time and place), and a plot (the events that happen in a story). Invite your student to complete the story map.

5 **EXPLORE** Explain to your student that stories usually have main ideas and supporting details. Distribute a copy of the Web found on page 354. Ask, *What do you think is the main idea in* Blackout? [blackouts may be fun at first but then they can be uncomfortable] Guide your student to identify a main idea based on the supporting details. Have your student write the main idea in the center of the Web. Then invite him or her to write details that support, or show, the main idea in the surrounding ovals.

GET ORGANIZED

Take this time to look through your family's emergency supplies and check to make sure your batteries work and so on.

6 **RELATE** Have your student think of a time when there was an emergency, such as a blackout. If your student keeps a journal, have him or her write how he or she felt during the emergency and what he or she did during it. If your student can't recall an emergency, have him or her imagine how he or she would have felt.

7 **DISCUSS** Have your student circle the words **portable, announcer,** and **suddenly** in the story. Ask your student to use the surrounding sentences to help him or her decide what each word means. Then review the definitions of each word. Ask your student to use each word in an original sentence.

8 **IDENTIFY** Explain that a cause tells why something happened, and an effect is what happened. Point out something that happened in the story and ask your student to explain why it happened. Tell your student that his or her explanation is the cause of the effect. Ask another question and have your student answer it orally.

9 **CONNECT** You may want to take this time to talk with your student about emergencies and how you'd prefer to handle them in your home. If you'd like, help your student find an article in a magazine or newspaper about a child who triumphs in an emergency situation.

FOR FURTHER READING

Kids to the Rescue!: First Aid Techniques for Kids, by Maribeth Boelts, Darwin Boelts, and Marina Megale, ill. (Parenting Press, Inc., 2003).

Police and Emergency Vehicles, by Arlene Bourgeois Molzahn (Enslow Publishers, Inc., 2002).

Super Storms, by Seymour Simon (SeaStar Books, 2002).

You Read to Me and I'll Read to You: Stories to Share from the 20th Century, by Janet Schulman, ed. (Knopf, 2001).

Branching Out

TEACHING TIP

Have your student retell the story orally to reinforce his or her comprehension.

CHECKING IN

To assess your student's understanding of the story, have him or her tell whether it's realistic fiction or fantasy and explain why.

Read Fiction

Blackout

by Anne and Harlow Rockwell

It was cold.

All the trees were covered with ice. Every branch of every tree was shining with ice.

"Oh, how pretty the trees look!" said Dan.

"Yes, they do," said Father. "But I hope the wind does not begin to blow."

The wind began to blow. The ice began to crack. The branches began to break.

CRASH!

One big branch fell down.

CRASH!

Another fell down.

The wind blew harder.

CRASH! CRASH!

The television went off. So did the light in the bathroom.

"Look," said Mother. "An electric power line is down. That is why the light went out. And the television, too."

Father built a fire in the fireplace. He used the wood Grandmother had given them for Christmas. Dan was glad they had a fire. It was nice and warm. It was pretty, too.

Father called the power company. Mother did, too. But the line was always busy. The wind blew.

(CONTINUED) ▶

Student Learning Page 1.A: Read Fiction

The branches cracked. And the house was cold and dark, except by the fireplace. "We can cook over the fire," said Mother.

And they did.

There were hot dogs, marshmallows and popcorn.

"This is fun," said Dan. "It is like a picnic."

"It is fun right now," said Father. "But I hope they fix the electric power soon."

"It is too dark to eat," said Mother. She found two candles. She lit them and they had light to eat by.

Father and Dan took a flashlight and found the sleeping bags in the attic.

Each of them put on three pairs of socks.

"This is like the North Pole," said Dan.

Then Father found the portable radio. It worked with batteries.

Everyone listened to the news. The radio announcer told them what to do during the blackout.

Mother went into the kitchen. She turned on the faucet in the sink. She filled big pots with water. Then she left the water running.

She went into the bathroom. She turned on the faucets in the sink and the tub. She flushed the toilet. She left all the faucets running.

Father turned off the water valve in the cellar. Soon all the faucets stopped running.

"Now," said Father, "there is no more water in our pipes. So our pipes cannot freeze."

The wind blew. A branch fell on the roof. Ice cracked. Father put more wood on the fire.

(CONTINUED)

Everyone told stories and jokes and sang songs until they fell asleep.

More ice cracked and the wind blew.

When they woke up, the wind had stopped. But it was cold. Ice still covered the trees.

All day everyone waited for the power to go on.

That night they had canned beans, canned tuna fish, crackers and cookies and water from the pots in the kitchen. There was ice on top of the water in the pots.

When Dan went to the bathroom, he could not flush the toilet. He could not wash his hands or brush his teeth. And it was icy cold in the bathroom.

They all got into sleeping bags. They listened to the radio. Suddenly the radio was quiet. The batteries were used up.

In the morning, it was not as cold. The ice began to melt in the sun.

Dan said, "We have one candle, two radio batteries, one flashlight and no wood. What will we do tonight?"

(CONTINUED) ▶

Student Learning Page 1.A: Read Fiction   **7**

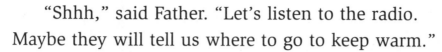

"Shhh," said Father. "Let's listen to the radio. Maybe they will tell us where to go to keep warm."

But suddenly the radio was quiet again. The last good batteries were all used up.

All day they waited. The ice dripped and melted in the sunshine.

Then the sun went down. It began to get darker and colder.

Suddenly, as the stars came out, a truck came. A truck from the power company!

"Hooray!" shouted Dan.

"Wow!" said Timmy, when he saw the lights on the truck.

"We sure are glad to see you," said Mother and Father and all the neighbors to the workers on the truck.

They worked hard and fast.

In a little while, the lights in all the houses went on.

Complete a Story Map

Write about the characters, setting, and plot in the boxes.

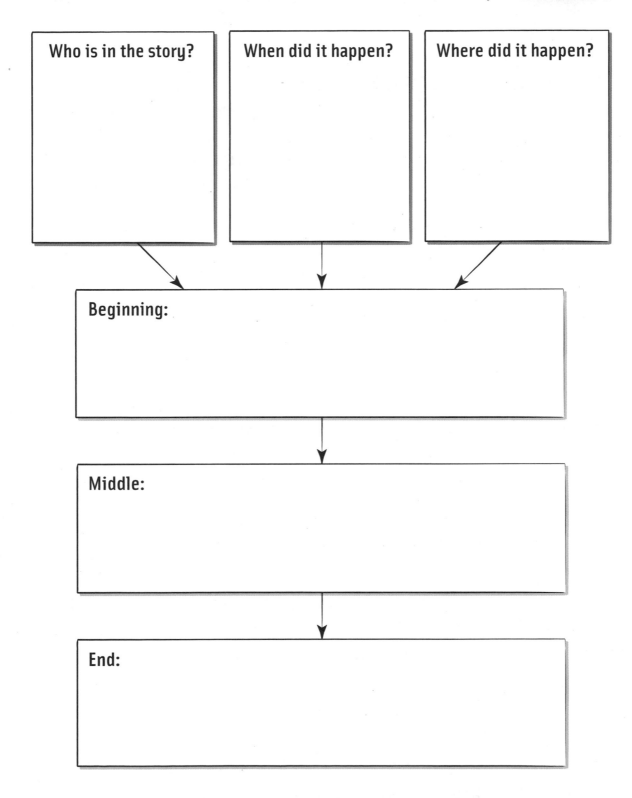

Who is in the story?

When did it happen?

Where did it happen?

Beginning:

Middle:

End:

What's Next? You Decide!

Now it's your turn to choose what to do next in the lesson. Read the activities and decide which one you want to do—you may want to try them both!

Create a Picture Book

MATERIALS

- ❑ 6–7 sheets construction paper
- ❑ crayons or markers
- ❑ 1 hole puncher
- ❑ yarn

STEPS

Make a picture book for *Blackout*.

- ❑ Write down the most important things that happened in the story.
- ❑ Draw a picture of each event on a sheet of construction paper.
- ❑ Write a sentence about each picture at the bottom of the page.
- ❑ Put the pages in the order that each event happened.
- ❑ Draw a cover for your book on a sheet of construction paper.
- ❑ Put the cover on top of the other pages. Then punch holes in all the pages of the book. Tie the pages together with yarn.

Make an Emergency Collage

MATERIALS

- ❑ 1 sheet construction paper
- ❑ old magazines
- ❑ 1 pair scissors
- ❑ glue

STEPS

Make a collage of things to do in an emergency.

- ❑ Ask an adult for some old magazines that you can cut up.
- ❑ Make a list of things you might need in an emergency, like a flashlight and batteries.
- ❑ Look through magazines for pictures of each thing on your list.
- ❑ Glue the pictures onto construction paper.
- ❑ Write the name of each thing under the picture.
- ❑ Hang up your collage for others to look at.

Understanding Creative Writing

Creative writing takes us as far as our imaginations allow.

OBJECTIVE	BACKGROUND	MATERIALS
To have your student use creative writing to express his or her imagination	Creative writing includes any type of literature that's written to express original ideas. The goal of most creative writers is to use words that help readers create images in their minds. Creative writing often appeals to a reader's senses and emotions. A vivid word or phrase can trigger connections to sounds, sights, tastes, smells, and feelings. In this lesson, your student will write a creative story. He or she will also practice organizing ideas in writing.	<ul><li>Student Learning Pages 2.A–2.B</li><li>3 pictures from a magazine</li><li>1 copy Writing Lines, page 355</li><li>1 copy Sequence Chain, page 354</li></ul>

VOCABULARY
COMMUNICATE to express or show ideas to others **DESCRIPTION** the use of words to tell about someone or something

Let's Begin

1 **INTRODUCE** Begin the lesson by showing your student three pictures from a magazine that show people interacting or doing something. Ask your student to choose which picture he or she finds the most interesting. Give your student the picture he or she chose. Then ask your student to make up a very short story for the picture. Encourage your student to be creative! Have your student share his or her ideas out loud. Distribute a copy of the Writing Lines found on page 355 and have your student write his or her story.

2 **SHARE** Tell your student that he or she is going to **communicate** his or her story through creative writing. Explain that the word *communicate* means to express or show ideas to others. Have your student begin by identifying the characters and setting of his or her story. If necessary help your student elaborate on ideas by naming the characters and the time and place of the story. Remind your student that creative writing includes **description.** Encourage your student to describe the characters and setting using words that will help readers connect to their senses of sight,

TAKE A BREAK

Bake some cookies or a healthy treat to provoke your student's sense of smell. Point out how he or she can use other senses as you make the food. Then invite your student to eat some of the finished product to practice using his or her sense of taste!

smell, sound, touch, and taste. Give these examples to your student: *Her skin was smooth like silk. The house smelled sweet like cookies. The fluffy, white clouds covered the sun.*

3 **DISTRIBUTE** Distribute a copy of the Sequence Chain found on page 356. Invite your student to think about the action in his or her story. Have him or her use the Sequence Chain to note the important events of the story in the order in which they will happen.

4 **WRITE** Invite your student to use the Sequence Chain to write the story. Point out that the story should have supporting details for each main idea. Tell your student that a main idea is the most important idea in a story. The supporting details tell the reader more about the main idea. Point out an example. Tell your student that a main idea might be: *Anna loves her cat.* Some supporting details might be: *Anna feeds her cat. Anna brushes her cat every day. Anna plays with her cat.* Ask your student to think of another supporting detail for this main idea.

5 **REINFORCE** Encourage your student to write in complete sentences. Tell him or her that each sentence should have a subject (a person or thing doing an action) and a verb (an action). Check your student's writing for correct sentence structure, grammar, and punctuation. To allow your student to concentrate on his or her sentences, you can also type as your student dictates his or her story to you.

6 **REVIEW** Distribute Student Learning Page 2.A. Ask your student to read the directions out loud, and encourage him or her to ask questions if necessary. Then invite your student to write in a notebook about what he or she has learned about creative writing.

Branching Out

TEACHING TIP

Tell your student that writers often like to use different words in their writing rather than repeat the same ones. Show your student how to use a children's thesaurus to vary word choice in his or her writing. Point out that he or she can also use a thesaurus to find colorful words that will help readers picture the story in their minds.

CHECKING IN

To assess your student's understanding of the lesson, invite your student to write a summary of his or her story. Remind your student that a summary is short and includes the most important information in a piece of writing.

FOR FURTHER READING

Month-by-Month Write and Read Books, by Veronica Robillard (Scholastic Professional Books, 1999).

Writer's Express: A Handbook for Young Writers, Thinkers, and Learners, by Dave Kemper, Patrick Sebranek, Ruth Nathan, and Chris Krenzke, ill. (Great Source Education Group, Inc., 2000).

Writing Activities Just for Young Learners, by Martin Lee and Marcia Miller (Scholastic Professional Books, 2001).

Write a Creative Story

Write a number between 1 and 4 on each line. Then make a sentence.
Match the numbers you chose with the numbers in the boxes.
Example:

Box 1: _____1_____   Box 2: _____2_____   Box 3: _____2_____

Sentence: _A big black cat ran high in the sky._

Box 1: _____   Box 2: _____   Box 3: _____

Sentence: _____

Box 1	Box 2	Box 3
1. A big black cat	**1.** walked	**1.** across the rose garden.
2. A man with a long beard	**2.** ran	**2.** high in the sky.
3. A snake with sharp teeth	**3.** danced	**3.** around the house.
4. A flying dragon	**4.** jumped	**4.** through the forest.

Now write a short story. Begin with the sentence you just made.
You may wish to use extra sheets of paper.

_____

_____

_____

_____

_____

What's Next? You Decide!

Now it's your turn to choose what to do next in the lesson. Read the activities and decide which one you want to do— you may want to try them both!

Make a Grab Bag

MATERIALS

- ❑ 1 brown paper bag
- ❑ 10 small objects that fit into the bag

STEPS

Write a story using something from your house.

- ❑ Find 10 objects in your house that fit into the brown paper bag.
- ❑ Place the 10 objects in the bag.
- ❑ Reach into the bag and pull out one object.
- ❑ Write a creative story that includes that object.
- ❑ Share your story with a family member or friend.

Picture It, Paint It, Write It

MATERIALS

- ❑ watercolor paints
- ❑ 1 paintbrush
- ❑ 1 sheet white paper

STEPS

When you write creative stories you use words to help readers paint pictures in their mind. Now it's time to actually paint the picture!

- ❑ Imagine a creative story.
- ❑ Use the watercolors to paint part of the story you imagined.
- ❑ Let your picture dry.
- ❑ Show family members and friends your picture. Tell them your story as you show the picture.
- ❑ Now write a story from the picture you painted.

Exploring Fantasy

*Fantasy takes us beyond our everyday world
and lets us dream the impossible.*

OBJECTIVE	BACKGROUND	MATERIALS
To have your student read and learn about stories that are fantasy	Many of the earliest stories children hear and read are fantasies. Nursery rhymes, fairy tales, cartoons, and animated movies are fantasies. In this lesson, your student will read a fantasy and identify the features of this genre.	■ Student Learning Pages 3.A–3.C ■ 1 copy Comparison Chart, page 353

VOCABULARY
FANTASY a story in which some characters or events are make-believe **CHARACTERS** the people or animals a story is about **PLOT** what happens in a story **SUMMARIZE** to tell what happens in a story in a short way

Let's Begin

1 **INTRODUCE** Tell your student that the selection he or she is about to read is a **fantasy** called *Ella's Games*. Explain that fantasy stories include make-believe. In them, animals and people do things that couldn't happen in real life. Point out that in many fantasies authors include realistic people or events to make the stories seem more believable. Challenge your student to name a fantasy story he or she has read.

2 **DISTRIBUTE, READ, AND MONITOR** Distribute Student Learning Page 3.A. Have your student read the story aloud. Tell him or her to pause every few lines to check his or her understanding. Suggest that your student ask himself or herself these questions: *What has happened so far? Did I miss anything?* Invite your student to pause and reread to clarify the text before he or she continues reading.

3 **DISCUSS** Talk with your student about the **characters** in the story. Ask, *Who is the story about?* [Ella and her brothers, Jack, Jim, and Joe] *What do you know about Ella?* [she is a mouse; she likes to make up games] *What do you know about Ella's brothers?* [they like to play in the honeysuckle tub] Then ask your student what the **plot** is, or what happens in the story.

Ask, *What happened first? What happened next?* Help your
student connect to the story. Then ask your student to write
about a time when he or she was too young to do something.

4 **DISCOVER AND DISTRIBUTE** Tell your student that the story
has parts that are real and parts that are make-believe. For
example, honeysuckle and dandelions are real parts of the story,
while talking mice are make-believe. Give your student a copy
of the Comparison Chart on page 353. Write these column
headings in the chart: "Story Part," "Real," "Make-Believe." Help
your student list story parts in the Story Part column. Then have
him or her decide whether each part is real or make-believe and
put a checkmark in the correct column. For additional practice,
construct a fantasy hideaway by draping a sheet over two chairs.
Climb inside with your student and have him or her describe the
make-believe place.

5 **INVESTIGATE AND PREDICT** Discuss how one thing in a story
can cause another thing to happen. Ask, *Why did Ella play on
her own and make up games?* [because her brothers wouldn't
let her play in the tub] *Why did Ella's brothers change their
minds and invite her to play in the tub?* [because they believed
Ella's make-believe games were real] Then ask your student to
guess what might happen next in the story.

6 **EXPLORE** Explain that some words have more than one meaning.
Point out the word *play* in the second sentence. The word *play*
can mean "to have fun in a game or sport." It also can mean
"a drama that is performed onstage." Ask, *Which meaning of*
play *is used in the story?* [to have fun in a game or sport]

7 **EXPLAIN AND DISTRIBUTE** Explain that a good way to review
what happens in a story is to **summarize,** or tell what happens
in a story in a short way. Distribute Student Learning Page 3.B.
Tell your student to draw a scene for the beginning, middle, and
end of the story. Then have him or her write a caption for each
picture that explains what is happening.

Branching Out

TEACHING TIP

A good way to reinforce comprehension is to have your student retell
the story out loud in his or her own words. Encourage him or her to use
transition words, such as *first, next, then,* and *after.*

CHECKING IN

To assess your student's understanding of the lesson, ask him or her to
choose a fantasy to read. When he or she is finished reading, ask why
the story is a fantasy. Then ask him or her to identify the characters and
summarize the plot.

Discover Fantasy

Ella's Games
by David Bedford and Peter Kavanagh

Ella's brothers played all morning in the honeysuckle tub.

Ella wanted to play too.

"You'd be scared!" said Jack.

"You're too small!" said Jim.

"You can't even climb!" said Joe.

So Ella went away to play on her own, and found . . .

(CONTINUED)

a cat's whisker.

And she made up a game.

"What's that?" asked Jack when Ella came back.

"I'll tell you . . ." said Ella.

"It's a whisker from a rainbow cat, who tried to chase me. But I didn't run. I plucked out one of her whiskers, and frightened her away!"

"Can I play in the honeysuckle tub now?" asked Ella. "I won't be scared—I can frighten cats!"

"You still can't play with us," said Jim, "because you're too small."

So Ella went to play on her own again, and found . . .

a fluffy dandelion.

And she made up a game.

(CONTINUED)

18   Making the Grade: Everything Your 2nd Grader Needs to Know

Ella's brothers were having a bath when Ella came back.

"Why are you so muddy?" asked Jim.

"I'll tell you . . ." said Ella.

"I found an elephant having a mud bath. He said, 'Help me, Ella, I'm stuck!' So I tickled his nose with a feathery flower, and he sniffed and snuffled and SNEEZED his way out."

"*Now* can I play in the honeysuckle tub?" asked Ella. "It doesn't matter if I'm small—I can save elephants!"

(CONTINUED)

"You still can't play with us," said Joe. "You can't climb."

So Ella went away to play on her own once more, and found . . .

a big stone.

And she made up a game.

Ella's brothers were getting ready for bed when Ella came back.

(CONTINUED) ➤

"What's that?" asked Joe.

"I'll tell you . . ." said Ella.

"It's a dragon's sore tooth. I climbed all the way up to the dragon's head, and plucked it out. He was so pleased, he took me flying around and around the clouds."

"Wow!" said Joe. "You play all the *best* games, Ella."

That night, Ella's brothers couldn't sleep.

"Ella," asked Jack, "will you play in the honeysuckle tub tomorrow? You won't be scared—you frightened a cat!"

"You're not too small," said Jim. "You saved an elephant!"

"And you *can* climb," said Joe. "You even climbed a dragon!"

"All right," said Ella happily.

"What shall we play?" asked Jack, Jim, and Joe.

"I'll tell you . . ." said Ella.

(CONTINUED) ➤

And the next day, Jack, Jim, and Joe made
ready to sail across the sea

in the fantastic new adventure of . . .

Captain Ella and her brave pirate crew!

Summarize *Ella's Games*

Draw a picture in the box for each part of the story. Write
a sentence below each picture telling what the picture
shows. Then write a paragraph about each picture on a
separate sheet of paper.

Beginning:

Middle:

End:

What's Next? You Decide!

Now it's your turn to choose what to do next in the lesson. Read the activities and decide which one you want to do—you may want to try them both!

Record a Fantasy Story

MATERIALS

- ❑ 1 audiocassette tape
- ❑ 1 audiocassette recorder

STEPS

- ❑ Make up your own fantasy story. It should have make-believe people, animals, or events.

- ❑ Write down your story on paper. Tell what happens in the story and how it ends.

- ❑ Ask someone to help you make an audio recording of your story.

- ❑ As you record your story, read it with expression. Show the characters' feelings. Change your voice to sound like the different people in the story.

- ❑ Play your fantasy story for your family!

Make Ella's Dragon

MATERIALS

- ❑ several sheets different colored construction paper
- ❑ 1 pair scissors
- ❑ tape
- ❑ glue
- ❑ aluminum foil
- ❑ brightly colored cloth
- ❑ crayons or colored pencils

STEPS

Make a dragon with a sore tooth.

- ❑ Cut a body, head, tail, and wings from construction paper.

- ❑ Glue bits of foil and cloth all over the dragon's body parts.

- ❑ Tape the body parts together.

- ❑ Draw the dragon's eyes, nose, and mouth.

- ❑ Remember to draw the dragon's sore tooth.

- ❑ Show your dragon to your family and friends.

PROMOTING LITERACY

ing LESSON 1.4

Comprehending Verbs

Without verbs, our world would be full of inanimate objects!

OBJECTIVE	BACKGROUND	MATERIALS
To help your student study verbs to develop grammar, phonics, and word skills	Your student may already know that most verbs show action. However, some verbs also show states of being or serve as helping verbs. In this lesson, your student will learn to use these types of verbs and about irregular action verbs.	■ Student Learning Pages 4.A–4.C

VOCABULARY
VERBS words that show action or states of being **IRREGULAR VERBS** verbs in which the past tense is not formed by adding *–ed* **CONTRACTION** shorter way to write two words

Let's Begin

1 **DEFINE** Begin the lesson by telling your student that most **verbs** show action. Read these sentences to your student:

> The dog jumped over the fence.
> My sister wants that toy.

Ask your student to name the action verb in each sentence. Invite him or her to tell whether the action is in the present tense (happening now) or in the past tense (already happened). Ask, *How can you tell if an action already took place?* [the verb will have an *-ed* at the end]

2 **EXPLAIN** Tell your student that some verbs don't end in *–ed* in the past tense. These verbs are called **irregular verbs.** Their spelling changes in the past tense. Two irregular verbs are *say* and *see*. Invite your student to read the sentences below. Ask him or her to complete the sentences in the past tense. Be sure he or she uses the past tense forms *said* and *saw*.

> I say hello to my friends.
> Yesterday, I _____ hello to my friends.
> He sees his neighbor.
> Yesterday, he _____ his neighbor.

Ask your student to write one sentence using the past tense form of *say* and one using the past tense form of *see*.

3 **REVEAL** Reveal that some verbs don't show action. The verb *be* tells what someone or something is or was. The words *am, are,* and *is* show the present tense of *be*. The words *was* and *were* show the past tense. Place a pen on the table and say, *The pen is on the table.* Then place several books on the floor and say, *The books are on the floor.* Ask your student to repeat the sentences in the past tense. Be sure he or she uses the past tense forms *was* and *were*. Then distribute Student Learning Page 4.A.

4 **DISCOVER** Tell your student that the verb *have* is a commonly used irregular verb. This verb shows possession, or what belongs to someone or something. Read these sentences aloud:

> I have cereal for breakfast.
> He has a new bike.

Ask your student to rewrite the sentences above in the past tense.

5 **INVESTIGATE** Encourage your student to think about the verbs and verb forms that he or she has learned in this lesson. Help him or her see that all of these verb forms tell about things that happened in the past or are happening in the present. Explain that when something is going to happen in the future, the verb *will* is often used with another verb. Ask your student to complete the sentences below. Then distribute Student Learning Page 4.B.

> Tomorrow, I will _____.
> On my birthday, I will _____.

6 **EXPLAIN** Tell your student that a **contraction** is a shorter way to write two words. They are formed by dropping letters and replacing them with an apostrophe. For example, the words *do not* form the contraction *don't,* and the words *can not* form the contraction *can't*. Show how the apostrophe replaces the *o* in *not* in both *don't* and *can't*. Have your student think of three contractions. [possible answers: isn't, won't, doesn't] Then have him or her tell you what words each is made from. Challenge your student to use two contractions in a sentence.

ENRICH THE EXPERIENCE

Set up a simple treasure hunt for your student. Hide a small prize and write a clue explaining where the prize is hidden. Try to use the verbs from the lesson in the clues.

Branching Out

TEACHING TIP

Encourage your student to keep a simple journal to practice using verbs correctly. Each night, ask your student to write a few sentences in a notebook about the events of the day.

CHECKING IN

Make a list of subject pronouns: *I, you* (singular), *he, she, it, we, you* (plural), and *they*. To assess your student's understanding of verbs, name the different verbs that were studied in this lesson. Ask your student to think of sentences using different subject pronouns with the verbs.

FOR FURTHER READING

Kites Sail High: A Book About Verbs, by Ruth Heller (Paper Star, 1998).

Little Book of Verbs, by Babs Bell Hajdusiewicz (Goodyear Publishing Company, 2000).

Verbs (Sentences), by Kelly Doudna (Sandcastle, 2002).

Use Forms of *Be*

Complete the chart by filling in the correct form of *be*.

	I	You	He, She, It	We	You (more than one)	They
Present tense of *be*						
Past tense of *be*						

Now use two of the verbs in a sentence. Draw a picture for each sentence.

Sentence: _____

Sentence: _____

Write Verbs in Sentences

Look at the pictures. Write two sentences about each of the people in the pictures. Use the verbs in the box. Use a contraction in the second sentence.

am	is
are	was
were	have
has	saw
said	will go

1. _____

_____

_____

_____

2. _____

_____

_____

_____

3. _____

_____

_____

_____

What's Next? You Decide!

Now it's your turn to choose what to do next in the lesson. Read the activities and decide which one you want to do—you may want to try them all!

Make a Book

MATERIALS

- ❏ 6 sheets construction paper
- ❏ crayons or markers
- ❏ yarn
- ❏ 1 hole puncher

STEPS

Make a book of things that you will do in the future!

- ❏ Make a list of things that you think you will do in the future.
- ❏ Choose five things from the list. Draw each thing on a separate sheet of construction paper.
- ❏ At the bottom of each page, write a sentence beginning with *I will* to explain what the picture shows.
- ❏ Make a cover for your book.
- ❏ Punch three holes through the pages. Tie the pages together with yarn.
- ❏ Share your book with your family and friends.

Act It Out

MATERIALS

- ❏ 10 index cards
- ❏ 1 box

STEPS

- ❏ Think of 10 action verbs. Write each verb on an index card.
- ❏ Place the cards in a box and mix them up.
- ❏ Play a game with two or more people. One person should choose an index card from the box and not tell what the verb is.
- ❏ The person with the index card should act out the action verb. The other players should try to guess the verb.
- ❏ Take turns choosing index cards and acting out the verbs!

(CONTINUED)

Play Who Has What?

MATERIALS

❑ 11 index cards

STEPS

❑ On 10 index cards, write five singular nouns (one person, place, or thing) and five plural nouns (more than one person, place, or thing).

❑ On one index card, write the verb *has* on one side. Write the verb *have* on the other side.

❑ Mix up the 10 noun cards. Place them facedown.

❑ Choose one of the noun cards. Read the noun out loud.

❑ Turn over the has/have card to show the verb you would use with the noun.

❑ Begin a sentence with the noun followed by *has* or *have*. Make up your own ending to the sentence. Say the whole sentence out loud.

❑ Invite another player to choose a noun card and repeat the steps.

❑ Keep playing until you've used all the nouns!

Make Before and After Pictures

MATERIALS

❑ 1 magazine

❑ 1 pair scissors

❑ 1 posterboard

❑ glue

STEPS

❑ Look in the magazine for a picture that shows an activity or some action.

❑ Imagine what might have happened before the picture was taken. Draw a picture of this scene.

❑ Imagine what might have happened right after the picture was taken. Draw a picture of this scene.

❑ Cut out all three pictures and glue them to the posterboard.

❑ Show your before and after pictures to your family and friends.

Using Articles

An article is a little word that is a big part of a sentence.

OBJECTIVE	BACKGROUND	MATERIALS
To have your student understand, identify, and use articles	The words *a, an,* and *the* are called articles. They are generally used before nouns in sentences and titles. Your student encounters articles in virtually any type of text he or she reads. Your student also uses articles in his or her writing. In this lesson, your student will learn how to identify and use articles.	▪ Student Learning Pages 5.A–5.B ▪ 3 index cards ▪ 1 favorite children's book

VOCABULARY

ARTICLES the words *a, an,* and *the*
SINGULAR NOUNS words that name one person, place, or thing
PLURAL NOUNS words that name more than one person, place, or thing

Let's Begin

1 **INTRODUCE** Begin this lesson by writing the words *a, an,* and *the* on index cards. Then ask your student to repeat the following lines:

> *A, an,* and *the* are articles we say.
> We use these little words every single day.
> *A, an,* and *the* are articles we use.
> Even as we write, they're words we often choose.

Have your student repeat each line after you read it.

2 **REVEAL** Share with your student that he or she is going to learn how to recognize and use **articles.** Explain that articles are the words *a, an,* and *the.* Point out that the articles *a* and *an* are used before **singular nouns.** Explain that singular nouns indicate just one person, place, or thing. Ask your student to look at the rhyme again and identify the three articles. Have your student write a sentence using each of the three articles in his or her notebook.

3 **EXPLAIN** Tell your student that there are rules for using *a* and *an* in sentences. Explain that the article *a* is used before words beginning with consonants. Write this example sentence for your student: *I saw a̲ dog running through my yard.* Then explain that the article *an* is used before words beginning with a vowel or

FOR FURTHER READING

Grammar Graphics and Picture Perfect Punctuation: A Fun and Easy Way to Learn Through Pictures, by Jerry Lucas (Lucas Educational Systems, 2000).

Grammar, Second Grade: Mastering Basic Skills, by Deborah Morris and Larry Morris (Rainbow Bridge Publishing, 2002).

Month-by-Month Phonics for Second Grade, by Patricia Cunningham and Dorothy Hall (Carson-Dellosa, 2000).

vowel sound. Now write another example for your student: *I saw an animal running through my yard.* Challenge your student to think about the rules for *a* and *an*. Then ask him or her to make up three sentences using *a* and three sentences using *an*. Have your student write one of the sentences in his or her notebook and explain why he or she used *a* or *an*. Then have your student choose one of the sentences that he or she wrote and write a paragraph about it.

4 **PRACTICE** Give your student the index cards for *a* and *an* from Step 1. Think of a sentence with *a* or *an*. Say the sentence out loud, but pause where the article *a* or *an* should be. Ask your student to hold up the card for the article that completes the sentence. For example, say, *Jim wrote* (pause) *letter to his grandma.* Your student should hold up the right card and then respond by repeating the sentence with the correct article: *Jim wrote a letter to his grandma.* Practice with at least five sentences that have *a* or *an*.

5 **CHALLENGE** Ask your student to write down three sentences that use the article *a* and three sentences that use the article *an*. Remind him or her that the article *a* is used before words beginning with consonants. The article *an* is used before words beginning with a vowel or vowel sound. Have your student read the sentences out loud.

6 **EXTEND** Tell your student that the article *the* points out specific nouns. Explain that *the* can be used with both singular nouns and **plural nouns.** Tell your student that plural nouns indicate more than one person, place, or thing. Give an example: *The boy ate the cookies.* Emphasize that *the* can refer to a specific person, place, or thing (such as the dog, the playground, the mayor, and so on). Ask your student to use *the* in two sentences, one with a singular noun and one with a plural noun.

7 **DISTRIBUTE** Distribute Student Learning Page 5.A. Invite your student to practice recognizing and using articles.

Branching Out

TEACHING TIP

It will help your student learn if you correctly demonstrate a concept. Point to different objects around the house. Have your student use *a*, *an*, or *the* before stating the name of the object. For *an*, you might use an egg, an ice cube, an air conditioner, an umbrella, and so on.

CHECKING IN

To assess your student's understanding of the lesson, ask him or her to point out *a*, *an*, and *the* in book and story titles. Help him or her see that the same rules apply for using articles in titles.

Use Articles

Complete the sentences with *a* or *an*.

1. We saw _____ clown at the circus.

2. She ate _____ ice-cream cone.

3. Wisconsin is _____ state in the Midwest.

4. _____ dog walked across the street.

5. She used _____ umbrella to stay dry.

6. I have _____ aunt.

7. _____ animal walked in front of us at the farm.

8. She made _____ pan of cookies.

These sentences have mistakes in them. Write each sentence the correct way.

9. A elephant has a long trunk.

   _____

10. The cat liked to chase an mouse.

   _____

11. We had a sandwich and a apple.

   _____

What's Next? You Decide!

Now it's your turn to choose what to do next in the lesson. Read the activities and decide which one you want to do—you may want to try them both!

Play a Game of That's Silly!

STEPS

Invite a family member or friend to play a game called That's Silly!

- ❑ One player makes up a sentence that uses an article either correctly or incorrectly. That person could say, "The cat ran from an dog."

- ❑ If the sentence is correct, then the other person says, "That's right!" If the sentence isn't correct, then the person says, "That's silly!"

- ❑ If the person says, "That's silly!" he or she needs to say the sentence the correct way. So that person would say, "That's silly! The correct way is 'The cat ran from a dog.'"

Read a Story

MATERIALS

- ❑ 1 children's story

STEPS

Writers use many articles in the stories they write.

- ❑ Fold a sheet of paper into three columns.

- ❑ Unfold the paper. Write "a" in the first column. Write "an" in the second column. Write "the" in the third column.

- ❑ Read a short children's story that you like.

- ❑ Look for *a, an,* and *the* in the story. When you see one of these articles, make a checkmark for it in the correct column on the paper.

- ❑ Keep doing this until you finish the story. Then count how many checkmarks you have in each column.

- ❑ Challenge a family member or friend to be an article finder, too!

Understanding Nouns

*Nouns surround us—we sleep on nouns, eat and drink nouns,
travel in nouns, and play with nouns!*

OBJECTIVE	BACKGROUND	MATERIALS
To help your student understand what nouns are and how they are used	Nouns are among the most important building blocks of the English language. Common nouns—those that aren't specific—are the general names of all the people, places, and things of our world. In this lesson, your student will learn what nouns are and what they name. He or she will also learn what plural nouns are and how to form them.	■ Student Learning Pages 6.A–6.B ■ 2 copies Writing Lines, page 355 ■ 1 copy Comparison Chart, page 353

VOCABULARY
NOUN a word that names a person, place, or thing **PLURAL NOUN** a word that names more than one person, place, or thing

Let's Begin

1 **INTRODUCE** Begin the lesson by explaining that a **noun** is a naming word. Nouns name people, places, and things. Ask, *Is the word* ball *the name of a person, place, or thing?* [yes] *Is* ball *a noun?* [yes] *Is the word* sing *the name of a person, place, or thing?* [no] *Is* sing *a noun?* [no] Ask your student to look around and name some of the objects he or she sees. Discuss the fact that the objects he or she named are things, and therefore, the words that name them are nouns. Give your student a copy of the Writing Lines found on page 355. Have your student spend 10 minutes writing the names of all nouns he or she can find in the room.

2 **DISCUSS** Talk with your student about the three categories of nouns. A noun can name a person, such as *mother* or *friend*. A noun can name a place, such as *hospital* or *park*. A noun can name a thing, such as *tree* or *book*. Have your student give his or her own examples of each noun category. Then invite your student to play a guessing game. Say, *I am a person. People come to me when they are sick. I try to cure them or make them feel better. Who am I?* [doctor] After your student guesses the answer, give another set of clues: *I am a thing. I have four legs and a tail. I can wag my tail. I like to eat bones. What am I?* [dog] Take turns with your student giving clues and guessing answers.

> **(!)**
> **A BRIGHT IDEA**
>
> Have your student choose a book. Give him or her enough time to read through the book. Then have your student look back over one of the pages in the book and point out the nouns in each sentence.

3 **ORGANIZE** In his or her notebook, have your student make a three-column chart titled "Nouns." Tell him or her to write the column headings "Person," "Place," and "Thing." Then have your student listen as you say the following words one by one: *chair, girl, city, table, father, mall, apple, airport,* and *neighbor.* Tell him or her to write each word in the correct column in his or her notebook. Invite your student to name additional words to categorize. Then distribute Student Learning Page 6.A.

4 **EXPLAIN** Explain that nouns can name more than one person, place, or thing. Such a noun is called a **plural noun.** For example, the noun *shoe* names one shoe. The noun *shoes* names more than one shoe. Ask, *What is the difference in spelling between the words* shoe *and* shoes? [*shoes* has an –*s* on the end] Explain that to make a noun plural, just add –*s* or –*es* to the end of the word. Use –*s* for most nouns. Use –*es* when the noun ends in *s, x, z, sh,* or *ch.* Have your student spell out the plural form of the nouns *watch, boat,* and *box.*

5 **DISTRIBUTE** To help your student understand plural nouns, give him or her a copy of the Comparison Chart found on page 353. Have him or her write these headings for the columns: "Noun," "One," and "More Than One." Help your student write these words in the Noun column: *dresses, brother, bus, dishes, aunt,* and *beach.* Then tell your student to put a check in the One column if the word names only one person, place, or thing. Have him or her put a check in the More Than One column if the word names more than one person, place, or thing.

6 **PRACTICE** Give your student more practice with plural nouns. On a second copy of the Writing Lines found on page 355, have your student write the plural form of each noun he or she wrote in Step 1.

Branching Out

TEACHING TIP

Many educators believe that children learn grammar best by seeing how words fit together in sentences. Reinforce the concept of nouns by having your student write sentences and then identify the nouns he or she wrote.

CHECKING IN

To assess your student's understanding of the lesson, ask him or her to make a list of all the nouns circled on Student Learning Page 6.A. Ask your student to tell whether the noun names a person, a place, or a thing. Then ask him or her whether the noun names one or more than one person, place, or thing.

Find the Nouns

Find the nouns in each sentence. Circle them. Then write the nouns in the box next to each sentence.

Sentences	Nouns
1. A brother and a sister like to go to the zoo.	
2. The boy always wants to see the lions.	
3. The girl likes to watch the seals play.	
4. Sometimes there are elephants.	
5. People eat in the park nearby.	

Draw your favorite zoo animal! Write its name below the picture. Then write a paragraph about the animal.

What's Next? You Decide!

Now it's your turn to choose what to do next in the lesson. Read the activities and decide which one you want to do—you may want to try them both!

Label Your Nouns!

MATERIALS

❑ sticky notes

STEPS

Make labels for things that are around you. They are all nouns!

❑ Look around. Decide what you want to label.

❑ Write the name of each thing on a sticky note. Use correct spelling.

❑ Put each label on the thing it names. Be sure to get permission before you put a label on anything!

❑ Show your family. Someone may want to take pictures!

❑ Take off all the labels. Stick them to sheets of paper.

❑ Display your labels where everyone can see them.

Play a Card Game

MATERIALS

❑ 24 index cards
❑ colored pencils

STEPS

Play a card game with nouns!

❑ Choose 12 nouns. Use two cards for each noun.

❑ On one card write a noun that names one person, place, or thing. On another card write the same noun so that it names more than one person, place, or thing.

❑ Play a game like Go Fish. Mix up your cards. Hand out six cards to each player. Put the rest of the cards facedown in a pile.

❑ Try to make pairs of nouns that match, such as *sock* and *socks*. Players ask for cards. For example, a player might ask, "Do you have *sock*?" Or players take cards from the pile.

❑ The first player to make three pairs wins the game!

Working with Compound Words

When you study compound words, you learn that some words are meant for each other.

OBJECTIVE	BACKGROUND	MATERIALS
To have your student identify and use compound words	Compound words are made by joining together two smaller words. For example, the word *cupcake* is a compound word. Understanding compound words will increase your student's vocabulary as well as improve his or her spelling skills. In this lesson, your student will identify and use compound words.	▪ Student Learning Pages 7.A–7.B ▪ children's books or magazines

VOCABULARY
COMPOUND WORDS words made by joining together two smaller words to make one new word

Let's Begin

1 **INTRODUCE** Begin this lesson by writing the following rhyme on a sheet of paper. Then read the rhyme out loud to your student.

> Football, rainbow, mailbox, and campground,
> Two words together can make a compound.
> Birdhouse, popcorn, bathtub, eyebrow,
> Listen, watch and we'll learn how.

Have your student repeat each line after you read it.

2 **REVEAL** Tell your student that he or she is going to learn how to recognize and make **compound words.** Explain that compound words are made by joining together two smaller words to make one new word. Ask your student to look at the rhyme and try to identify all eight compound words. [*football, rainbow, mailbox, campground, birdhouse, popcorn, bathtub,* and *eyebrow*]

3 **MODEL** Ask your student to write the eight compound words in the rhyme. Then challenge him or her to identify the smaller words that make up the compound words. Have your student

ENRICH THE EXPERIENCE

Some children have kinesthetic and auditory learning styles. Reading the rhyme to your student will help him or her learn by using auditory skills. You can also make up hand movements to go along with the words if your student is a kinesthetic learner.

verbally create a word equation for each compound word. For example, your student would say, *the word* football *equals* foot *plus* ball.

4 **EXTEND** Tell your student that knowing the meaning of the smaller words can help them learn the meaning of the compound words they form. For example, if your student knows what the words *bird* and *house* mean, he or she can figure out that a birdhouse is a house or shelter for a bird. Review some other compound words with your student. Challenge him or her to use the meanings of the smaller words to figure out the meanings of the compound words they form.

5 **THINK** Invite your student to think of some compound words and share them out loud. To make the activity more interactive, take turns identifying compound words with your student. Write down the words to create a list of at least eight compound words.

6 **DISCUSS** Discuss with your student how many texts we read have compound words. Give your student some children's books or magazines. Ask him or her to look through some passages and find compound words.

7 **REVIEW** Have your student explain to you what a compound word is. Then distribute Student Learning Page 7.A. Invite your student to practice recognizing and using compound words.

Branching Out

TEACHING TIP

Explain to your student that compound words must be real words that make sense. For example, *book* and *cup* are real words. However, when these words are joined, they form *bookcup*, which is not a real word and doesn't make sense.

CHECKING IN

To assess your student's understanding of the lesson, give him or her index cards on which are the words *cup, book, snow, out, mark, cake, side,* and *man*. Ask your student to match two cards to make a compound word. Your student will create the compound words *cupcake, bookmark, snowman,* and *outside*.

FOR FURTHER READING

Grammar Skills: 2nd Grade Mastering Basic Skills, by Deborah Morris and Larry Morris (Rainbow Bridge Publishing, 2002).

Jumpstart Reading and Writing: 2nd Grade, by Lisa Trunbauer (Scholastic Trade, 2000).

Write Away, by Dave Kemper, Ruth Nathan, Patrick Sebranek, and Carol Elsholz (Houghton Mifflin, 2002).

Explore Compound Words

Divide the compound word into two smaller words. Draw a picture for each part. The first one has been done for you.

1. cupcake   =   <u>cup</u>   +   <u>cake</u>

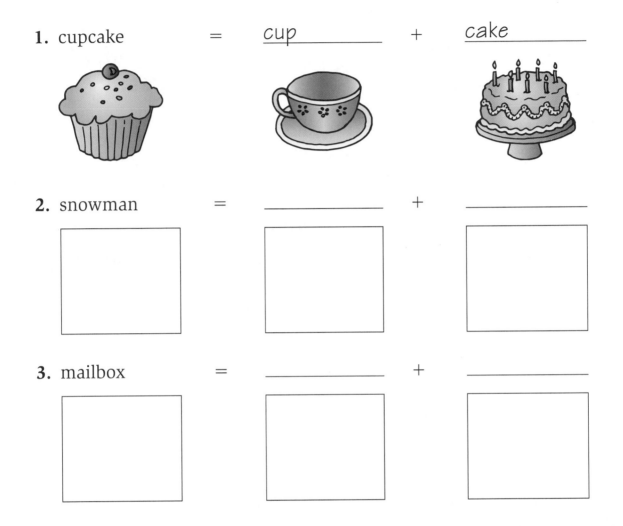

2. snowman   =   _____   +   _____

3. mailbox   =   _____   +   _____

Match the words to make compound words. Check each word in a dictionary.

4. star _____   **A.** brush

5. tooth _____   **B.** wear

6. sand _____   **C.** fish

7. under _____   **D.** time

8. day _____   **E.** box

Student Learning Page 7.A: Explore Compound Words   **41**

What's Next? You Decide!

Now it's your turn to choose what to do next in the lesson. Read the activities and decide which one you want to do— you may want to try them both!

Play a Compound Word Game

MATERIALS

❏ index cards

STEPS

Invite a family member or friend to play this compound word game.

❏ Write these words on index cards: *rain, coat, snow, flake, paint, brush, star, fish, ice, cream, bath, tub, pop, corn, play,* and *ground.*

❏ Mix up the cards. Give eight cards to each player.

❏ Each player should make as many compound words with his or her cards as possible.

❏ Write down the number of compound words each player makes in a round. Each real compound word scores one point.

❏ Play three more rounds. Repeat the steps above.

❏ The player with the most points after four rounds wins!

Write a Compound Word Poem

MATERIALS

❏ 1 sheet construction paper
❏ markers or crayons

STEPS

Practice using compound words in poetry.

❏ Write a poem about anything you wish. You can write about your favorite things, your family, your pet, a certain place—anything.

❏ Use as many compound words as you can in your poem.

❏ You can use words that rhyme in your poem, such as *see* and *tree.* Or your poem doesn't have to rhyme at all.

❏ Decorate your poem when you're done. Make a fun border. Draw pictures to show the compound words or other things in the poem.

❏ Read the poem to family and friends. Tell them to listen for the compound words.

Reading Folktales

Folktales teach us pearls of wisdom that are timeless.

OBJECTIVE	BACKGROUND	MATERIALS
To help your student read a folktale and write an ending for a story	Folktales are an important part of many cultures. Many of these stories are told from generation to generation as part of an oral tradition. Folktales often teach a lesson or moral, so they may also reflect the values and beliefs of the cultures they come from. In this lesson, your student will read a folktale and learn about the characteristics of the genre.	■ Student Learning Pages 8.A–8.C ■ 1 dictionary

VOCABULARY
FOLKTALE a traditional story told from generation to generation

Let's Begin

1 **INTRODUCE** Tell your student that the story he or she is about to read is a **folktale** called *The Secret Room*. A folktale is a traditional story that is told from generation to generation. A folktale often teaches a lesson or shows a value or belief. Explain to your student that he or she can sometimes guess what a story will be about by reading the title. Ask him or her to predict an idea that may be in the selection based on its title. [a mystery; finding out about something that was hidden]

2 **READ** Distribute Student Learning Page 8.A. Invite your student to read the selection out loud. Provide guidance as necessary.

3 **REFLECT** Explain to your student that most stories have characters, a setting, and a plot. Remind your student that to identify these elements he or she should consider the following questions: Ask, *Who is in the story?* [the king, man with a beard, chief counselor] *Where did the story happen?* [in the desert, in the kingdom] *What happened in the beginning of the story?* [the bearded man answered a question for the king] *What happened in the middle of the story?* [the bearded man is invited to be treasurer, the chief counselor becomes jealous and accuses him of stealing] *What happened at the end of the story?* [the king saw how wise the bearded man was and made him chief counselor]

4 **BUILD VOCABULARY** Point out to your student that he or she will sometimes read a story with unfamiliar words. Ask your student to name a way he or she can learn the meanings of new words. [look up the words in a dictionary] Explain that sometimes the other words in a sentence give clues about the meaning of an unknown word. Invite your student to look for these words in the text: *shrewd, influence, envy,* and *clever.* Ask him or her to circle each word and think about what it might mean. Have him or her give a possible definition based on the words around it. Then help your student look up these three words in a dictionary and compare his or her guess with a dictionary definition.

5 **EXPAND** Tell your student that sometimes "sayings" or phrases that he or she reads don't mean exactly what they say. Point out the phrase "because my head is older than my beard" at the beginning of the reading selection. Explain that literally this phrase would mean that his beard isn't old enough to turn gray yet. The actual meaning of the phrase refers to how wise the man is. Now look at the saying toward the end of the selection, "But I must not get too full of myself." Ask your student what he or she thinks it means. Then reveal that this saying means that the man doesn't want to think that he is better than anyone else because he has these honors and riches. Together with your student think of common sayings and help him or her determine their literal and actual meanings.

6 **RETELL** Distribute Student Learning Page 8.B. Explain that sometimes it's easier to understand a story by retelling it through pictures or words.

7 **CONCLUDE AND CONNECT** Explain to your student that authors don't always explain everything to the reader. The reader can use clues from the story to draw conclusions, or figure out information. Ask, *What kind of person is the king?* [smart, trusting] *What is most important to the chief counselor?* [being the best] *What is most important to the bearded man?* [being himself] Have a discussion about why it was important to the bearded man to be himself.

A BRIGHT IDEA

Go to the library with your student and find more than one version of the same folktale. Read the different versions and compare and contrast them with your student.

FOR FURTHER READING

Adventures of Spider: West African Folktales, by Joyce Cooper Arkhurst (Little Brown and Company, 1999).

Golden Tales: Myths, Legends, and Folktales from Latin America, by Lulu Delacre (Scholastic Paperbacks, 2001).

Stories to Solve: Folktales from Around the World, by George Shannon, R. A. Katcher, ed., and Peter Sis, ill. (HarperCollins Children's Books, 2000).

Branching Out

TEACHING TIP

Talk with your student about what the moral of the story is. Talk about what the moral means to us today, in everyday life.

CHECKING IN

To assess understanding of the lesson, read another folktale with your student. Ask him or her to identify the setting, characters, and plot.

Enjoy a Folktale

The Secret Room
by Uri Shulevitz

One day a king was traveling through the desert. There he met a man. "Why is your head gray and your beard black?"

"Because my head is older than my beard." The king was pleased with the man's reply. "You must not tell this to anyone until you have seen my face ninety-nine times," the king ordered.

When the king returned home, he asked his chief counselor: "Why does a man's hair turn gray before his beard?" The chief counselor didn't know why. And he was not clever enough to figure it out. But he was shrewd. He asked one of the king's companions where they had traveled. Then he rode out into the desert and found the man. "Why is your head gray and your beard black?"

"I cannot tell you," said the man.

"I am the king's chief counselor. If you don't tell me, I'll have you thrown in prison. If you do, I'll give you one thousand gold coins."

"Ninety-nine copper coins will do," said the man. The chief counselor gave him the money and got the answer. "What a fool that man is, to have asked for so little."

When the chief counselor answered the king's question, the king summoned the man at once. "You have disobeyed me."

(CONTINUED) ➤

"But, your Majesty, I followed your orders," said the man.

"How so?" asked the king.

"I did not tell him until I'd seen your Majesty's face ninety-nine times—on these coins," said the man. The king was so impressed with the man's cleverness that he appointed him treasurer. And the man served the king diligently. In time, the king came to value his advice in all matters and rewarded him handsomely. As the man's influence grew, so did the chief counselor's envy. Day and night he thought: I must get rid of that man.

So he accused the man of stealing gold from the treasury and hiding it in his house. When the king heard this, he went to the man's house. They searched for a long time but found nothing. Then the chief counselor discovered a door that was locked. "Aha!" he said. "A secret room!" The king ordered the man to unlock the door. But the room was empty.

The king was astonished. "What is this secret room?"

"Your Majesty, I am grateful for all the honors and riches you have given me," said the man. "But I must not get too full of myself.

"So I come every day to this room to remind myself that I am still the same man with the gray head and the black beard whom you once met in the desert."

"I knew you were clever," said the king. "Now I know you are wise." He dismissed the chief counselor and appointed the man in his place.

Draw a Story Map

Draw pictures in the squares or fill in the missing words to tell the story of *The Secret Room*.

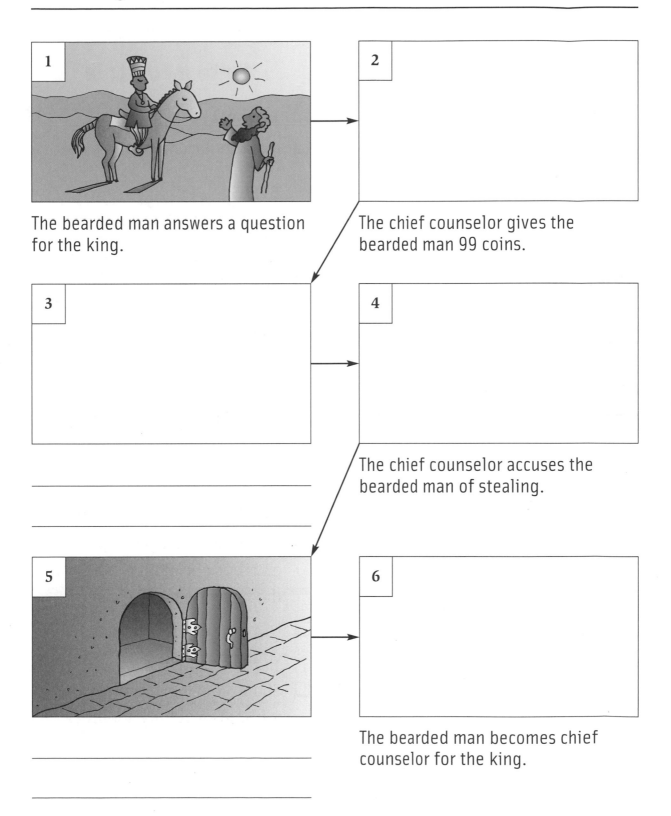

1

The bearded man answers a question for the king.

2

The chief counselor gives the bearded man 99 coins.

3

_____

_____

4

The chief counselor accuses the bearded man of stealing.

5

_____

_____

6

The bearded man becomes chief counselor for the king.

What's Next? You Decide!

Now it's your turn to choose what to do next in the lesson. Read the activities and decide which one you want to do—you may want to try them both!

Act It Out

MATERIALS

❏ 1 blanket or sheet

❏ 1 walking stick

❏ 1 crown made from construction paper

STEPS

Act out *The Secret Room*.

❏ Gather the materials you need.

❏ Use the blanket as a costume for the chief counselor, the walking stick for the bearded man, and the crown for the king.

❏ Act out the story.

❏ Use a different voice for each character and change costumes.

❏ Perform the play for your family.

Write a Folktale

MATERIALS

❏ markers or crayons

STEPS

Write a folktale that you have heard.

❏ Think about a story that someone told you that teaches a lesson.

❏ Write down your idea of the story. You can change some of the characters and things that happen.

❏ Make sure you start each sentence with a capital letter.

❏ Make sure you put a period or other end punctuation at the end of each sentence.

❏ Draw a picture that goes with your new ending.

❏ Share your new ending with a friend or family member.

Examining Poetry and Writing in a Journal

A poem grows from a person's unique response to our world.

OBJECTIVE	BACKGROUND	MATERIALS
To have your student interpret a poem and write his or her own poem	Poetry is a condensed form of literature. Poets often use vivid words and descriptions to express strong feelings and to help readers form images. A poem is usually made up of groups of lines called stanzas. There are many different ways to write a poem. Poems may include words that rhyme or words that don't rhyme. In this lesson, your student will interpret a poem and write a poem in response to the world around him or her.	■ Student Learning Pages 9.A–9.B

VOCABULARY
POETRY a type of writing that uses images and patterns to express feelings

Let's Begin

1 **INTRODUCE** Invite your student to think about when he or she sneezes. Then have your student describe the experience in a short journal entry. Ask, *Does your nose tickle? Do you sneeze when you smell certain things?* When your student has finished, ask him or her to read the journal entry out loud.

2 **EXPLAIN** Tell your student that writing a journal entry and drawing a picture are two ways to show one's feelings or ideas. Explain that another way to express emotions and thoughts is through writing **poetry.** Tell your student that poetry is a type of writing that uses images and patterns to express feelings. Explain that many poems include rhyming words. Tell your student that rhyming words have the same ending sound, such as *bat* and *hat.* Invite your student to say a word that rhymes with *run.* Then ask him or her to write four pairs of rhyming words.

3 **DISTRIBUTE** Distribute Student Learning Page 9.A. Read the title of the poem and the poet's name out loud. Tell your student that when reading poetry it's important to watch for commas and other punctuation. Have your student circle all of the punctuation in the poem.

Examining Poetry and Writing in a Journal **49**

4 **READ** Invite your student to read the poem out loud twice. Ask your student to pause when he or she comes to a punctuation mark. Remember to be patient as he or she encounters any new words. You may want to help your student sound out the words that he or she found challenging. After the poem has been read, ask your student to write how he or she feels about the poem in a journal entry.

5 **EXPLORE** Have your student write down all the rhyming words he or she can find in the poem. Encourage your student to see that there are five sets of rhyming words [those that rhyme with *tickle*; those that rhyme with *shiver*; those that rhyme with *wiggle*; those that rhyme with *tease*; and those that rhyme with *guess*] Now read the poem out loud to your student. Before reading, tell him or her to listen to the different rhyming sounds that he or she hears, and to see if he or she can notice how they're grouped together.

6 **PRACTICE** Tell your student that now it's his or her turn to write a poem. Have your student write a poem about anything he or she chooses. If your student can't think of a topic right away, suggest writing about a hobby, a pet, a favorite place, or an animal. If you'd like, go to http://www.gigglepoetry.com for fun ideas. Allow time for your student to write. Review your student's work for correct spelling and punctuation. Help him or her make changes if necessary. Ask your student to read his or her finished poem out loud.

TAKE A BREAK

Poetry often reflects how people respond to the world around them. Take your student for a walk outside and ask him or her to pay attention to what he or she sees, hears, smells, and feels. Invite your student to describe his or her reactions to you.

Branching Out

TEACHING TIP

If your student is lacking motivation for learning a particular concept, it's probably because he or she is struggling with it. Offer your student a lot of praise at each step of the lesson so he or she realizes that progress is being made.

CHECKING IN

To assess your student's understanding of the lesson, play a rhyming game. Write the word *play* at the top of a sheet of paper. Invite your student to write down all the words he or she can think of that rhyme with *play*. Be sure your student writes actual words that rhyme with *play*, rather than made-up words (such as *stay* not *zay*).

FOR FURTHER READING

The Random House Book of Poetry for Children, by Jack Prelutsky (Random House, 2000).

Stories and Poems for Extremely Intelligent Children of All Ages, by Harold Bloom (Scribner, 2001).

Writing Activities Just for Young Learners, by Martin Lee and Marcia Miller (Scholastic Professional Books, 2001).

Discover Poetry

Sneeze
by Maxine Kumin

There's a sort of a tickle
the size of a nickel,
a bit like the prickle
of sweet-sour pickle;

it's a quivery shiver
the shape of a sliver,
like eels in a river;

a kind of a wiggle
that starts as a jiggle
and joggles its way to a tease,

which I cannot suppress
any longer, I guess,
so pardon me, please, while I sneeze.

What's Next? You Decide!

Now it's your turn to choose what to do next in the lesson. Read the activities and decide which one you want to do— you may want to try them both!

Sing a Poem

MATERIALS

❏ 1 audiocassette recorder (optional)

❏ 1 audiocassette tape (optional)

STEPS

Songs are poems that are sung. See (and sing) for yourself!

❏ Think of the words to your favorite song.

❏ Read the words out loud without singing them. Does it sound like a poem?

❏ If possible, sing the song or say the song as you record it on a tape recorder.

❏ Play, say, or sing the song for your friends and family.

Write an Acrostic Poem

MATERIALS

❏ markers, crayons, or colored pencils

STEPS

The first letters of the lines of an acrostic poem are the letters of a name. Write an acrostic poem for your name or for someone else's name.

❏ Write each letter of the person's first name in a column. Look at the example for the name *Kim*.

❏ Write a poem about the person. Each line of the poem should begin with a letter in the name.

❏ Write the first letter of each line in a different color so the name stands out.

❏ Share your acrostic poem with family and friends.

Kind and sweet

Is nice to meet

My best friend, Kim

Exploring Biographies

The lives of brave and fascinating people have shaped the history of our world.

OBJECTIVE	BACKGROUND	MATERIALS
To have your student learn about biographies and read an excerpt from a biography	Biographies tell us more than the mere facts and events of someone's life. They give us a picture of the culture and historical time period in which the person lived. In this lesson, your student will read an excerpt from a biography and identify the elements of the genre.	■ Student Learning Pages 10.A–10.C ■ 1 favorite biography or book (with a title page, a table of contents, and images with captions)

VOCABULARY

BIOGRAPHY a true story about a person's life

EVENTS things that happen

SETTLERS people who make their home in a new place

SETTLEMENT the village or town where settlers live

Let's Begin

1 **INTRODUCE** Begin the lesson by telling your student that the name of the story he or she is going to read is *Pocahontas*. Explain that the story is a **biography.** A biography is a true story about a person's life. It gives facts about the person and tells about the **events** the person experienced. Then distribute Student Learning Page 10.A. Have your student read the story out loud. Be prepared to guide his or her reading as necessary.

2 **DISCUSS** Talk with your student about the meanings of any words in the story he or she doesn't know. Point out the words **settlers** and **settlement** in the story. Tell your student that both of these words have the word *settle* in them. Ask, *What does* settle *mean?* [to make a home in a new place] *What does* settlers *mean?* [people who make their home in a new place] *What does* settlement *mean?* [the village or town where settlers live] Have your student write these words and their definitions in his or her notebook.

3 **CONNECT** Have your student discuss what he or she learned about Pocahontas's life. Ask, *When was she born?* [around 1595]

! A BRIGHT IDEA

Visit the Biography.com Web site at http://www. biography.com and follow the link to the classroom section where you can find biographies about famous people to read with your student.

Where did she live? [in the area that's now Virginia] *What happened when she was about 12?* [men from England came and built Jamestown] Invite your student to share ideas about how his or her life is similar to and different from Pocahontas's life.

4 **DISCOVER** Explain that a main idea is one of the most important ideas about a topic. Details are facts about a main idea. Ask, *What is one main idea in the biography you just read?* [Pocahontas was a Native American girl in early American history] *What are some details about the main idea?* [her father was Powhatan, a great chief; she was born around 1595; her real name was Matoaka]

5 **REVIEW AND RELATE** Review with your student the most important facts and events about Pocahontas's life. Discuss how he or she would summarize what happened when Pocahontas was young and what happened when she got older. Then have your student retell the most important parts of the biography, including the way it ended, in his or her own words.

6 **WRITE** Distribute Student Learning Page 10.B. Invite your student to write a biography about his or her hero. Encourage your student to write the events of the person's life in the order in which they happened. Help your student check his or her biography for correct spelling, grammar, and sentence structure.

7 **EXPAND** Have your student look at one of his or her favorite biographies or books. Introduce your student to the different parts of a book. Begin with the title of the book. Show your student the title and the author's name on the title page. Show your student the table of contents and tell him or her that this is a list of the things that can be found in the book. Finally, show your student the captions found near images in the book. Have your student go through the book and identify and explain the title page, the table of contents, and the captions.

Branching Out

TEACHING TIP

Help your student connect reading with his or her own interests. For example, if your student is interested in horses, you might help him or her find biographies about famous jockeys or Pony Express riders.

CHECKING IN

To assess your student's understanding of the lesson, ask him or her to choose a biography to read. Ask your student to explain why the story is a biography. Then ask him or her to identify the main ideas and supporting details.

ENRICH THE EXPERIENCE

Your student might enjoy the PBS animated adventure series called *Liberty's Kids.* It introduces children to the people and stories behind the birth of our nation.

FOR FURTHER READING

Author: A True Story, by Helen Lester (Houghton Mifflin, 2002).

Don't Know Much About the Presidents, by Kenneth C. Davis (HarperCollins Children's Books, 2001).

Salt in His Shoes: Michael Jordan in Pursuit of a Dream, by Deloris Jordan (Simon and Schuster, 2000).

Read a Biography

Pocahontas
by Lucia Raatma

Pocahontas was the daughter of a Native American chief. She helped the English **settlers** who came to live in America. She was an important person in early American history.

Pocahontas was born around 1595, before the United States became a country. She lived in an area that is now called Virginia.

Her father, Powhatan, was a great Indian chief. He ruled thirty tribes.

(CONTINUED)

Student Learning Page 10.A: Read a Biography

Pocahontas's real name was Matoaka. Only members of her tribe called her by that name. *Pocahontas,* her nickname, meant "playful little girl." She loved to play in the woods near her village.

When Pocahontas was about twelve years old, her life changed. Men from England came from across the sea. They built a **settlement** called Jamestown. It was near Pocahontas's village.

For a few years, Pocahontas helped to keep peace between the English settlers and her people. The English did not have enough food. Pocahontas brought food to Jamestown.

Write About Your Hero

Write a biography about your hero. A hero is a person who has done something great. Your hero can also be a person you want to be like.

_____

_____

_____

_____

_____

_____

_____

_____

_____

_____

_____

_____

_____

What's Next? You Decide!

Now it's your turn to choose what to do next in the lesson. Read the activities and decide which one you want to do—you may want to try them both!

Make a Pocahontas Poster

MATERIALS

❑ 1 posterboard
❑ markers, crayons, or colored pencils

STEPS

Show the story of Pocahontas's life on a poster.

❑ Reread the story of Pocahontas. Decide what events you would like to show on your poster.
❑ Draw pictures that show the events.
❑ Write a sentence under each picture telling what the picture shows.
❑ Color the pictures with markers, crayons, or colored pencils.
❑ Ask to display your poster so everyone in your family can see it.

Interview a Person

MATERIALS

❑ 1 audiocassette recorder (optional)
❑ 1 audiocassette tape (optional)

STEPS

You can learn about a person's life by asking him or her questions. This is called an interview.

❑ Think of a family member or friend you would like to learn more about. Ask the person if you can interview him or her.
❑ Think of some questions to ask the person.
❑ Write or have an adult help you write the questions.
❑ Meet with the person for your interview. Then ask your questions.
❑ If you can, record your interview on a tape recorder. Ask an adult to help you.
❑ If you can't record the interview, write a paragraph that tells what you learned.

Reading Nonfiction

*The world is an amazing place. Discover
more about it by reading nonfiction!*

OBJECTIVE	BACKGROUND	MATERIALS
To have your student read and summarize a piece of nonfiction writing	Nonfiction writing tells about real people, places, things, and events. Students often read nonfiction writing in subject areas, such as science, history, as well as literature. In this lesson, your student will read a nonfiction piece of writing and learn to identify the characteristics of the genre.	■ Student Learning Pages 11.A–11.C ■ markers, crayons, or colored pencils

VOCABULARY

NONFICTION writing that tells about real people, places, things, and events

FACTS information about something that is true

OPINIONS beliefs or thoughts about something

Let's Begin

1 **INTRODUCE** Begin this lesson by writing the heading "Bat" at the top of a sheet of paper. Divide the area below the heading into a three-column KWL Chart. At the top of the first column write "What I Know." At the top of the second column write "What I Want to Know." Finally, above the third column write "What I Learned." Ask your student what he or she knows about bats and write his or her ideas in the first column.

2 **QUESTION** Ask your student to think of questions he or she has about bats. Write his or her questions in the middle column of the chart. If your student isn't really clear on what a bat is, show him or her a picture of one from the Internet or an encyclopedia. Tell your student that he or she is going to read a **nonfiction** article about bats. Explain that nonfiction writing tells about real people, places, things, and events. Invite your student to name something a person might learn from reading a nonfiction article.

3 **READ** Direct your student to Student Learning Page 11.A. Read out loud the selection's title, *Beautiful Bats*. Tell your student that words in titles and headings can sometimes help readers guess information. Ask your student to guess something that he

FOR FURTHER READING

Jump Start Entering 2nd Grade, by Lisa Trumbauer (Scholastic, 2002).

A Life Like Mine: How Children Live Around the World, by Amanda Rayner (DK Publishing, 2002).

What the Moon Is Like, by Franklyn M. Branley (HarperCollins Children's Books, 2000).

or she might learn from reading the article. Then guide your student as he or she begins reading the selection. Invite your student to pause if he or she doesn't understand a word. Encourage your student to use the words around an unfamiliar word to guess its meaning.

4 **DRAW CONCLUSIONS** Explain that readers can use clues in a text to figure things out. Help your student use textual information to draw conclusions about bats. For example, the author writes that bats sleep during the day. Point out this detail. Ask, *What can you figure out about bats if you know they sleep during the day?* [bats are active at night] Then ask, *The author writes that bats have wings. What can you figure out about bats if you know they have wings?* [they can fly]

5 **CONNECT AND COMPARE** Invite your student to share what he or she has learned about bats by reading the selection. Write his or her responses in the third column of the chart. Look at all three columns with your student. Invite your student to connect his or her prior knowledge of bats to the new knowledge. Help your student identify how his or her ideas about bats have changed after reading *Beautiful Bats.* Then have your student use the third column of the chart to summarize the selection. Ask your student to use his or her own words to tell you the most important parts of *Beautiful Bats.*

6 **EXPAND** Introduce **facts** and **opinions** to your student. Explain that a fact is information about something that is true, and an opinion is a person's belief or thought about something. For example, the information about bats in this lesson's selection, *Beautiful Bats,* is factual. If you were to make the statement, "Bats are scary," that would be an opinion. Ask your student to make a few statements of fact about bats that he or she learned. Then have him or her make a few statements of opinion about bats. Then distribute Student Learning Page 11.B. Invite your student to write a book report for *Beautiful Bats.* Tell him or her that the book report should explain the most important information in the selection.

Branching Out

TEACHING TIP

Comparing and contrasting information can help your student build background and context. Ask your student to tell how bats are similar to and different from another type of flying animal, such as a bird.

CHECKING IN

Ask your student to suppose he or she works at a library. There is a reader at the library who doesn't understand nonfiction. Ask your student to tell how he or she would explain nonfiction to this reader.

Investigate Nonfiction

Beautiful Bats
by Linda Glaser

Little Brown Bats are shy, gentle animals with strong toes and big ears and round black eyes. On both sides of their small, furry bodies, they have wings that open large and wide.

Their wings don't have feathers like a bird's. Their wings have a stretchy, rubbery skin. And when bats fly, they shape their wings to swoop and soar and dart and dive.

Bats are found in all parts of the world.

(CONTINUED)

They zip and zigzag through the air swirling spirals in the sky.

Little Brown Bats sleep during the day, hanging upside down from their toes.

Their wings look like tiny umbrellas that are neatly folded closed.

They sleep inside caves or hollow trees, in empty attics or wooden bat houses.

They fly out of their roosts and into the air, flitting in and out of sight.

They zip and swoop and dart and dive, hunting for little bugs to eat.

They catch hundreds of mosquitoes and other bugs, and they eat them as they fly.

To zip around in the black of night, they use their ears and their voices.

They click-click-click and chatter and chirp. Then they listen for the echoes of their calls.

They follow the echoes of their click-click-clicks to find their way through the darkness.

But their clicks are too high for people to hear.

Write a Book Report

PROMOTING
LITERACY

ing 11.B

Write a book report for *Beautiful Bats* on the lines. Then draw a picture in the box or on a separate sheet of paper.

Beautiful Bats is about _____

_____

_____

_____

_____

_____

_____

_____

_____

_____

_____

_____

_____

_____

_____

What's Next? You Decide!

Now it's your turn to choose what to do next in the lesson. Read the activities and decide which one you want to do—you may want to try them both!

Write Nonfiction

■ MATERIALS

- ❏ several sheets construction paper
- ❏ 1 stapler

■ STEPS

Share what you know by writing nonfiction.

- ❏ Choose something you know how to do. Do you know how to make a sandwich or brush your teeth?
- ❏ Now explain how to do the activity you chose. Write each step of the activity on a separate sheet of construction paper.
- ❏ Draw pictures next to each step to show what you have to do.
- ❏ Make a cover for your book. Then ask an adult to help you staple each sheet of paper together.
- ❏ Share your nonfiction book with a family member or friend.

Work at the Zoo

■ MATERIALS

- ❏ 1 posterboard
- ❏ markers, crayons, or colored pencils
- ❏ 1 small sheet construction paper
- ❏ tape

■ STEPS

Suppose you are a zookeeper at a zoo.

- ❏ Draw a large bat on posterboard.
- ❏ Write your name on a small sheet of construction paper.
- ❏ Tape it to your shirt so visitors at the zoo know who you are.
- ❏ Invite friends and family to visit your zoo.
- ❏ Show them the picture of the bat.
- ❏ Then tell your visitors everything you know about bats.

Using Conjunctions

*Conjunctions allow us to connect a stream
of ideas as we speak and write.*

OBJECTIVE	BACKGROUND	MATERIALS
To teach your student how common conjunctions are used in sentences	A conjunction is a word that connects other words, phrases, or sentences. Some examples of frequently used conjunctions are *and, or,* and *but.* It's important to know how to use conjunctions correctly because they allow writers to smoothly combine ideas in sentences. In this lesson, your student will learn how to identify and use conjunctions.	■ Student Learning Pages 12.A–12.B ■ glue ■ 13 index cards (optional)

VOCABULARY
CONJUNCTIONS words that connect other words, phrases, or sentences

Let's Begin

1   **REVIEW** Ask your student to give an example of a noun and a verb. Remind him or her that nouns name a person, place, or thing. A verb shows the action of a sentence. (Refer to Lessons 1.4, 1.6, and 1.7 for a review of nouns and verbs.) Read the following sentence out loud to your student and invite him or her to write it in a notebook.

>   Tomas and Ava swim and run every day.

   Ask your student to circle the nouns [*Tomas, Ava, day*] and underline the verbs [*swim, run*] in the sentence.

2   **DEFINE** Explain to your student that he or she will be learning about a part of speech called **conjunctions,** which are words that connect other words, phrases, or sentences. As a visual aid, break a pencil in half. Help your student see that each of the two pieces can still be sharpened and used to write, but they work better as a whole. Invite your student to use glue to reconnect the two pieces. Explain that conjunctions act like glue, connecting words, phrases, and sentences. Ask your student to repeat: *Conjunctions are like glue.*

3   **IDENTIFY** Invite your student to look back at the sentence from Step 1. Point out the words that are not circled or underlined. Tell your student that the word *and* is a conjunction. In this

---

ENRICH THE EXPERIENCE

Your student might enjoy the Kidnews.com Web site, which can be found at http://www. kidnews.com. This site includes articles and stories written by children. Have your student identify conjunctions in what he or she reads on the site.

sentence, it's used to connect two nouns and two verbs. Invite your student to point out which nouns and verbs are connected by the conjunction *and*.

4 **EXTEND** Explain that *or* is another conjunction that often appears between two nouns or verbs. Tell your student that *or* is sometimes used to point out a choice. Ask your student to listen as you read the following sentences:

> You can have an orange and an apple.
> You can have an orange or an apple.

Tell your student that the meaning of the second sentence changes when the conjunction *and* is replaced by *or*. Have a discussion with your student about the differences caused by changing the conjunctions.

5 **EXPAND** Inform your student that *but* is another commonly used conjunction. It's usually used to combine two sentences with different or contrasting ideas. An example is *Marissa wants to go to the party, but she has to work.* Invite your student to use the word *but* to combine the following pairs of sentences:

> I want to get ice cream. I don't have any money.
> Jake fed the dog. The dog won't eat the food.

Then provide practice in using conjunctions by distributing Student Learning Page 12.A.

6 **PLAY** Play a conjunction game with your student. Write five nouns and five verbs on ten separate index cards. Then write the conjunctions *and, or,* and *but* on three separate index cards. Lay the cards facedown in three separate piles. Have your student choose one card from each pile and use the words to make up a sentence. Have your student write the sentence in his or her notebook. Replace and mix up the cards between each turn. Encourage your student to be creative when making his or her sentences.

Branching Out

TEACHING TIP

Help your student understand the importance and frequency of conjunctions in everyday language. Call attention to the conjunctions that he or she uses. Invite your student to rephrase sentences without conjunctions and note the differences in meaning and sense.

CHECKING IN

To assess your student's understanding of the lesson, make a copy of a poem or short story that has conjunctions. Invite your student to read through the excerpt and highlight the places where conjunctions are used.

GET ORGANIZED

As your student learns about different parts of speech, record them in a chart on a poster. List the parts of speech, their definitions, and example sentences with the parts of speech underlined. Your student can use this resource throughout his or her grammar instruction.

FOR FURTHER READING

Fantastic! Wow! And Unreal! A Book About Interjections and Conjunctions, by Joy Peskin, ed. (Puffin, 2000).

Parts of Speech (*Classroom Helpers*), by Sara Freeman, Mary Hassinger, Alyson Kieda, and Kathryn Wheeler, eds. (Frank Schaffer Publications, 2002).

Silly Sentences: Grammar Skills Practice for the First Three Years of School (DK Publishing, 2000).

Write Sentences
with Conjunctions

Read the phrases. Each has an *and* or an *or*. Write sentences using each phrase on the lines.

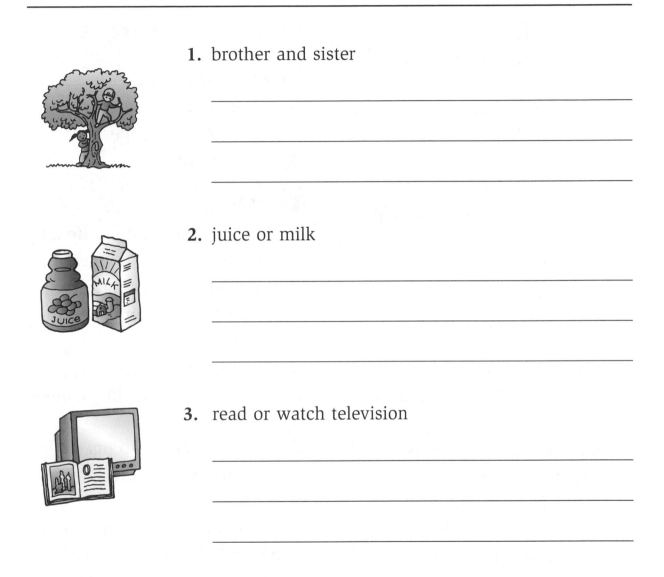

1. brother and sister

_____

_____

_____

2. juice or milk

_____

_____

_____

3. read or watch television

_____

_____

_____

4. shoes and socks

_____

_____

_____

What's Next? You Decide!

Now it's your turn to choose what to do next in the lesson. Read the activities and decide which one you want to do—you may want to try them both!

Make a Conjunction Mobile

MATERIALS

❏ 1 bottle glue
❏ 1 hanger
❏ 1 piece cardboard
❏ markers, crayons, or colored pencils
❏ string
❏ 1 hole puncher
❏ 1 pair scissors

STEPS

❏ Trace the bottle of glue three times on the cardboard. Cut out the glue-bottle shapes.
❏ Write a different conjunction on the front of each cutout.
❏ On the back of each cutout, write a sentence with each conjunction.
❏ Decorate both sides of the glue-bottle cutouts.
❏ Punch a hole through the top of each cutout. Thread string through each hole and tie it. Tie the other end to the hanger.

Create a Sentence Puzzle

MATERIALS

❏ sentence strips (or long sheets of construction paper)
❏ 1 pair scissors

STEPS

❏ On a sentence strip, write a sentence with a conjunction.
❏ Cut the sentence apart. Each word should be on its own section.
❏ Mix up the words.
❏ Give them to a family member or friend.
❏ Ask your partner to put the sentence back in the correct order.
❏ Then have your partner make a puzzle for you.
❏ Think of some silly sentences to write.
❏ Who can come up with the silliest sentence?

PROMOTING LITERACY

LESSON 1.13

Exploring Prepositions

If your words and phrases can't relate,
introduce them to some prepositions!

OBJECTIVE	BACKGROUND	MATERIALS
To help your student identify prepositions and use them correctly	A preposition is a word that shows a relationship to another word in a sentence. Prepositions begin phrases that provide more details in a sentence. In this lesson, your student will explore several common prepositions and learn to use them in speaking and writing.	■ Student Learning Pages 13.A–13.B ■ 1 pair scissors

VOCABULARY

PREPOSITIONS words that connect nouns or pronouns to the rest of a sentence
OBJECT OF THE PREPOSITION a noun or pronoun that's connected to a sentence by a preposition

Let's Begin

1 **INTRODUCE** Review with your student the parts of speech that he or she has learned so far. Nouns, verbs, and conjunctions are all important parts of sentences. Explain that today your student will be learning about another part of speech called **prepositions.** Tell your student that a preposition provides more information in a sentence. Invite your student to copy the following words in his or her notebook:

in   on   by   to   from   at

2 **EXAMINE** Explain to your student that the words he or she just wrote are all prepositions. Ask your student to look at the words and think of something they all have in common. [they all tell location] Point out that many prepositions are helpful because they give information about location or place. Ask your student to copy these sentences in his or her notebook and circle the preposition in each:

My bike is in the garage.

James walked home from the park.

My friend's apartment is by the video store.

Alyssa's markers are on her desk.

Grandpa loves going to the zoo.

John is at the store.

A BRIGHT IDEA

To help your student understand how to use prepositions of place, play a hide-and-seek game. Select an object to hide, then invite your student to look for it. Guide him or her with "hot" and "cold" clues. When your student has found the object, invite him or her to describe where it was. Point out that by describing an object's location, your student uses prepositions naturally.

3 **CONNECT** Define *preposition* for your student. Tell him or her that prepositions connect nouns and pronouns to the rest of a sentence. The noun or pronoun that's being connected by the preposition is called the **object of the preposition.** Invite your student to look back at the sentences from Step 2. Invite him or her to underline the noun that's being connected by the preposition in each sentence.

4 **EXPAND** Point out to your student that not all prepositions tell location. For example, the words *with* and *of* are common prepositions that don't show location. However, they are still used to connect words to the rest of a sentence to provide more information. Ask your student to identify the preposition and object in these sentences:

> I eat dinner with my family.
> I read the rest of the book.

5 **ENGAGE** Play a preposition game with your student. Call out a direction and have your student complete the action. For example, say, *Stand next to the door. Sit under the table. Sit on the chair.* Then have your student call out directions for you.

6 **DISTRIBUTE** Distribute Student Learning Page 13.A. Read the directions with your student, and then guide him or her in completing the page. When he or she has finished, have him or her write a poem using prepositions.

Branching Out

TEACHING TIP

Prepositions are often confusing to students because they are used in many different ways. For example, a student lies *in* his or her bed, but sits *on* a couch. Encourage your student to say prepositional phrases out loud to hear if they sound right before writing them in a sentence.

CHECKING IN

To assess your student's understanding of the lesson, invite him or her to write in a notebook six places that he or she sometimes goes. Then you should write the prepositions of place on slips of paper and mix them up. Invite your student to select a slip of paper and use the preposition to create a sentence about one of the locations he or she listed. Ask your student to say the new sentence out loud.

FOR FURTHER READING

Behind the Mask: A Book About Prepositions (World of Language), by Ruth Heller (Paper Star, 1999).

Under, Over, By the Clover: What Is a Preposition?, by Brian P. Cleary (Lerner Publishing Group, 2002).

Writing Skills Made Fun: Parts of Speech, by Karen Kellaher (Scholastic, Inc., 2001).

Pick a Preposition

Pick prepositions from the tree to complete the poem!
Use each preposition once.

The little bird sat _____ the old oak tree,

she spread her wings and flew _____ me.

She flapped and landed _____ my arm,

and said she moved _____ a northern farm.

When winter came _____ air that chills,

she flew to a tree _____ the southern hills.

Student Learning Page 13.A: Pick a Preposition   **71**

What's Next? You Decide!

Now it's your turn to choose what to do next in the lesson. Read the activities and decide which one you want to do—you may want to try them both!

Make a Preposition Book

MATERIALS

❑ 6 sheets construction paper

❑ markers, crayons, or colored pencils

❑ 1 stapler

STEPS

❑ Write a phrase with each of these words: *in, on, by, to,* and *from.*

❑ Write each phrase at the bottom of a sheet of construction paper.

❑ Draw a picture of each phrase on the paper.

❑ Make a cover for your book. Give it the title "Where Is It?"

❑ Staple your cover and other sheets of paper together.

❑ Share your book with a family member or friend.

Play in the Box

MATERIALS

❑ 1 large box

❑ items from the room you're in

STEPS

Play this game with a friend or family member.

❑ Ask your partner to leave the room.

❑ Choose something from the room you're in and put it in the box.

❑ When your partner comes back, ask him or her to guess what's in the box. Have him or her ask questions you can answer to provide clues.

❑ When your partner guesses the object, open the box.

❑ Now ask your partner to put something in the box. You guess what it is!

Understanding Prefixes and Suffixes

The more words you know, the easier it is to express exactly what you want to communicate.

OBJECTIVE	BACKGROUND	MATERIALS
To help your student understand what prefixes and suffixes are, what they mean, and how they're used	Many English words have prefixes, suffixes, or both. When these word parts are added to the beginning or end of a word, they change the meaning of the word. Knowing what a prefix or suffix means is key to figuring out what the entire word means. In this lesson, your student will learn what prefixes or suffixes are, what some of the most common ones mean, and how they're used in sentences.	■ Student Learning Pages 14.A–14.D

VOCABULARY
BASE WORD the central part of a word that other word parts may be attached to
PREFIX a word part attached to the beginning of a base word
SUFFIX a word part attached to the end of a base word

Let's Begin

1 **INTRODUCE** Explain to your student that a **base word** is the central part of a word. It may have other word parts attached to it. A word part attached to the beginning of a base word is a **prefix.** A word part attached to the end of a base word is a **suffix.** Adding a prefix or a suffix changes the meaning of a word. Write the word *thankful* and show it to your student. Ask, *What is the base word?* [thank] Then ask, *What word part is attached to* thank? [–*ful*] *What kind of word part is* –ful? [suffix] Now write the words *sadly* and *unlock*. Have your student underline each base word, name the word part, and tell what kind of word part it is.

2 **EXPLAIN** Talk to your student about the suffixes –*er* and –*est*. Tell him or her that these suffixes are used when two or more things are being compared. The suffix –*er* means "more." The suffix –*est* means "the most." Help your student make a three-column chart of comparative words in his or her notebook. Write the column headings "Base Word," "More (–*er*)," and "The Most (–*est*)." Have your student write these base words and their comparatives

ENRICH THE EXPERIENCE

Check out http://www.
funbrain.com/kids
center.html with your
student. You and your
student can find links to
grammar and word games.

A BRIGHT IDEA

Have a scavenger hunt!
Choose two pages from a
newspaper or magazine.
Tell your student to circle
every suffix and prefix he
or she can find and total
the number of words.
Then it's your turn to see
if you can find more
words than your student.

FOR FURTHER READING

*Phonics and Word Skills:
Inventive Exercises to
Sharpen Skills and Raise
Achievement* (*Basic, Not
Boring Grades 2–3*), by
Imogene Forte, Marjorie
Frank, and Laurie Grupe
(Incentive Publications,
1998).

*Words Their Way: Word
Study for Phonics,
Vocabulary, and
Spelling Instruction*,
by Donald R. Bear
(Prentice Hall, 1999).

in the chart: *kind, soft, light, fresh,* and *fast.* Ask him or her to use each comparative word in a sentence.

3 **EXPLAIN AND DISTRIBUTE** Explain that some base words change spelling when *–er* or *–est* are added. Help your student add these comparatives to the chart in his or her notebook: *big/bigger/biggest, sad/sadder/saddest, funny/funnier/funniest,* and *happy/happier/happiest.* Have him or her underline the base word and identify the spelling changes—the final consonant is doubled in *big* and *sad* and the *y* changes to *i* in *funny* and *happy.* Then distribute Student Learning Page 14.A.

4 **DISCUSS** Introduce the suffixes *–ly* and *–able.* Write the word *loudly.* Ask, *What is the base word?* [loud] *What does* loudly *mean?* [in a loud way] Write the word *washable.* Ask, *What is the base word?* [wash] *What does* washable *mean?* [able to be washed] Ask your student if he or she can name any more words that end in *–ly* and *–able.* If so, challenge him or her to tell what the words mean.

5 **DISCUSS AND DISTRIBUTE** Discuss the suffixes *–ful, –less,* and *–ness.* Write the words *hopeful, helpless,* and *softness.* Have your student underline the base words. Have him or her tell the meaning of each word and use it in a sentence. Ask your student if he or she can name other words that have the suffixes *–ful, –less,* and *–ness.* Then distribute Student Learning Page 14.B.

6 **EXPLAIN AND DISTRIBUTE** Explain that many words have the prefixes *un–* and *re–.* The prefix *un–* means "not" or "the opposite of." The prefix *re–* means "doing it again" or "back." Point out that knowing what these prefixes mean is a big help in figuring out the meanings of longer words. Have your student write these two words: *uneven* and *rebuild.* Tell him or her to underline the base words. He or she should apply his or her knowledge of the meanings of *un–* and *re–* and write the definitions of the two words. Then distribute Student Learning Page 14.C.

Branching Out

TEACHING TIP

A lesson about suffixes is a good opportunity for your student to practice his or her dictionary skills. Suggest that he or she look up base words to see if their spellings change when suffixes are added.

CHECKING IN

To assess your student's understanding, ask him or her to write two words each using the prefixes and suffixes in the lesson. Ask him or her to say the words out loud and use them in sentences.

Write Comparing Words

The word in each top block is a base word. In the middle block, add –er to the base word. Write the word. In the bottom block, add –est to the base word. Write the word.

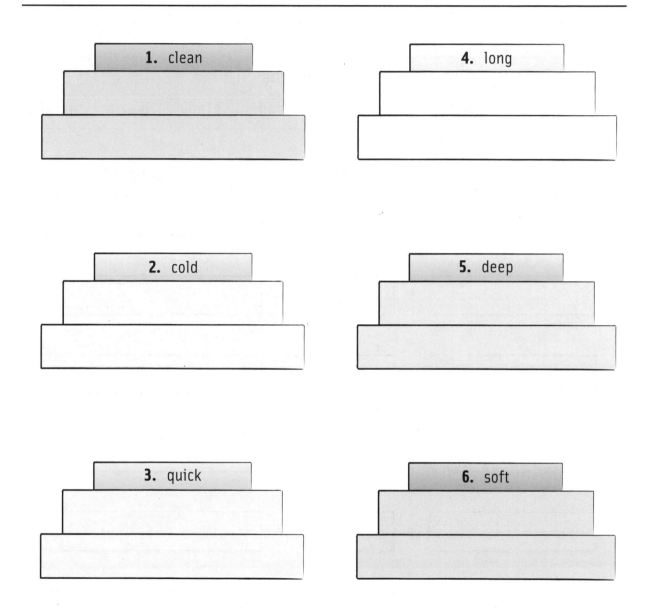

1. clean

4. long

2. cold

5. deep

3. quick

6. soft

Now write a sentence using at least one of the words you made.

_____

_____

_____

Make New Words with Suffixes

Choose a base word that can go with the suffix. Write it in the first box. Combine it with the suffix. Write the new word.

Base Words							
hope	chew	care	treat	sad	kind	help	quiet

Word	+	**Suffix**	=	**New Word**
1.	+	–ly	=	
2.	+	–able	=	
3.	+	–ful	=	
4.	+	–less	=	
5.	+	–ness	=	
6.	+	–ly	=	
7.	+	–ful	=	
8.	+	–able	=	

Find Meanings of
Un– and *Re–* Words

Read the meanings. Find a word in the oval that has the
same meaning. Write the word.

| untie | unhappy | unlock | untrue |
| repay | revisit | replace | retest |

Word	Meaning
1.	false
2.	to put something back
3.	to loosen
4.	to give money back
5.	sad
6.	to take an exam again
7.	open
8.	to go see again

Now write a sentence using at least one word from the oval.

_____

_____

_____

_____

What's Next? You Decide!

Now it's your turn to choose what to do next in the lesson. Read the activities and decide which one you want to do— you may want to try them both!

Make a Comparing Poster

Compare

big   bigger   biggest

long   longer   longest

MATERIALS

❏ 1 posterboard
❏ markers, crayons, or colored pencils

STEPS

Make a poster to show *–er* and *–est* words.

❏ Choose comparing words you want to show. Here are some ideas: *big, bigger, biggest; long, longer, longest;* or *scary, scarier, scariest.*

❏ Draw pictures that show what each word means.

❏ Under each picture write the word it shows.

❏ Hang your poster where everyone in your family can see it.

Make a Suffix-Prefix Game

MATERIALS

❏ 21 index cards
❏ 1 dictionary

STEPS

❏ Write each of these words, suffixes, and prefixes on an index card:

help	pass	–less
kind	–ful	loud
–ly	lock	play
care	wash	un–
friend	–ness	quick
–able	sad	fair
hope	real	re–

❏ Ask friends to play your game.

❏ Spread out the cards. Tell players the game is to make new words. Use one word card and one suffix or prefix card to make a new word.

❏ Look up words in the dictionary to make sure they are real words.

❏ The player who makes the most words wins the game.

Investigating Antonyms and Synonyms

*Learning words with similar and opposite meanings
leads to greater fluency in reading and writing.*

OBJECTIVE	BACKGROUND	MATERIALS
To help your student understand and use antonyms and synonyms	Antonyms are words with opposite meanings. Synonyms are words with the same or almost the same meaning. Learning to recognize antonyms and synonyms helps increase a reader's vocabulary, and using them makes writing more interesting. In this lesson, your student will learn what antonyms and synonyms are and how to recognize and use them.	■ Student Learning Pages 15.A–15.D ■ 1 copy Web, page 354

VOCABULARY

ANTONYMS words with opposite meanings

SYNONYMS words with the same or almost the same meanings

ADJECTIVES words that describe nouns

Let's Begin

1   **DEFINE** Explain to your student that words with opposite meanings are **antonyms.** Say common pairs of antonyms out loud, such as *hot/cold, new/old,* and *dark/light.* Challenge your student to say additional pairs of common antonyms that he or she knows. Then give your student a copy of the Web found on page 354. Tell your student to write "Opposites" in the center of the Web. Have him or her write a pair of antonyms in each circle.

2   **DISCUSS AND DISTRIBUTE** Tell your student that a prefix can sometimes make a word have an opposite meaning. Say the word *happy.* Ask, *What new word is formed when you add the prefix* un– *to the word* happy? [*unhappy*] *Are* happy *and* unhappy *antonyms?* [yes] Have your student create two more antonyms in the same way with the words *kind* and *fair.* Then distribute Student Learning Page 15.A. Give your student time to work through the page. After your student has completed the activity on the page, have him or her write a short story about balloons using at least four of the sets of opposite words.

3 **DEFINE AND EXPLAIN** Tell your student that words with the same or almost the same meaning are **synonyms.** Say pairs of synonyms out loud, such as *big/large, quick/fast,* and *small/tiny.* Encourage your student to say pairs of synonyms that he or she might know. Point out that it's often possible to replace one synonym for another in a sentence. Have your student write these two sentences in his or her notebook: *The girl found a big rock. Here is a warm slice of pizza.* Direct him or her to underline the words *big* and *warm.* Tell him or her to replace *big* and *warm* with synonyms and rewrite the sentences using the new words.

4 **DISCUSS AND DISTRIBUTE** Point out to your student that many synonyms have similar but not exact meanings. One word might fit in a sentence better than another. Some words that have similar meanings help readers make different pictures in their minds. Discuss how the synonyms *large* and *huge* give these two sentences different meanings: *That is a large building. That is a huge building.* Then distribute Student Learning Page 15.B.

5 **EXPLAIN AND DISTRIBUTE** Tell your student that the antonyms and synonyms in this lesson are **adjectives.** Adjectives are words that describe nouns. Demonstrate how antonyms and synonyms function as adjectives in sentences. Give this sentence to your student: *There is a big dog.* Ask, *Which word is the noun?* [dog] *Which word is the adjective describing the noun?* [big] *Which word is a synonym or means the same thing as* big? [large] *Which word is an antonym or means the opposite of* big? [little] Distribute Student Learning Page 15.C. Tell your student that on this page the antonyms and synonyms in the sentences are adjectives.

6 **CONNECT** Play an antonym/synonym game with your student. Call out an adjective, then say *same* or *opposite,* and have your student call out a word that means the same or the opposite. Then switch and have your student call out words.

Branching Out

TEACHING TIP

As you talk about antonyms and synonyms with your student, keep in mind that your student probably hasn't yet absorbed all the connotations of words. For example, he or she might not know that *slender* and *skinny* have different connotations and are used in different ways.

CHECKING IN

To assess your student's understanding, ask him or her to choose two pairs of antonyms and two pairs of synonyms from the lesson. Ask him or her to say the words out loud and use each of them in a sentence.

Find the Opposites

Each word in a balloon has an opposite word in the cloud.
Find the opposite word. Write it in the blank balloon.

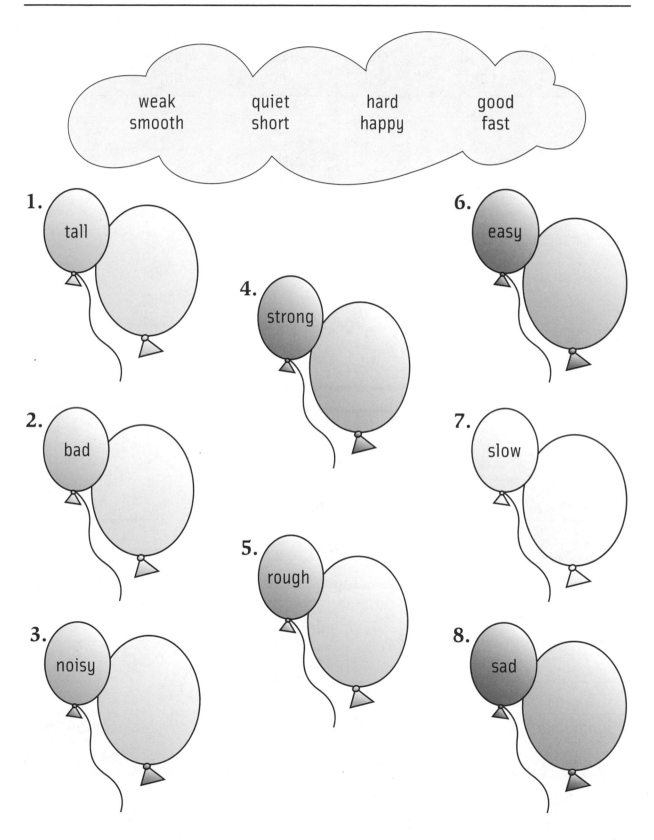

Cloud words: weak, smooth, quiet, short, hard, happy, good, fast

1. tall

2. bad

3. noisy

4. strong

5. rough

6. easy

7. slow

8. sad

PROMOTING LITERACY

ing 15.B

Climb the Mountain

Write a synonym and an antonym for the words in the mountain. Use the words from the word box. Follow the signs!

| quick | laugh | cry | short | whisper | high |
| slow | cold | yell | hot | big | small |

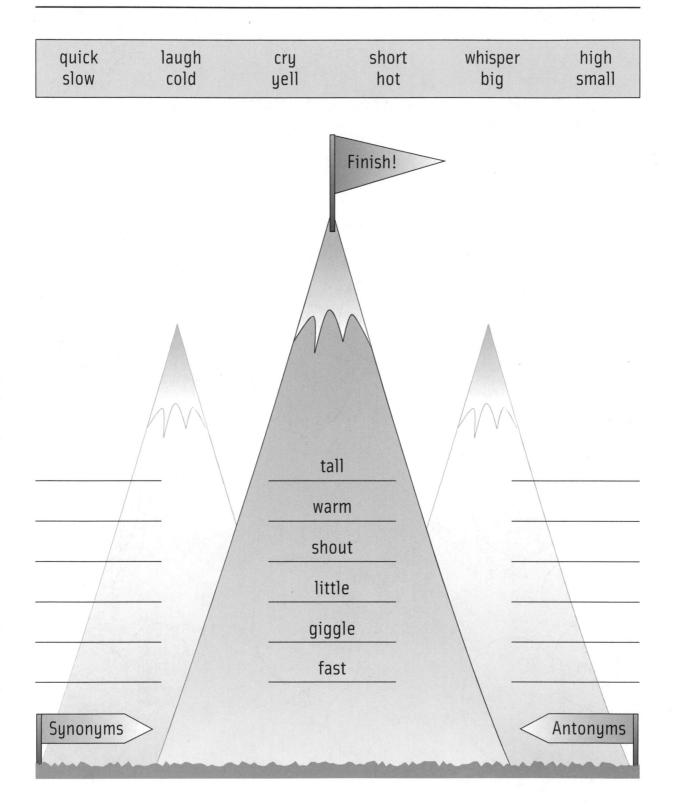

Finish!

tall

warm

shout

little

giggle

fast

Synonyms ▷

◁ Antonyms

Making the Grade: Everything Your 2nd Grader Needs to Know

Replace Antonyms and Synonyms

| nice | quiet | loud | clean |
| dark | messy | bright | unpleasant |

Rewrite each sentence. Replace the underlined word with a synonym from the word box.

1. Carla's room is always <u>neat</u>.

   _____

2. The room was large and <u>sunny</u>.

   _____

3. Jason had a <u>noisy</u> party last week.

   _____

4. Our bus driver has a <u>pleasant</u> voice.

   _____

Rewrite each sentence. Replace the underlined word with an antonym from the word box.

5. Carla's room is always <u>neat</u>.

   _____

6. The room was large and <u>sunny</u>.

   _____

7. Jason had a <u>noisy</u> party last week.

   _____

8. Our bus driver has a(n) <u>pleasant</u> voice.

   _____

What's Next? You Decide!

Now it's your turn to choose what to do next in the lesson. Read the activities and decide which one you want to do—you may want to try them both!

Make a Find-the-Opposites Poster

MATERIALS

- ❑ old magazines and newspapers
- ❑ 1 pair scissors
- ❑ 1 sheet construction paper
- ❑ glue
- ❑ markers, crayons, or colored pencils

STEPS

Make a poster that shows opposites!

- ❑ Find pictures in old magazines and newspapers. Here are some ideas to get you started: a beach in summer and a ski hill in winter, a tall man and a short man, an old person and a baby.
- ❑ Cut out the pictures. Paste them on the construction paper.
- ❑ Draw your own opposites, too. Fill up the paper.
- ❑ Show your picture to friends. Ask them how many opposites they can find.

Write a Funny Story

STEPS

- ❑ Write a story about a character you make up.
- ❑ Have your character do exactly the opposite of what people expect! For example, if a sign says "Quiet Please," your character yells. When it's time to go to sleep, your character gets out of bed.

- ❑ Give your character a funny name.
- ❑ Write your story in complete sentences using correct spelling.
- ❑ You may want to draw pictures to show what happens in your story.
- ❑ Read your story to your friends and family!

Comprehending Homophones

*You can't always judge a word by its sound—
especially when it's a homophone!*

OBJECTIVE	BACKGROUND	MATERIALS
To have your student understand, identify, and use homophones	Words that are pronounced the same but have different spellings and meanings are called homophones. Examples of homophones include *to/too/two, know/no, red/read, buy/by, for/four, there/their,* and *write/right.* In this lesson, your student will learn how to identify and use homophones.	■ Student Learning Pages 16.A–16.B ■ 9 index cards

VOCABULARY

HOMOPHONES words that are pronounced the same but have different spellings and meanings

Let's Begin

1 **INTRODUCE** Begin this lesson by having your student write the following sentence in his or her notebook:

>   I brought four cookies for my friends.

Ask your student to underline the two words that sound the same in the sentence—*four* and *for.*

2 **EXPLAIN** Share with your student that these two words are called **homophones** because they sound the same but have different spellings and meanings. Write the words *red* and *read* on a sheet of paper. Share that these two words are also homophones. Challenge your student to tell you the meaning of each word. [*red*: a color; *read*: understood words that are written]

3 **SHARE** Tell your student that *to/too/two* is another example of homophones. Show your student the following sentences. Point out the words *to, too,* and *two.*

>   I am going to the store.
>   You can come, too.
>   I will buy two apples.

A BRIGHT IDEA

Have your student read one of his or her favorite books. Then have him or her identify and record pairs of homophones in the book. Have your student write his or her own sentences using each pair of homophones.

Tell your student that *to, too,* and *two* are used in different ways in a sentence. The word *to* is often used to connect parts of a sentence. In the sentence, it joins two sentence parts to show location. Share that the word *too* means "also." *Too* can also mean "a lot" or "very much." Finally, share that *two* indicates the number. Ask your student to use the words *to, too,* and *two* in three different sentences.

4 **PRACTICE** Tell your student that *know/no, buy/by, there/their,* and *write/right* are all homophones. Use each word in a sentence. Then ask your student to spell each word in his or her notebook.

5 **DRAW** Ask your student to draw a picture of two homophones. Some possible homophones to illustrate are *pair/pear, red/read,* and *ant/aunt.* Instruct your student to write a sentence with each word below the picture he or she draws. Then have your student write a paragraph, using the homophones he or she chose.

6 **BRAINSTORM** Challenge your student to brainstorm some other homophones. On a sheet of paper, write as many homophones as your student can think of. You may need to say one of the homophones and ask your student to come up with another. For example, you could say, *The room is bare without any pictures.* Then ask your student to explain the meaning of the word *bare.* Next, guide your student in coming up with the homophone *bear* and ask him or her to tell the word's meaning. Then distribute Student Learning Page 16.A.

7 **EXPAND** Have your student create a song of homophones. First go to the PBS Kids Web site at http://www.pbskids.org, then click on the Between the Lions link and go to the Songs page. Encourage your student to write his or her own song about homophones.

A BRIGHT IDEA

Helping your student form associations with other words may help him or her grasp meanings. For example, tell your student that he or she can remember the meaning of *there* by thinking about the word *here,* whose letters are in the word *there.* Both words indicate a place.

Branching Out

TEACHING TIP

Tell your student that it's easy to recognize homophones when they are written down because they're spelled differently. However, when we hear a homophone, we have to use context to understand the correct meaning. Remind your student that paying attention to the words in a sentence will help him or her understand the meaning of homophones that are spoken out loud.

CHECKING IN

To assess your student's understanding of the lesson, give your student index cards with the words *to, too, two, know, no, there, their, write,* and *right* written on each one. Place the index cards facedown and ask your student to choose a card. Instruct your student to use the chosen homophone in a sentence correctly.

FOR FURTHER READING

Reading Puzzles and Games, by Martha Cheney (RGA Publishing Group, 1998).

Spectrum Spelling: Grade 2, by Nancy Roser (McGraw-Hill Children's Publishing, 2002).

Writing: Grade 2 (McGraw-Hill Children's Publishing, 2001).

Busy as a Bee

Use the homophones to help Busy Bee complete the story.

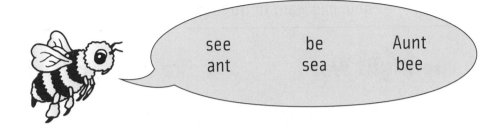

see   be   Aunt
ant   sea   bee

I spent the day with my _____ Milly. She took

me to the beach by the _____. I played in the sand

and made a castle. A tiny _____ marched across

the small tower I built, so I called it Little Prince of the

Sand Castle. Then a _____ buzzed by and landed

on the other tower I made. "Who will this _____?"

I thought. "Well, this must be the Queen Bee!" Soon,

it was time to go home. I had so much fun at the beach.

Most of all, I was happy to _____ my Aunt Milly!

Draw a picture of the underlined homophone in each sentence.

The <u>sun</u> shone brightly.   He played with his <u>son</u>.

What's Next? You Decide!

Now it's your turn to choose what to do next in the lesson. Read the activities and decide which one you want to do— you may want to try them both!

Write the Right Word

MATERIALS

❑ markers, crayons, or colored pencils

STEPS

❑ Write a story using as many homophones as you can.

❑ When you have finished your story, underline the pairs of homophones.

❑ Use one color to underline each pair of homophones. For example, if you used the homophones *to* and *two,* then you could underline both words in red.

❑ Read your story to a family member or friend.

❑ How many homophones did your family member or friend count?

❑ Write another homophone story, or have someone write a story for you.

❑ See how many homophones you can find!

Make a Homophone Book

MATERIALS

❑ old magazines or newspapers
❑ 1 pair scissors
❑ several sheets construction paper
❑ glue
❑ 1 stapler

STEPS

❑ Look through old magazines and newspapers for pictures of things that are homophones.

❑ Use scissors to cut out the pictures. For example, you could cut out a picture of a *pear* and a *pair* of socks.

❑ If you have trouble finding some pictures of things that are homophones, you may draw them.

❑ Glue each pair of homophones to the same sheet of construction paper.

❑ Under each picture, write the name of the homophone.

❑ Staple your book together and share it with a friend.

In Your Community

To reinforce the skills and concepts taught in this section,
try one or more of these activities!

Making Inferences

Inferring is often a difficult task for a second grader, yet it's a critical reading skill that your student needs to practice. Your student may be timid about making inferences for fear of being wrong. To help your student become more comfortable practicing this skill, provide real-word experiences your student is familiar with. Take a field trip in your community and allow your student the opportunity to practice guessing. Have your student use his or her prior experience to guess where you will be going or how long it will take to get there. If you're at the grocery store, ask your student to guess what you're having for dinner based on what you're buying. Use your creativity as you spend an afternoon devoted to honing your student's ability to infer in a safe environment.

Phonics and Word Skills Scavenger Hunt

Many second graders have some difficulty pronouncing particular letter sounds. Make a list of these problems and embark on a scavenger hunt at the park or the grocery store. Ask your student to locate items that begin with the letter sounds from your list. For example, if your student has difficulty pronouncing the letter combination *ch*, ask your student to find things such as children at the park or cheese at the grocery store. At the end of the scavenger hunt, have your student point out all the items that were found with the proper letter sounds from the list. This useful activity is a way for your student to strengthen his or her phonics skills.

Research and Share a Biography

Have your student research and orally share a biography about someone in your community. Allow your student to pick anyone as the subject. It could be the mayor of your town, a police officer, a teacher, or another person your student might be interested in learning more about. Once your student has selected a person to focus on, arrange an interview so your student can ask him or her questions. Encourage your student to take notes, or help him or her record the interview. Then invite your student to write the biography based on the interview. Arrange another meeting with the subject and have your student orally share the biography.

Visit a Nature Preserve

Creative writers often get their inspiration from nature. With a notebook and pen in hand, take your student to a nature preserve near your home. Walk the trails and take in the scenes of nature. Have your student write descriptive words and sketch a little scene. Remind your student that the words and drawing should connect to the five senses. When you return home, have your student use the experience to begin writing a creative story.

Tour a Local Newspaper Company

Most communities have weekly or daily newspaper publications. Arrange for you and your student to tour a facility where a local publication is printed. Explain to your student that the reporters need to use all types of words in their writing—including homophones. Ask your student to write a few sentences about his or her trip using the homophones *to/too/two, there/their,* and *write/right.*

We Have Learned

Use this checklist to summarize what you and your student
have accomplished in the Promoting Literacy section.

❑ **Fiction**
❑ reading and analyzing fiction
❑ understanding characteristics and
elements of fiction

❑ **Folktales**
❑ reading and analyzing folktales
❑ understanding characteristics and
elements of folktales
❑ writing an ending for a folktale

❑ **Fantasy**
❑ reading and analyzing fantasy
❑ understanding characteristics and
elements of fantasy

❑ **Poetry**
❑ reading and analyzing poetry
❑ understanding characteristics and
elements of poetry
❑ writing a poem

❑ **Writing**
❑ writing in a journal/diary,
independent writing
❑ writing a book report

❑ **General Nonfiction**
❑ reading and analyzing general
nonfiction
❑ understanding characteristics and
elements of general nonfiction

❑ **Creative Writing**
❑ understanding the need for
communication
❑ using main ideas, supporting details,
and sequencing in a logical manner

❑ **Biography**
❑ reading and analyzing biography
❑ understanding characteristics and
elements of biography
❑ writing about a hero

❑ **Grammar, Phonics,
and Word Skills**
❑ nouns, plural nouns, compound
words
❑ understanding the articles *a, an, the*
❑ understanding the verbs *am, is,
are, have, has, said, saw, will go*
❑ understanding antonyms and
synonyms
❑ understanding common homophones
❑ understanding the conjunctions *and,
or, but*
❑ understanding the prepositions *in,
on, by, to, from, with, at, of*
❑ understanding suffixes and prefixes

We have also learned:

_____

_____

_____

Math

Math

Key Topics

Number Sense
Pages 93–98

Patterns and Numbers to 100
Pages 99–104

Addition and Subtraction of Two-Digit Numbers
Pages 105–112

Patterns and Numbers to 1,000
Pages 113–118

Addition and Subtraction of Three-Digit Numbers
Pages 119–124

Money and Fractions
Pages 125–134

Multiplication, Division, and Algebraic Methods
Pages 135–144

Geometry and Measurement
Pages 145–156

Calendars, Time, and Data Collection
Pages 157–164

Generating Number Sense

A good teacher sees potential in correct answers. A great teacher sees potential in incorrect answers.

OBJECTIVE	BACKGROUND	MATERIALS
To give your student a visual sense of numerical values and how to compare them	Comprehending numerical values will prepare your student for addition and subtraction. In this lesson, your student will use pictures, objects, and numbers to learn and develop his or her number sense.	■ Student Learning Pages 1.A–1.D ■ 50 marbles ■ several groups of objects, such as dry beans, straws, and craft sticks ■ 50–100 pennies

Let's Begin

1 **PREVIEW** Display 10 marbles to your student. Have him or her count the number of marbles out loud. Then have your student write the number 10 in his or her notebook.

2 **DEMONSTRATE** Explain that your student can use a value he or she knows to estimate amounts. Keep the set of 10 marbles close by for reference. Make three new sets with 3, 9, and 20 marbles each and show them to your student. Ask, *Without counting, which pile has about 10 marbles?* [the pile of 9] *Explain how you used a value that you know to get the answer.* [I compared each pile to the pile of 10; the pile of 3 was too small; the pile of 20 was too large] To verify his or her answer, have your student go ahead and count the exact number in each of the three sets and write the totals in his or her notebook.

3 **PRACTICE** Repeat the activity in Step 1 and Step 2 using different objects, such as building blocks, dry beans, straws, or craft sticks. As in Step 1, have your student make a pile of 10 first, and then estimate the number of items in a larger pile without counting. You can also do the exercise with different reference amounts, such as 5, 15, or 20.

4 **EXTEND** Using building blocks, dry beans, straws, craft sticks, or other household items, create six different sets of objects in front of your student. Half of the sets should have more than 15 pieces and the other half should have less than 15 pieces.

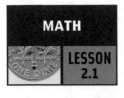
Ask, *Can you point to the sets that have more than 15?* Review your student's answers. If your student has trouble choosing the correct sets without counting, create a set of 15 items off to the side for a reference. Once your student has selected the correct sets, repeat the exercise with different types and sizes of objects. This time have your student choose the sets that are *less than* a certain amount.

5 **DISTRIBUTE** If your student is able to complete the number sense exercises correctly, distribute Student Learning Pages 1.A and 1.B and have him or her complete the exercises. If your student is having difficulty with the concept, refer to the margin tip.

6 **RELATE** Show your student six separate sets of 10 objects each displayed on a table. Ask, *How could you find out how many total objects are here without counting all of them?* Guide your student to see that each set has about the same number of objects and that there are six sets total. Your student can count the number of items in one of the sets [10] and then count by tens to estimate the total. [60]

7 **DISTRIBUTE** Distribute Student Learning Page 1.C. Have your student complete the exercise. Review his or her work.

Branching Out

TEACHING TIP

The next time you're at the mall or grocery store with your student, take a number sense break. Together, stand back and observe the people standing in front of you or in each check-out line. Ask your student to decide about how many people he or she sees.

CHECKING IN

Check your student's understanding of the lesson in real-world situations like at the grocery store. Ask your student to tell you about how many oranges are in a bag, or how many bananas are on the table. Have your student check periodically to see if his or her estimates are reasonable by counting the items.

A BRIGHT IDEA

Show your student a large pile of pennies. Have your student suppose that he or she wants to know how much money he or she has but doesn't have time to count it. Explain that your student can estimate the number of pennies. First have him or her count out a group of 10 pennies. Then have your student compare the group of 10 pennies to the larger group of pennies to reach an estimate.

FOR FURTHER READING

Easy Math Art Projects and Activities: Delightful Art Projects for Young Learners That Teach and Reinforce Math Concepts and Skills, by Cecilia Dinio Durkin (Scholastic, Inc., 1999).

Hot Math Topics: Number Sense, by Carol Greenes, Linda Schulman Dacey, and Rika Spungin (Dale Seymour Publications, 1999).

Teaching Number Sense, by Julia Anghileri (Continuum, 2001).

Talk About Number Sense

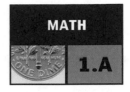
Look at the picture. Then answer the questions.

1. The top box has 20 triangles. Without counting, which boxes contain

   about 20 triangles? _____

20 Triangles

A.	B.	C.	D.

Complete the sentence with the best answer.

2. _____ is the smallest number of triangles that look like
   about 20 triangles.

   A. 43   **B.** 16   **C.** 8

3. _____ is the largest number of triangles that look like
   about 20 triangles.

   A. 58   **B.** 12   **C.** 24

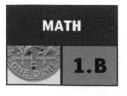
See Number Sense

Look at the crayons. Circle the sets that have more than 10 crayons.

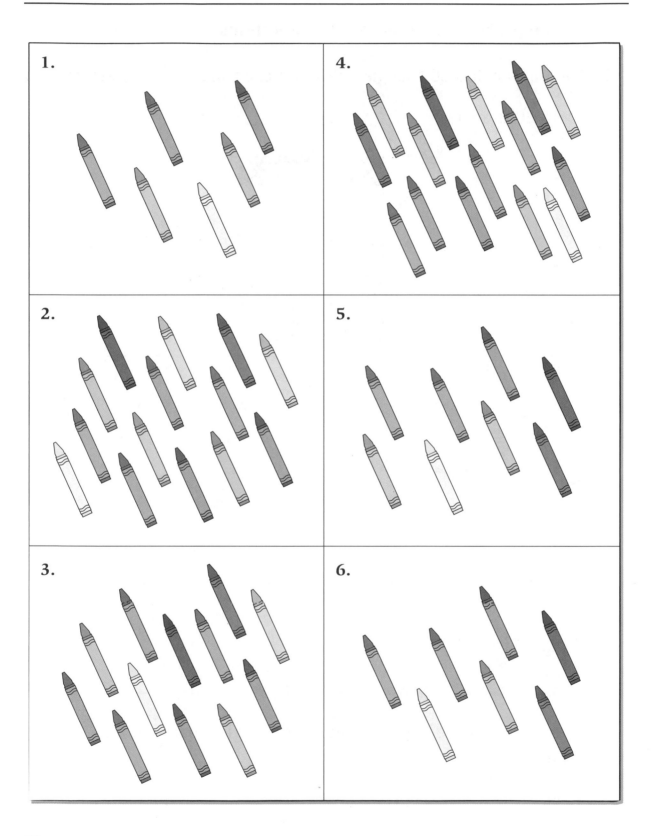

1.

2.

3.

4.

5.

6.

Find the Total

Look at the pictures. Then answer the questions.

1. About how many people are in the buses together?

_____

2. How did you get your answer without counting?

_____

_____

What's Next? You Decide!

Now it's your turn to choose what to do next in the lesson. Read the activities and decide which one you want to do— you may want to try them both!

Guess the Marshmallows!

MATERIALS

❑ 1 bag marshmallows

❑ 1 large cookie sheet

❑ 1 spoon

STEPS

❑ Open the bag of marshmallows and spill them onto the cookie sheet.

❑ Use a spoon and take 10 marshmallows off the cookie sheet.

❑ Guess the number of marsh-mallows left on the cookie sheet. Use the 10 marsh-mallows to help you estimate.

❑ Have a friend or a family member guess the number of marshmallows, using the same steps as you.

❑ Then count the number of marshmallows on the cookie sheet. Whose guess was closest?

Draw a Shape Problem

MATERIALS

❑ crayons or markers

STEPS

❑ Choose a shape to draw.

❑ Draw 30 of these shapes on a sheet of paper. Use crayons or markers to color your shapes.

❑ Divide another sheet of paper into four boxes by drawing two intersecting lines.

❑ In two of the boxes, draw about 30 of your shapes.

❑ In the other two boxes, draw amounts that are much less than 30.

❑ Now have a friend or family member solve the problem. Have him or her look at the first sheet of paper. Then give the person the second sheet of paper. Ask which boxes show about 30 of your shape.

❑ Check to see if the person gets the correct answer.

MATH

LESSON
2.2

Exploring Patterns and Numbers to 100

Patterns are everywhere—on bedspreads, wallpaper, even in numbers!

OBJECTIVE	BACKGROUND	MATERIALS
To teach your student to identify and use patterns found in numbers up to 100	The more that your student understands numbers, the more successful he or she will be as a mathematician. If your student knows how tens and ones are combined to build numbers, he or she will better understand addition, subtraction, multiplication, division, and other math concepts. In this lesson, your student will learn about place value and comparing numbers in a variety of ways. He or she will also explore regrouping.	■ Student Learning Pages 2.A–2.B ■ place-value blocks ■ several counters or buttons ■ crayons or markers

Let's Begin

PLACE VALUE

1 **MODEL** Explain to your student that to understand how big a number is, he or she needs to understand place value. Help your student count to 100 by tens: 10, 20, 30, 40, 50, 60, 70, 80, 90, 100. Show your student 2 tens blocks, or two groups of ten. Ask, *How many tens do you see?* [2] *What is the value of 2 tens?* [20] Point to each tens block as you count by tens with your student. Invite him or her to count more sets of tens.

2 **TEACH** Show your student 2 tens and 1 one. Ask him or her to count with you as you say, *ten, twenty, twenty-one.* Instruct your student to write the number 21 in his or her notebook. Point to each digit as you model saying *twenty-one is 2 tens and 1 one.* Have your student count out the following: 3 tens and 4 ones [34]; 5 tens and 2 ones [52]; and 2 tens and 9 ones [29].

3 **PRACTICE** Tell your student to write the numbers 49, 17, 30, and 55 on a sheet of paper. Ask him or her, *Which number has 7 ones?* [17] *Which number has 4 tens?* [49] *How many tens are in 30?* [3] Continue asking your student similar questions. Have him or her write five numbers with 6 ones in his or her notebook.

4 **MODEL** Using place-value blocks, counters, or buttons, place 7 tens and 4 ones where your student can see them. Ask, *How many tens and ones do you see?* [7 tens, 4 ones] Tell your student, *We can write the number as 7 tens, 4 ones.* Ask, *How much is 7 tens?* [70] *How much is 4 ones?* [4] Explain that 70 + 4 is another way to write the number. Ask, *What is another way we can write the number?* [74] Display tens and ones for other numbers and have your student write the numbers in three ways.

REGROUPING

1 **EXPLAIN** Model for your student how 13 ones can also be described as 1 ten and 3 ones. Explain that knowing this fact will help in adding and subtracting numbers. Place 10 ones blocks in front of your student. Ask, *How many ones do you see?* [10] *Can you think of another way to describe the blocks?* Guide your student to discover that 10 ones is the same as 1 ten. Explain that grouping 10 ones to form 1 ten is called *regrouping*. Have your student regroup other groups of ones into tens, such as 20 or 30.

2 **PRACTICE** Ask your student to count out 16 ones. Ask, *Is it possible to regroup?* [yes] Have your student count out 10 ones and trade them for 1 ten. Ask, *How many tens and ones are in 16?* [1 ten, 6 ones] Ask your student to name other numbers that have 1 ten.

3 **EXPAND** Have your student count out 3 tens and 12 ones. Ask, *Do you have enough ones to regroup?* [yes] Ask, *What can 12 ones be regrouped as?* [1 ten, 2 ones] *You started with 3 tens and 12 ones. Now what do you have?* [4 tens, 2 ones] Ask, *In what other ways can you write 4 tens and 2 ones?* [40 + 2; 42] Repeat the activity with other sets of tens and ones. Ask, *How many ones do you need to regroup?* [10 or more]

NUMBER PATTERNS

1 **INTRODUCE** Explain to your student that understanding number patterns will help him or her add, subtract, multiply, and divide larger numbers. Tell your student that being able to skip count by tens from any starting point will help him or her add groups of 10 to a number. Model how 6 + 2 relates to 60 + 20. Ask your student to tell you the sums of 6 + 2 and 60 + 20. [8; 80]

2 **EXPLORE** Ask your student to count out a group of 3 ones and a group of 4 ones. Ask, *What is 3 + 4?* [7] Have your student count out a group of 3 tens and a group of 4 tens. Ask, *What is 3 tens + 4 tens?* [7 tens] *How much is 7 tens?* [70] Model how knowing the value of 3 tens, 4 tens, and 7 tens can help your student add those values. Ask, *What is 30 + 40?* [70] Continue this activity with other basic addition facts. Have your student practice adding the following in his or her notebook: 20 + 30 = _____; 10 + 80 = _____; 30 + 50 = _____; and 50 + 20 = _____. [50; 90; 80; 70]

> **?**
> **DID YOU KNOW?**
>
> It's very important to have your student physically trade ones blocks for tens blocks so that he or she fully understands the concept of regrouping.

3   **EXPAND** Have your student count out a group of 1 ten and a group of 3 tens and 5 ones. Ask, *What is 1 ten + 3 tens?* [4 tens] *So what do you think 1 ten + 3 tens and 5 ones will be?* [4 tens, 5 ones] *What is the value of 4 tens and 5 ones?* [45] If needed, help your student model these equations by having him or her move the counters or place-value blocks. Add the 1 ten to the group of 3 tens and 5 ones to help your student see the total of 4 tens and 5 ones. Explain to your student that adding 1 ten to a number will increase the tens by one number. Ask, *What do you get if you add 1 ten to 22?* [32]

4   **ILLUSTRATE** Have your student write the numbers 1 to 30 in his or her notebook. Ask him or her to circle groups of two consecutive numbers, such as 1 and 2, 3 and 4, 5 and 6, and so on. Point to the second number in each group as you say the numbers with your student. [2, 4, 6, 8, and so on] Explain that you are counting by twos. Ask, *If you want to count by threes, how many numbers would you circle?* [3] Repeat the activity with your student for counting by threes and fives. Instruct your student to skip count aloud.

5   **PRACTICE** Have your student write the following in his or her notebook:

     6, 9, 12, _____, _____, _____
     25, 30, 35, _____, _____, _____

    Instruct your student to fill in the missing numbers of each pattern, giving him or her help if necessary. Tell your student to explain which number is being added in each pattern. [3, 5] Ask, *Do you think it would be faster to count to 100 by twos, threes, or fives? Why?* [fives, because 5 is greater than 3]

ODD AND EVEN NUMBERS

1   **EXPLORE** Explain to your student that many math rules and shortcuts depend on being able to distinguish between odd and even numbers. Tell your student that rules such as an odd number plus an odd number equals an even number and an even number plus an odd number equals an odd number can help him or her decide if an addition answer is reasonable. Give your student six counters. Ask him or her to arrange the counters into two rows, matching each counter with another counter across from it. Ask, *Do you have any counters left over, or do you have two equal rows?* [equal] Continue the activity with different numbers of counters, such as 7, 8, 9, 10, and so on. Have your student keep track of the numbers that made two equal groups and the numbers that had one counter left over.

2   **EXPLAIN** Ask, *What do you notice about all the numbers that had no counters left over?* [all these numbers have a digit in the ones column that you can count to by twos] Explain that your student cannot count by twos to get to any of the numbers that had one counter left over. Say that all of the numbers with none

    Exploring Patterns and Numbers to 100   **101**

left over come out even, so they are called even numbers. Tell your student that the numbers with one left over are called odd numbers. Have your student explain how counting by twos helps him or her tell if a number is odd or even.

COMPARING AND ORDERING NUMBERS

1 **EXPLAIN** Tell your student that comparing numbers is a skill that people use every day, such as when they're shopping for the best bargains, planning the shortest way to get somewhere, and playing games. Ask your student, *Which is greater, 25 or 31?* [31] Encourage your student to explain how he or she knows which number is greater. Have him or her practice choosing the greater number with various number pairs. Direct your student to write equations using greater-than (>) and less-than (<) symbols, such as 25 < 31.

2 **EXPAND** Have your student write the numbers 56, 16, and 26 in his or her notebook. Ask him or her to rewrite the numbers in order from greatest to least. If your student has difficulty, show him or her how to check the tens column of each number. Ask, *Which number has the most tens?* [56 has the most tens, so it is the greatest number] When your student has correctly placed the numbers in order [56, 26, 16], have him or her repeat the activity with the numbers 27, 18, and 29. [29, 27, 18]

3 **RELATE** Have your student order the numbers 34, 37, and 31 from greatest to least. [37, 34, 31] Say, *We ordered these numbers from greatest to least. Which number is first?* [37] *Which is second?* [34] *Which is third?* [31] Have your student reorder the numbers from least to greatest in his or her notebook. [31, 34, 37] Then distribute Student Learning Page 2.A to your student.

Branching Out

TEACHING TIP

Use manipulatives, such as place-value blocks, counters, or drawings, as much as possible to model skills for your student. He or she may need concrete examples to fully experience these number concepts.

CHECKING IN

Give your student three two-digit numbers. Ask him or her to put the numbers in order from greatest to least. Then have him or her add 10, 20, and 30 to each number. Ask your student to tell you if each number is even or odd.

Practice with Number Patterns

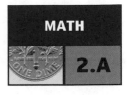

Fill in the blanks.

1.

_____ tens = 30

2.

_____ tens _____ ones = _____

3. 7 tens = _____

4. 6 tens 2 ones = _____

5. 6 ones + 8 ones = _____ tens _____ ones

6. 5 tens 2 ones + 9 ones = _____ tens _____ ones

7. 9, 10, 11, 12, _____, _____, 15, _____

8. 20, _____, 30, 35, _____, 45, _____

Circle the even numbers.

9. 8 9 10 11 12 13 14 15 16 17 18 19 20 21 22 23 24 25

Compare. Use > or <.

10. 19 _____ 40

11. 56 _____ 73

Put the numbers in order from greatest to least.

12. 43, 66, 61 _____

What's Next? You Decide!

Now it's your turn to choose what to do next in the lesson. Read the activities and decide which one you want to do—you may want to try them both!

Make a Hundreds Chart

MATERIALS

- ❏ 1 sheet construction paper
- ❏ 1 ruler
- ❏ crayons or markers

STEPS

- ❏ Have an adult help you draw a grid on construction paper. The grid should have 10 rows and 10 columns.

- ❏ Write the number 1 in the box in the upper left-hand corner. Number the boxes in the first row from 1 to 10.

- ❏ Number the first box in the second row 11. Continue numbering the boxes in the second row from 11 to 20.

- ❏ Fill out the rest of the boxes in the same way, starting the third row with 21 and so on.

- ❏ Count by tens. Color all of the numbers you counted blue.

- ❏ Color the boxes orange as you count by fives. Color the boxes red as you count by twos.

- ❏ Color box 37 brown.
- ❏ Find the box that is 10 more than 37 and color it green.
- ❏ Why can some boxes be colored more than one color?

Count Money Patterns

MATERIALS

- ❏ pennies, nickels, and dimes

STEPS

- ❏ Gather a small group of each kind of coin and arrange them in a row.

- ❏ Place the nickels first, then dimes, and then pennies.

- ❏ Nickels are worth 5 cents. Touch each nickel as you count by fives.

- ❏ Dimes are worth 10 cents. Add another 10 as you touch each dime.

- ❏ Pennies are worth 1 cent. Add one more for each penny.

- ❏ Have a friend or family member count other combinations of pennies, nickels, and dimes.

Adding Two-Digit Numbers

It's often the most basic lessons that we carry with us the longest.

MATH

LESSON 2.3

OBJECTIVE	BACKGROUND	MATERIALS
To teach your student to use addition facts to add two-digit numbers	Knowing how to add two-digit numbers will prepare your student for complex arithmetic. In this lesson, your student will learn various ways to add two-digit numbers.	■ Student Learning Pages 3.A–3.B ■ place-value blocks

Let's Begin

1. **PREVIEW** Tell your student that he or she can use simple addition facts to add multiples of 10. Have him or her write this problem in his or her notebook: 2 + 5 = _____. Have your student use ones blocks to represent the problem. Then ask him or her to solve it. [7]

2. **MODEL** Together with your student make a set of 2 tens blocks and a set of 5 tens blocks. Point to each set and ask your student which number is represented. [20 and 50] Direct your student to write 20 + 50 = _____ beneath the first problem in his or her notebook. Then ask, *If 2 + 5 = 7, what is 20 + 50?* [70]

3. **ASK** Ask, *What is similar about the two problems?* [both use the digits 2 and 5] *What is different about the two problems?* [the numbers in the second problem end in zero] *How did knowing the answer to 2 + 5 help you solve 20 + 50?* [2 tens + 5 tens = 7 tens, and 7 tens is equal to 70] *What addition fact can help you solve 50 + 40?* [5 + 4] *What is 50 + 40?* [90]

4. **EXPLAIN** Tell your student that a number line can help him or her count on. Explain the number line to your student, showing him or her that each tick mark between the tens is equal to 1. Then have your student write this problem in his or her notebook: 5 + 3 = _____. Ask, *What place value are you adding?* [ones] Say, *This means you must count on by ones.* Model counting on by ones by starting at 5 and counting up 3 to 8.

> **! A BRIGHT IDEA**
>
> If your student is having difficulty adding multiples of 10, suggest that he or she count the tens blocks in both sets and add a zero to the end of that number.

0   10   20   30   40   50   60   70   80   90   100

5 **DISCUSS** Explain to your student that adding two-digit numbers requires counting on by tens. Give your student this problem: 50 + 30 = _____. Tell him or her to write the problem in his or her notebook. Ask, *What place value are you adding?* [tens] Have your student point to the tens on the number line. Then invite him or her to count on by tens to find the sum. [80]

6 **EXPAND** Have your student write this problem in his or her notebook: 50 + 33 = _____. Model how to solve the problem on the number line. (First count on by tens from 50 to 80, then count on by ones to get 83.) Ask your student to use the number line to add 41 + 30. [71] Have your student verbally explain how he or she arrived at the solution.

7 **MODEL** Explain that your student can use place-value blocks to count on by tens. Show him or her 1 ten and 4 ones. Have your student say the number these blocks represent. [14] Instruct your student to add tens until he or she reaches 64.

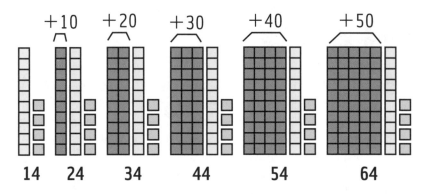

Have your student say each number in the chart. Ask, *What is similar about the numbers?* [each of the numbers has 4 ones] *How do the numbers increase?* [by 10] Show your student how to write an equation using this method. [14 + 20 = _____] Have him or her count on by tens to solve it. [34] Then distribute Student Learning Page 3.A.

FOR FURTHER READING

100 Days of School, by Trudy Harris (Millbrook Press Trade, 2000).

Developing Number Concepts: Addition and Subtraction, by Kathy Richardson (Dale Seymour Publications, 1998).

Mission: Addition, by Loreen Leedy (Holiday House, Inc., 1999).

Branching Out

TEACHING TIP

Visual learners will benefit from using pictures. Have your student draw 10 squares and 20 circles on a sheet of paper. Ask him or her to write the correct number beneath each group of shapes. Ask, *How many shapes are there in all?* [30]

CHECKING IN

Ask your student to use the number line to add groups of two-digit numbers. Observe to make sure he or she understands how to use the number line to add.

Practice Addition

Use the pictures to solve.

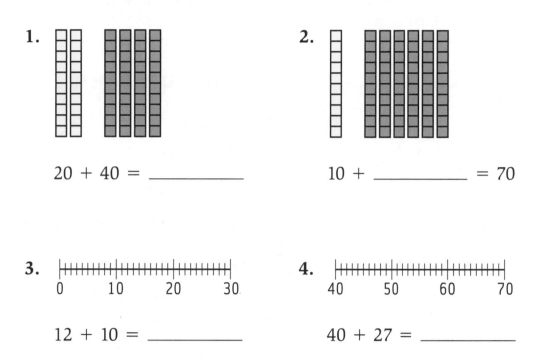

1. $20 + 40 =$ _____

2. $10 +$ _____ $= 70$

3. $12 + 10 =$ _____

4. $40 + 27 =$ _____

Add. Then write the addition fact that helped you.

5. $80 + 10 =$ _____

   Addition fact: _____

6. $20 + 30 =$ _____

   Addition fact: _____

Help Joe by choosing the correct answer.

7. Joe said, "I want to visit Tammy and Michael. Tammy lives 10 miles away. Michael lives 25 miles away. How many miles will I have to go to visit both people?" What equation should Joe use to answer his question? _____

   A $1 + 2$ **B** $10 + 25$ **C** $1 + 25$

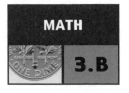

What's Next? You Decide!

Now it's your turn to choose what to do next in the lesson. Read the activities and decide which one you want to do—you may want to try them both!

Teach How to Count On

MATERIALS

❑ crayons or markers

STEPS

❑ Have an adult help you make a copy of the number line you used in this lesson.

❑ Explain to a friend or family member how to count on by tens to solve these problems:

- 10 + 10 = _____

- 50 + 30 = _____

- 17 + 40 = _____

- 20 + 77 = _____

❑ Use crayons or markers to draw pictures to help you explain counting on by tens.

Build and Solve

MATERIALS

❑ 9 index cards

❑ crayons or markers

❑ place-value blocks or counters

STEPS

❑ Use crayons or markers to write the numbers 1 to 9 on the index cards. Each card should have only one number.

❑ Place each number card facedown.

❑ Choose six number cards.

❑ Make a multiple of 10 from each number you chose. For example, use the card with the number 7 to make 70.

❑ Make three addition problems using the multiples of 10 you made. Each problem should have two numbers. An example is 70 + 10. Use each number only once.

❑ Solve each problem. Then check your answers.

Subtracting Two-Digit Numbers

There isn't one right way to teach. Just as children learn in different ways, teachers teach in their own style.

MATH

LESSON 2.4

OBJECTIVE	BACKGROUND	MATERIALS
To teach your student to subtract two-digit numbers and to understand how subtraction relates to addition	No matter where people go or what they do, they will always need to know how to subtract. A solid beginning in basic math facts will help your student as he or she begins to subtract greater numbers. In this lesson, your student will learn to subtract two-digit numbers using a variety of methods.	■ Student Learning Pages 4.A–4.B ■ place-value blocks ■ several counters or buttons

Let's Begin

1 **EXPLAIN** First tell your student that he or she can learn to subtract tens by relating what he or she already knows about subtracting ones. Ask your student to count out 7 ones using counters or place-value blocks. Have him or her remove 3 of the ones from the group. Ask your student to illustrate this with a subtraction sentence. [7 − 3 = 4] Next have your student count out 7 tens. Instruct him or her to remove 3 of the tens from the group. Ask, *How many tens do you have left?* [4] *Can we say 7 tens − 3 tens = 4 tens?* [yes] *How much is 7 tens? How much is 3 tens?* [70 and 30] *What is 70 − 30?* [40] Repeat the activity with other subtraction facts.

2 **TEACH** Draw a number line from zero to 100 with increments of tens. Model how to use the number line to count up from zero to 100 by tens and then backward from 100 to zero by tens. Have your student count backward by tens starting at various points on the number line. Then have your student write the problem 90 − 30 = _____ in his or her notebook. Model for him or her how to count back to answer the problem. Say, *If I take away 30, I am really taking away 3 tens. I can take away 3 tens by hopping back 3 tens on the number line.* Have your student touch 90 on the number line and then hop back 3 tens. Say, *Now you're at 60. So, 90 − 30 = 60.* Have your student use the number line to solve similar problems.

ENRICH THE EXPERIENCE

Draw pictures of subtraction problems for your student and have him or her write the number sentence that goes with each picture.

3 **MODEL** Explain to your student that he or she will better understand subtraction if given a number of ways to find an answer. Have your student write the problem 36 − 12 = _____ in his or her notebook. Have your student show 36 with place-value blocks or counters. Then have him or her remove 1 ten and 2 ones. Ask, *How many do you have left?* [24] Continue solving other problems in the same fashion.

4 **DRAW** Have your student revisit the problem 36 − 12. Ask, *What kind of picture could you draw to help you solve this problem?* Show him or her the examples below. Have your student practice using pictures to solve subtraction problems.

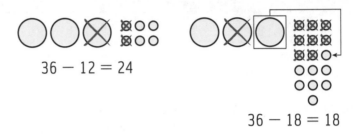

$$36 - 12 = 24$$

$$36 - 18 = 18$$

Then show your student how to write and solve subtraction problems vertically. Explain how to cross out the tens and ones as you regroup and replace the numbers with the new amount of tens and ones.

5 **EXPLORE** Explain that it's important for your student to have a way to check his or her work. Ask, *What is 14 − 9?* [5] *How can you prove to me that 14 − 9 is really 5?* Discuss your student's ideas. Guide your student to discover that because 5 + 9 = 14, addition can be used to check subtraction. Then distribute Student Learning Page 4.A to your student.

Branching Out

TEACHING TIP

The more concrete experiences—such as handling place-value blocks and drawing pictures—your student encounters, the more he or she will understand subtraction concepts.

CHECKING IN

Ask your student to solve the problem 43 − 28 and show you how to check his or her work. Then have your student verbally describe how he or she found the solution.

Subtract Two-Digit Numbers

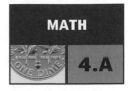

Subtract. Use any method.

1.   80
     − 10

2.   70
     − 30

3.   65
     − 20

4.   18
     − 12

5.   36
     − 14

6.   93
     − 45

7.   82
     − 19

8.   61
     − 40

9.   55
     − 38

Find the difference in the first glove. Then write an addition problem in the second glove to check your answer.

10.

11.

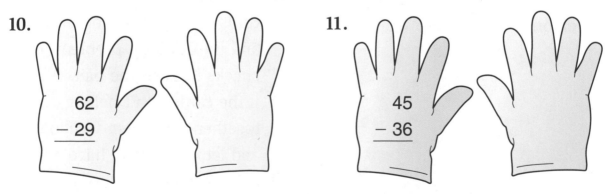

    62
− 29

    45
− 36

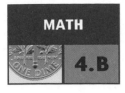

What's Next? You Decide!

Now it's your turn to choose what to do next in the lesson. Read the activities and decide which one you want to do—you may want to try them both!

Play the Subtraction Race

MATERIALS

❏ 1 die

STEPS

Play this game with an adult or a friend.

❏ Each person begins with 99 points. Write 99 at the top of a sheet of paper.

❏ On your first turn, throw the die and subtract the number you roll from 99. You can use counters or draw pictures to help.

❏ Now have your friend throw the die and subtract his or her number from 99.

❏ Keep taking turns. The first person to get to zero wins!

Make a Memory Game

MATERIALS

❏ index cards
❏ crayons or markers

STEPS

❏ Give a friend five index cards. Ask him or her to write a subtraction problem on each card.

❏ Solve the problem on each of the cards. You can use counters to help.

❏ Use the remaining five cards to check your answers. Write addition problems on the cards to check the subtraction.

❏ Now mix up the cards and place them facedown in rows.

❏ Turn over two cards. If the two cards are a subtraction problem and the addition problem that checks it, keep the pair.

❏ If the cards don't belong together, turn them facedown and let your friend have a turn.

❏ Take turns until all of the matches have been made.

Investigating Patterns and Numbers to 1,000

Every child is born with a capability for learning. The teacher's task is to help the child bring out what's already inside.

OBJECTIVE	BACKGROUND	MATERIALS
To help your student expand his or her understanding of place values in numbers up to 1,000	Understanding the place value of digits in numbers is the foundation of all mathematics. Grasping the concept of place value also lays the groundwork for reasoning and problem solving. In this lesson, your student will expand his or her understanding of patterns in three-digit numbers.	■ Student Learning Pages 5.A–5.B ■ counters to represent 100 ones, 10 tens, and 10 hundreds (such as 100 pennies, 10 dimes, and 10 dollar bills) ■ 4 index cards with the numbers 1, 2, 3, and 4 written on them ■ 1 spinner with numbers (0–9 is ideal, but any numbered spinner will work) ■ 1 newspaper

Let's Begin

PATTERNS WITH ONES, TENS, AND HUNDREDS

1 **REVIEW** Use the counters to review number patterns. Have your student count out 10 pennies. Ask, *How many ones are in 1 ten?* [10] Add a penny. Ask, *How many ones are there now?* [11] Have your student write the number 11 in his or her notebook. Ask, *How many tens are in this number?* [1] *How many ones are in this number?* [1 or 11] Continue with other two-digit numbers: 18, 23, 46, and so on. Have your student use dimes and pennies to model the numbers. Then direct him or her to explain the number of tens and number of ones in each.

2 **MODEL AND EXPLAIN** Continue to use pennies, dimes, and dollar bills to model patterns with ones, tens, and hundreds. Ask your student to count out 10 dimes. Say, *You know that 10 ones is 1 ten. How much are 10 tens?* [1 hundred] *Let's skip count by tens to 100.* [10, 20, 30, 40 . . . 100] Have your student count out the dimes as you skip count together. Put a dollar bill in

GET ORGANIZED

If you choose to use pennies, dimes, and dollar bills as counters for this lesson, be sure to refer to dimes as "10 cents" and dollars as "one hundred cents," rather than "one dime" or "one dollar." This will help your student connect the coins to the place values.

place of the 10 tens. Say, *Let's add 3 more tens.* Have your student add 3 dimes. Ask, *How many hundreds do we have?* [1] *How many tens do we have?* [3] Have your student write the number 130 in his or her notebook. Ask him or her to underline the hundreds place, circle the tens place, and place an X over the ones place in 130. [hundreds: 1; tens: 3; ones: 0]

3 **DISCUSS** Continue the activity with the three-digit numbers 321, 206, and 583, using pennies, dimes, and dollar bills to model the ones, tens, and hundreds in each. Ask, *What digit tells the number of tens in 321?* [2] Ask your student to skip count by hundreds to 900 and finish the activity by writing 947 in his or her notebook. Say, *Use dollars, dimes, and pennies to show 947. How many dollar bills do you need?* [9] *How many dimes?* [4] *How many pennies?* [7]

THREE-DIGIT NUMBERS

1 **EXPLAIN** Explain to your student that knowing place values means he or she can name any number. Use this place-value table to review hundreds, tens, and ones:

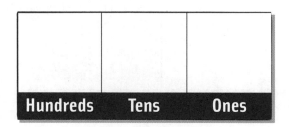

Hundreds	Tens	Ones

Ask your student to use a pencil to write the number 123 in the hundreds, tens, and ones places in the table. Ask him or her to name the number of hundreds, the number of tens, and the number of ones in 123. Together use a dollar bill, two dimes, and three pennies to model 123. Then have your student erase 123 and write 213 in the table. Ask, *What digit is in the hundreds place in this number?* [2] Ask your student to model 213 with counters or coins.

2 **DISCUSS** Give your student four index cards with the numbers 1, 2, 3, and 4 written on them. Ask, *What is the least three-digit number you can make with the index cards?* [123] Have your student write the number in his or her notebook. Ask him or her to identify the place value of each digit. [1 hundred, 2 tens, 3 ones] Then ask, *What is the greatest three-digit number you can make with the index cards?* [432]

WRITING THREE-DIGIT NUMBERS

1 **EXPLAIN** Remind your student that he or she already knows more than one way to write a number. Explain that there are three different ways to write any of the three-digit numbers your student has been forming. Help your student draw place-value

A BRIGHT IDEA

If your student is an action learner who will benefit from acting out a learning activity, draw a place-value chart for hundreds, tens, and ones on the sidewalk or with tape on the floor. Have him or her hop from square to square, clapping to demonstrate the digits and their place values.

blocks for 123 in his or her notebook, as shown below. Ask, *How do you say this number?* [one hundred twenty-three]

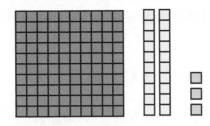

Say, *Let's write the number in three different ways.* Have your student write the number in his or her notebook in the following three ways: 1 hundred, 2 tens, 3 ones; 100 + 20 + 3; and 123.

2 **DISCUSS** Remind your student to pay attention to where zeros appear in three-digit numbers. Explain that a zero holds a place in a place-value chart when there are no tens or ones in a three-digit number. Ask, *Can you write two hundred four in three different ways?* [2 hundreds, 0 tens, 4 ones; 200 + 0 + 4; 204] Ask your student to pronounce each of the following numbers with you: seven hundred forty, three hundred sixty-five, and nine hundred eight. Then have him or her write each number in three different ways in his or her notebook. [7 hundreds, 4 tens, 0 ones; 700 + 40 + 0; 740; 3 hundreds, 6 tens, 5 ones; 300 + 60 + 5; 365; 9 hundreds, 0 tens, 8 ones; 900 + 0 + 8; 908]

COMPARING THREE-DIGIT NUMBERS

1 **EXPLAIN** Remind your student how to use place values when ordering two-digit numbers. Encourage him or her to recall that numbers are compared from left to right by their place values. The number with the greatest digit in the tens place is the greatest two-digit number. Explain that the same is true with three-digit numbers: The number with the greatest digit in the hundreds place is the greatest number. Ask your student to decide which of the following numbers is greater and to explain how he or she knows: 603 or 498. [603 is greater; it has a 6 in the hundreds place and 498 has a 4 in the hundreds place]

2 **ASK** Remind your student of how he or she made greater and lesser numbers with index cards. Ask your student to again form the number 123 with the index cards. Ask, *If we are counting by ones, what number comes before 123?* [122] *What number comes after 123?* [124] Now say, *I am going to say a number. Write the number in your notebook. Then write the number that comes before it, counting by ones, and the number that comes after it. The number is 329.* [328, 330]

3 **EXPAND** Draw 10 columns for your student in his or her notebook. Have him or her label the columns "0–99," "100–199," "200–299," and so on to "900–999." Give your student a spinner numbered from 0 to 9. Explain that your

Investigating Patterns and Numbers to 1,000 **115**

student will spin the spinner three times and write the digits in order to form a three-digit number. Then he or she must decide in which column the number he or she has formed should be listed. Have your student continue to play the spinner game and write the numbers in the correct columns.

ORDERING NUMBERS TO 1,000

1 **PREVIEW** Help your student prepare for ordering three-digit numbers by having him or her skip count by hundreds and tens. Say, *Begin at 200. Count by hundreds to 1,000.* [300, 400, 500 . . . 1,000] *Begin at 400. Count by tens to 500.* [410, 420, 430 . . . 500]

2 **COMPARE** Resume the spinner game. Explain that this time your student will spin the spinner three times and write the three digits in his or her notebook. Once your student has spun three times, have him or her use the three digits to make two different numbers. One should be the greatest possible number using the three digits and the other should be the least possible number. Then have him or her find a third number using the three digits that's between the greatest and least numbers.

3 **EXPAND** Have your student order a series of three-digit numbers. Shuffle the index cards with the numbers 1, 2, 3, and 4. Have your student draw three of the cards and write the three-digit number that the three cards form. Shuffle again and repeat. Challenge your student to write the new number above the first number if it's less than the first number or below the first number if it's greater than the first number.

Branching Out

TEACHING TIP

Throughout this lesson, check frequently that your student is comparing numbers by hundreds, then tens, then ones. As needed draw place-value tables and have your student write the digits in the proper cells.

CHECKING IN

To check your student's understanding of the lesson, give your student a list of four or five local area codes or three-digit telephone prefixes of family members. Have him or her order the numbers from least to greatest.

GET ORGANIZED

Adjust the columns you make according to the spinner you're using. For example, if the spinner has only the numbers 1, 2, 3, and 4, draw only four columns with the headings "100–199," "200–299," "300–399," and "400–499." You may want to make a spinner using construction paper, a pencil, and a paper clip. Put the paper clip over the point of the pencil and hold the pencil tip in the center of the spinner. Flick the paper clip with your finger to model for your student how the spinner works.

FOR FURTHER READING

Exploring Numbers, by Andrew King (Copper Beech Books, 1998).

Pattern Fish, by Trudy Harris (Millbrook Press, 2000).

Practice with Three-Digit Numbers

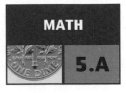
Write the number three different ways.

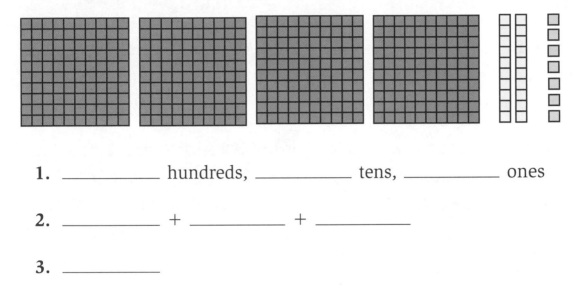

1. _____ hundreds, _____ tens, _____ ones

2. _____ + _____ + _____

3. _____

Draw a picture to show each number on a separate sheet of paper.
Circle the number that is greater.

4. 335   282

5. 114   479

Read each question. Then write the answer.

6. What number is in the tens place?

   841   _____

7. What number is in the ones place?

   103   _____

8. What number is in the hundreds place?

   577   _____

What's Next? You Decide!

Now it's your turn to choose what to do next in the lesson. Read the activities and decide which one you want to do— you may want to try them both!

Sneak In Between

MATERIALS

❑ 10 index cards marked with the numbers 0–9

STEPS

❑ Spread the cards facedown.

❑ Choose three cards. Turn them over. Use them to write a three-digit number.

❑ Choose three more cards and write a different three-digit number.

❑ Choose three more cards. This time, the number you write must fit between the first two numbers.

❑ Have an adult check your numbers.

Stack Up Numbers

MATERIALS

❑ 10 index cards marked with the numbers 0–9

STEPS

You can play this game by yourself or with someone else.

❑ Spread the cards facedown.

❑ Each player chooses three cards.

❑ Use the numbers on the cards to write as many two-digit and three-digit numbers as you can on a sheet of paper.

❑ On another sheet of paper, write all your numbers in order from least to greatest.

❑ Each player gets one point for each number he or she makes.

❑ Each player loses one point for each number that's out of order.

❑ The player with the most points wins.

❑ Have an adult check your numbers.

Adding and Subtracting Three-Digit Numbers

Many people fear that they are doing nothing of value in their lives.
A good teacher never faces this fear.

OBJECTIVE	BACKGROUND	MATERIALS
To teach your student to add and subtract three-digit numbers	Mastering the basics of regrouping to add numbers creates the foundation for regrouping in subtraction. Tying together the two skills will help your student strengthen both. In this lesson, your student will review addition and subtraction strategies and apply the skills to three-digit numbers.	■ Student Learning Pages 6.A–6.B ■ counters, coins, or place-value holders to represent 100 ones, 10 tens, and 10 hundreds

Let's Begin

REGROUPING IN ADDITION

1 **REVIEW** Help your student recall regrouping and place values when adding. Begin by giving him or her the problems $8 + 5$ and $6 + 9$. Help him or her solve each problem, putting a 1 in the tens place in each solution.

$$
\begin{array}{r}
1 \\
8 \\
+\ 5 \\
\hline
13
\end{array}
\qquad
\begin{array}{r}
1 \\
6 \\
+\ 9 \\
\hline
15
\end{array}
$$

2 **EXPAND** Make sure your student understands when to regroup when adding. Ask, *What will change if the numbers are tens?* [a zero will be in the ones place in each number] Have him or her solve these problems using place-value blocks.

8 tens + 5 tens = _____ [13 tens, or 130]

130 = _____ hundred, _____ tens [1, 3]

6 tens + 9 tens = _____ [15 tens, or 150]

150 = _____ hundred, _____ tens [1, 5]

MATH

LESSON 2.6

ADDITION WITH HUNDREDS

1 **DEMONSTRATE** Remind your student of how he or she added numbers. Have him or her solve these addition problems in his or her notebook: 3 + 5 and 300 + 500.

Model for your student how to find the answer to the second problem using place-value blocks. Then have him or her use the same procedure to solve additional problems.

2 **DISCUSS** Guide your student to recognize the relationship between the answers to 33 tens + 28 tens and 33 + 28. Ask, *How is adding three-digit numbers similar to adding two-digit numbers?* [regrouping is used for both] Then create additional problems for your student to solve in his or her notebook.

ADDITION WITH THREE–DIGIT NUMBERS

1 **MODEL** Use place-value blocks to model how to solve 287 + 489. [776] Discuss how adding these three-digit numbers is similar to adding two-digit numbers in that regrouping is used. Help your student work through each step of this addition problem in his or her notebook:

$$\begin{array}{r} 287 \\ + 489 \end{array}$$

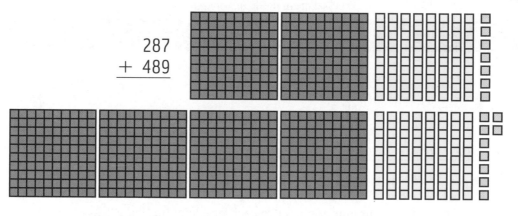

2 **PRACTICE** Invite your student to use place-value blocks to demonstrate the process of regrouping as he or she solves the problem 325 + 299 in his or her notebook.

3 **DISCUSS** Review each step in the preceding problem with your student. Ask, *How many place-value blocks did you have at first?* [3 hundreds, 2 tens, 5 ones and 2 hundreds, 9 tens, 9 ones] *How did you regroup first?* [5 ones + 9 ones made a group of 1 ten and 4 ones] *How did the groups of tens regroup?* [2 tens + 9 tens + 1 ten regrouped as 1 hundred and 2 tens] Continue through the process to the solution. Then have your student complete 146 + 715 in his or her notebook.

SUBTRACTION STRATEGIES

1 **REVIEW** Remind your student that there are different methods he or she can apply when subtracting numbers. Counting

forward or backward are common methods. Give your student the subtraction problems 12 − 9 and 43 − 2 to write in his or her notebook.

2 **DECIDE** Have your student decide which method would work best. Ask, *Would you count forward or backward to solve 12 − 9? Why?* [12 and 9 are close on a number line, so counting up from 9 is an easy way to find the answer, 3] *How about 43 − 2?* [it's easier to count back from 43 to find the answer, 41] Help your student write a fact family for each problem in his or her notebook. [12 − 9 = 3, 12 − 3 = 9, 9 + 3 = 12, 3 + 9 = 12; 43 − 2 = 41, 43 − 41 = 2, 2 + 41 = 43, 41 + 2 = 43]

3 **DISCUSS** Explain that there are other quick ways to subtract that can help. Inform your student that another strategy is to regroup. For example, you can make 1 ten with place-value blocks. Give your student 12 ones blocks and tell him or her to make a group of 9 and a group of 3. Then have your student write the problems 9 + 3 and 12 − 9 in his or her notebook.

Ask, *How can you solve the addition problem by regrouping to make 1 ten? Show me with your place-value blocks.* Your student should take 1 ones block from the group of 3 to make the group of 9 into a group of 10. This makes the addition problem easier: 10 + 2 = 12.

REGROUPING IN SUBTRACTING HUNDREDS

1 **DISCUSS** Ask your student to consider how subtraction problems change when the numbers include hundreds and tens instead of tens and ones. Have him or her write the problems 120 − 90 and 430 − 20 in his or her notebook.

Ask, *Do you need to regroup to solve 120 − 90? Demonstrate with place-value blocks.* [yes; 20 is less than 90, so 1 hundred and 2 tens must be regrouped as 12 tens to find the answer, 30] *Do you need to regroup to solve 430 − 20?* [no; each place value in the larger number is greater than the same place value in the smaller number, so simple subtraction will find the answer, 410]

2 **EXPAND** Have your student write the problem 320 − 180 in his or her notebook. Ask, *Will this problem require regrouping?* [yes] *Use place-value blocks to show me how you will regroup to solve the problem.* Your student should regroup 3 hundreds and 2 tens as 2 hundreds and 12 tens to find the solution, 140.

SUBTRACTION WITH THREE-DIGIT NUMBERS

1 **REVIEW** Remind your student that a subtraction problem with three-digit numbers must be set up correctly to see if regrouping is needed. Describe this situation to your student: *Anna has 221 seashells. She also has a collection of 119 buttons. How many more seashells than buttons does Anna have?*

Adding and Subtracting Three-Digit Numbers   **121**

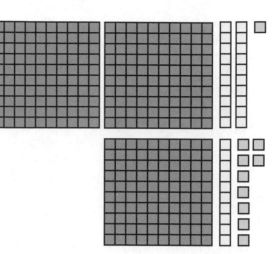

2 **ASK** Have your student write the problem in his or her notebook. Ask, *Will this problem require regrouping?* [yes] Have your student subtract the two numbers. [102] Observe his or her regrouping methods. Then have your student complete Student Learning Pages 6.A and 6.B.

Branching Out

TEACHING TIP

Use the regrouping and borrowing processes in addition and subtraction to reinforce related fact families.

CHECKING IN

To assess your student's understanding of this lesson, have your student use a number sentence to write his or her own word problem. Observe as your student uses regrouping to solve the problem.

FOR FURTHER READING

Counting Sheep (Step Into Reading + Math), by Julie Glass (Random House, 2000).

Math Made Easy: Second Grade Workbook, by Sean McCardle (Dorling Kindersley, 2001).

Subtraction, by Sheila Cato and Sami Sweeten (Lerner Publishing Group, 1999).

Practice with Three-Digit Numbers

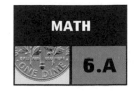

Climb up and down the mountain! Solve the addition problems to climb to the top. Solve the subtraction problems to climb back down. What number is Base Camp? (Hint: Both the addition and subtraction problem in Base Camp have the same answer.)

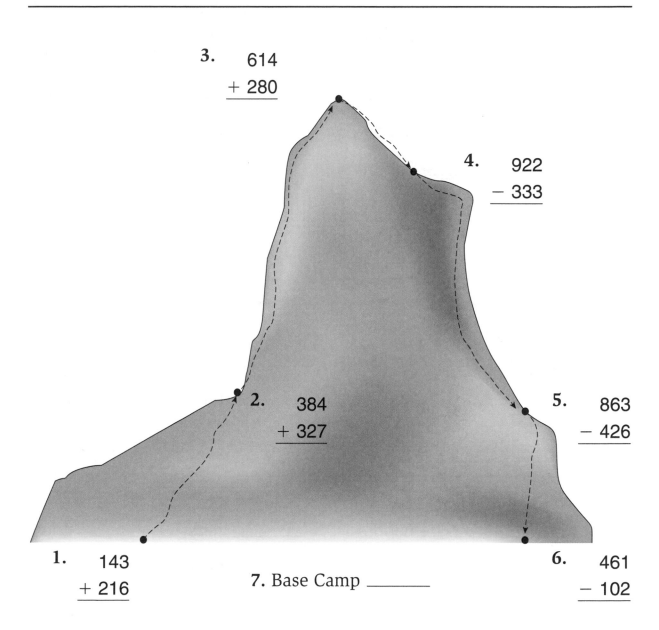

3. 614
  + 280

4. 922
  − 333

2. 384
  + 327

5. 863
  − 426

1. 143
  + 216

7. Base Camp _____

6. 461
  − 102

Explore Three-Digit Numbers

Rewrite and add.

1. 149
    + 163

    _____ hundred, _____ tens, _____ ones
    _____ hundred, _____ tens, _____ ones
    _____ hundreds, _____ ten, _____ ones

2. 682
    + 213

    _____ hundreds, _____ tens, _____ ones
    _____ hundreds, _____ ten, _____ ones
    _____ hundreds, _____ tens, _____ ones

Add.

3. 240
    + 313

4. 525
    + 415

5. 718
    + 112

Rewrite and subtract.

6. 674
    − 515

    _____ hundreds, _____ tens, _____ ones
    _____ hundreds, _____ ten, _____ ones
    _____ hundred, _____ tens, _____ ones

7. 587
    − 263

    _____ hundreds, _____ tens, _____ ones
    _____ hundreds, _____ tens, _____ ones
    _____ hundreds, _____ tens, _____ ones

Subtract.

8. 360
    − 333

9. 881
    − 216

10. 294
    − 104

Understanding Money

Family, friends, love, kindness . . . there are many forms of wealth.

OBJECTIVE	BACKGROUND	MATERIALS
To teach your student to count coins to $1.00 and to make change	Buy the groceries, pay the rent, use the toll bridge, call from a pay phone—everywhere we turn money is involved. In this lesson, your student will learn to count money, compare money values, and make change.	■ Student Learning Pages 7.A–7.B ■ real or play money (dollar bills, half-dollar coins, quarters, dimes, nickels, pennies)

Let's Begin

COINS

1 **DISCUSS** Explain to your student that he or she will encounter money in many ways, such as saving an allowance, spending birthday money, or finding coins in the sofa. Tell your student that knowing the value of money will help him or her make good decisions about money. Give your student one of each kind of coin: a penny, nickel, dime, quarter, and half-dollar. Make sure your student knows the names and values of each coin. Ask, *Which coin is the nickel? How much is a quarter worth? What is the name of this coin?*

2 **TEACH** Have your student count groups of only pennies. Then have him or her continue by counting groups of only nickels and of only dimes. Give your student two dimes, one nickel, and one penny. Tell him or her to line up the coins beginning with the greatest coin value. Count with your student as you touch each coin: 10, 20, 25, 26. Have your student practice counting other groups of pennies, nickels, and dimes.

3 **EXPAND** Introduce your student to quarters and half-dollars once he or she is comfortable with pennies, nickels, and dimes. Have your student practice counting groups of coins that contain one quarter. Then have the groups include two quarters and three quarters. Allow time for your student to practice counting money with quarters and half-dollars.

4 **EXPLORE** Ask your student to choose coins that total 27 cents. Encourage him or her to show 27 cents in more than one way. [1 quarter, 2 pennies; 1 dime, 2 nickels, 7 pennies; and so on]

A BRIGHT IDEA

Counting with quarters is often difficult for the younger student. Practice counting combinations of quarters and half-dollars to 75 cents before mixing them with other coins. When working with quarters, some children find it easier to count a quarter and nickel first, so they can add dimes to 30 cents.

5 **COMPARE** Give your student two sets of coins totaling amounts such as 79 and 89 cents. Ask him or her to count each set and tell you which is the greater amount of money. Have your student repeat the activity using different amounts of money. Ask, *Does having more coins mean having more money?* [no]

6 **LABEL** Ask your student to count out 81 cents. Ask, *How can I write 81 cents?* [81 cents; 81¢; $0.81] Model for your student how to write the amount in the three different ways. Explain that the zero in $0.81 holds the place for dollars. Have your student count groups of coins and write the amount in three ways.

DOLLARS

1 **EXPLORE** Introduce dollar bills to your student. Tell him or her that a set of coins can have a value greater than $0.99. Ask your student, *What comes after $0.99?* [$1.00] Ask, *Can you choose some coins that equal $1.00?* [yes] Have your student use coins to show $1.00 in different ways.

2 **TEACH** Read this problem to your student: *Maria purchased three notebooks for $0.90. She paid with a $1.00 bill. How much change did she receive?* [$0.10] Ask your student to solve the problem and explain how he or she reached the solution. Tell your student that he or she can count up to one dollar when making change. Say, *Suppose I spent $0.78 at the market. If I paid with a $1.00 bill, how much change would I receive?* Show your student how to count up from $0.78. Say, *Two pennies would make $0.79, $0.80. Two dimes would make $0.90, $1.00. The change would be $0.22.* Have your student practice making change from $1.00 with other amounts of $0.99 or less in his or her notebook.

3 **DISTRIBUTE** Distribute Student Learning Page 7.A to your student and have him or her complete it for more practice.

Branching Out

FOR FURTHER READING

The Coin Counting Book, by Rozanne Lanczak Williams (Charlesbridge Publishing, 2001).

Monster Money, by Grace MacCarone and Margaret A. Hartelius (Cartwheel Books, 1998).

TEACHING TIP

Counting money tends to be a difficult concept for this age group. Most children will benefit from repeated practice with real or play money.

CHECKING IN

To assess your student's understanding of the lesson, give your student an amount of money to count that is less than $1.00. Ask him or her to show the same amount using different coins and to write the amount in three different ways. Then say, *Suppose you spent that amount of money, but paid with a $1.00 bill. How much change would you receive?*

Count Money

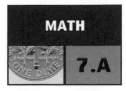

Count each set of coins. Write each amount three ways.

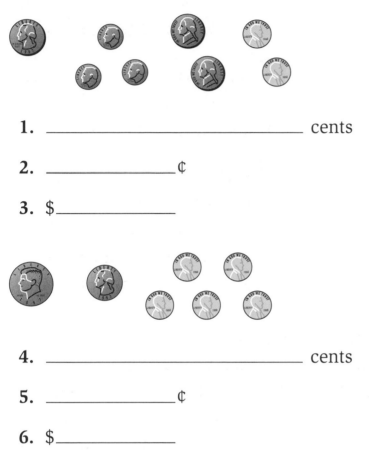

1. _____ cents

2. _____ ¢

3. $_____

4. _____ cents

5. _____ ¢

6. $_____

Circle the set of coins with more money.

7.

Read the problem. Then solve.

8. Alex bought $0.82 worth of peanuts at the fair. He paid with a $1.00 bill. How much change did he receive? _____

What's Next? You Decide!

Now it's your turn to choose what to do next in the lesson. Read the activities and decide which one you want to do—you may want to try them both!

Make a Poster

◉ MATERIALS

- ❑ 1 posterboard
- ❑ markers or crayons
- ❑ old magazines
- ❑ 1 pair scissors
- ❑ glue

◉ STEPS

Make a poster to teach other people about money.

- ❑ Draw and color pictures, or cut pictures from magazines, and glue them to your posterboard.
- ❑ Use markers or crayons to write words and numbers about money on your poster.
- ❑ Write the values of different coins. Then show ways to write different amounts of money.
- ❑ Draw different groups of coins that add up to $1.00.
- ❑ Draw a picture of a toy. Write the cost of the toy. Make sure it's less than $1.00. Then write how much change you would get from $1.00 if you bought the toy.

Open a Store

◉ MATERIALS

- ❑ play money
- ❑ small toys and other objects

◉ STEPS

Be the owner of a store!

- ❑ Gather small toys and other items to sell in your store.
- ❑ Use paper to make price tags for the items.
- ❑ Give each item a price less than $1.00.
- ❑ Give play money to your family and friends. Invite them to buy something from your store.
- ❑ Count up to $1.00 to give each person the correct amount of change.
- ❑ Have your family and friends find more items to sell in your store.

Using Fractions

Get ready for fraction action!

OBJECTIVE	BACKGROUND	MATERIALS
To teach your student to recognize and use fractions	Understanding parts of a whole and parts of a set will prepare your student for division and geometry. In this lesson, your student will use pictures and objects to become familiar with fractions.	▪ Student Learning Pages 8.A–8.C ▪ markers, crayons, or colored pencils ▪ 12 counters or buttons

VOCABULARY
SET a group made up of separate equal parts

Let's Begin

1 **ILLUSTRATE** Explain to your student that whole objects can be divided into equal parts. Tell him or her that a good example of a whole is a large square. Have your student draw a square in his or her notebook. Say, *You and I want to color this square. How can we separate it so we both color the same amount?* [split it into two equal parts] Have your student draw a line to divide the square in half. Then have him or her color half of the square.

2 **MODEL** Explain to your student that he or she can define halves as two equal parts. Point to the colored part of the square. Say, *One half of the square is colored.* Then model for your student how to see thirds using a circle. Have your student draw a circle in his or her notebook. Help him or her divide the circle into three equal parts. Instruct him or her to color a third of the circle.

3 **EXPAND** Help your student draw pictures of equal parts for fourths, fifths, sixths, sevenths, and eighths in his or her notebook. Have him or her draw circles, squares, triangles, rectangles, or other shapes. Direct your student to divide the shapes into four, five, six, seven, and eight parts, respectively. Then have him or her color one part of each shape to illustrate $\frac{1}{4}, \frac{1}{5}, \frac{1}{6}, \frac{1}{7}$, and $\frac{1}{8}$.

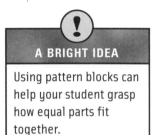

! A BRIGHT IDEA

Using pattern blocks can help your student grasp how equal parts fit together.

4   **EXPLAIN** Help your student write $\frac{1}{2}$ next to the square he or she made into equal halves earlier. Explain to him or her that this fraction shows the colored part of the square. Give your student this rule for forming fractions: The top (1) describes the colored part. The bottom (2) describes the total number of equal parts. Then have your student write a fraction for the shaded part of the circle.

5   **ILLUSTRATE** Tell your student that fractions can also name part of a **set.** Show your student the picture below. Explain that it's a set of gifts. Ask, *How many gifts are in the set?* [7] *How many are blue?* [3] Tell your student that $\frac{3}{7}$ of the gifts are blue. Say, *Explain how I got this fraction.* [the number of blue gifts is on top; the total number of gifts is on the bottom] Then ask, *What fraction shows the number of green gifts?* [$\frac{4}{7}$]

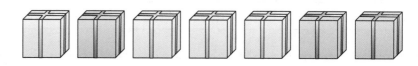

6   **EXPLORE** Explain that your student can make smaller equal sets out of a larger set. Display eight counters. Model for him or her how to make equal halves out of the counters. Ask, *How many counters are in each half?* [4] Explain that each half of the counters includes $\frac{4}{8}$ of the counters, so the fraction for each group is $\frac{4}{8}$ of the total set. Have your student use other groups of counters to explore different fractions of a group, such as $\frac{1}{6}$, $\frac{2}{5}$, $\frac{6}{10}$, and so on. Then distribute Student Learning Pages 8.A and 8.B to your student.

Branching Out

FOR FURTHER READING

Can You Eat a Fraction? (Yellow Umbrella Books: Math), by Elizabeth D. Jaffe (Pebble Books, 2002).

Fraction Jugglers: Game and Work Book and Math Game Cards, by Ruth Bell Alexander (Workman Publishing Company, 2001).

TEACHING TIP

Discuss with your student real-life situations that make use of fractions, such as writing a report that is $\frac{1}{2}$ page long.

CHECKING IN

To assess your student's understanding of the lesson, direct your student to the picture of the gifts. Ask, *Which is larger, $\frac{3}{7}$ or $\frac{4}{7}$?* [$\frac{4}{7}$] *How do you know?* [$\frac{4}{7}$ is the green gifts; $\frac{3}{7}$ is the blue gifts; there are more green gifts] Observe your student's technique of comparing fractions.

Work with Fractions

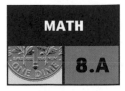

Look at the objects. Match the first three objects with the correct fractions from the box. Then color the other three objects to show the same fractions.

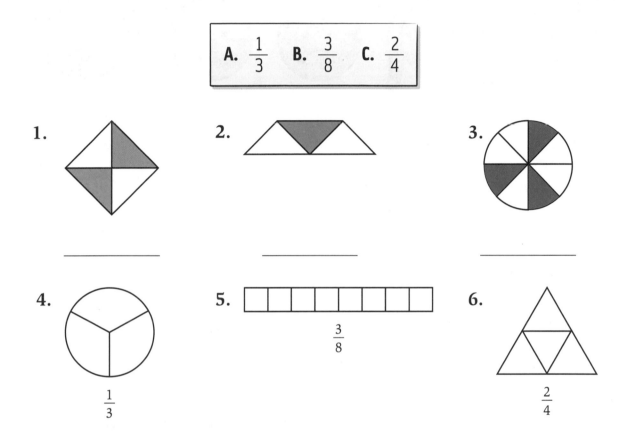

A. $\frac{1}{3}$ B. $\frac{3}{8}$ C. $\frac{2}{4}$

1. _____

2. _____

3. _____

4. $\frac{1}{3}$

5. $\frac{3}{8}$

6. $\frac{2}{4}$

Read each word problem. Then solve.

7. There are 8 people at a party. Everyone wants the same amount of cake. How many pieces should they cut the cake into? What fraction of the cake will each person get? _____

8. A sandwich has 4 equal parts. Eric eats $\frac{1}{4}$ of the sandwich. Monica eats $\frac{3}{4}$ of the sandwich. Who eats a greater amount of the sandwich?

_____

Practice Fractions

Look at the faces. Then answer the questions.

1. What fraction of the faces have hair? _____

2. What fraction of the faces are smiling? _____

3. What fraction of the faces are orange? _____

4. What fraction of the faces are frowning? _____

5. Which is greater, the fraction of blue faces or the fraction of green faces? _____

6. Which is less, the fraction of faces without hair or the fraction of smiling faces? _____

Read each word problem. Then solve. Use counters to help you.

7. Mary has 4 dogs. One half of her dogs are brown. How many of her dogs are brown? _____

8. Sri has 9 flowers. One third of his flowers are roses. How many of his flowers are roses? _____

What's Next? You Decide!

Now it's your turn to choose what to do next in the lesson. Read the activities and decide which one you want to do—you may want to try them all!

Make a Fraction Pizza!

MATERIALS

- ❏ 1 sheet construction paper
- ❏ 1 pair scissors
- ❏ 1 ruler
- ❏ crayons, markers, or colored pencils

STEPS

Ask an adult to help you with this activity.

- ❏ Use fractions to make a pizza with different toppings.
- ❏ Cut a large circle out of the construction paper. This is your pizza dough.
- ❏ Draw lines to divide the circle into eight equal parts. Use the ruler to make your lines straight.
- ❏ Choose three toppings that you want on your pizza.
- ❏ Draw the first topping on $\frac{4}{8}$ of the pizza.
- ❏ Draw the second topping on $\frac{1}{8}$ of the pizza.
- ❏ Draw the third topping on $\frac{3}{8}$ of the pizza.

Eat a Fraction Treat

MATERIALS

- ❏ 1 peeled banana
- ❏ 1 graham cracker
- ❏ 1 chocolate bar
- ❏ 1 plate
- ❏ 1 fork or spoon

STEPS

- ❏ Put $\frac{1}{2}$ of the graham cracker on a plate.
- ❏ Put $\frac{1}{4}$ of the banana on top of the graham cracker. Press the banana down with a fork or spoon.
- ❏ Put $\frac{1}{8}$ of the chocolate bar on top of the banana.
- ❏ Use the rest of the ingredients to make another treat.
- ❏ Make a new treat with other foods. Have an adult help you find foods to use. Write a recipe using fractions of the foods. Share your treat with a friend or family member.

(CONTINUED)

Choose a Card

ONE **MATERIALS**

- ❑ 4 index cards with the numbers 8, 10, 12, 14
- ❑ 12 counters or buttons

ONE **STEPS**

- ❑ Shuffle the index cards. Then lay them facedown.
- ❑ Choose one card.
- ❑ Count out the same number of counters as the number on the card. This is your set. Write the number in your notebook.
- ❑ Rearrange the counters to turn the set into two equal sets.
- ❑ What is half the set? Write the number in your notebook.
- ❑ Repeat for the rest of the cards.

Build and Answer

ONE **MATERIALS**

- ❑ 1 sheet construction paper
- ❑ 1 pair scissors
- ❑ crayons, markers, or colored pencils

ONE **STEPS**

- ❑ Cut two large squares out of construction paper.
- ❑ Have an adult help you cut one of the squares into nine equal squares.
- ❑ Cover the large square with the nine small squares.
- ❑ Use the small squares to answer these questions:
- ❑ How many equal parts are in the large square?
- ❑ Take away one small square. What fraction do you have?
- ❑ Which is greater, $\frac{1}{9}$ or $\frac{8}{9}$? (Hint: Take away eight squares to get $\frac{1}{9}$.)
- ❑ Would you rather have $\frac{2}{9}$ or $\frac{7}{9}$ of your least favorite food? Why?
- ❑ Would you rather watch $\frac{3}{9}$ or $\frac{9}{9}$ of your favorite movie? Why?

Exploring Multiplication and Division

A teacher is not only a great speaker, but also a great listener.

OBJECTIVE	BACKGROUND	MATERIALS
To introduce your student to multiplication and division using pictures, objects, and math facts	Teaching multiplication and division using visual tools and concrete examples will help your student master these functions. In this lesson, your student will use pictures and objects to answer multiplication and division problems.	■ Student Learning Pages 9.A–9.B ■ 30 counters or buttons ■ 10 connecting cubes ■ 3 index cards ■ 9 crayons

VOCABULARY

PRODUCT the answer to a multiplication problem

ARRAY an arrangement of rows and columns that helps demonstrate multiplication facts

Let's Begin

MULTIPLICATION

1 **PREVIEW** Introduce your student to multiplication by reviewing the concept of a set. Have him or her set up 3 equal sets of 6 counters or buttons. Ask, *How many counters are there in total?* [18] *How did you figure this out?* [I counted all the counters in all the sets]

2 **RELATE** Have your student write 6 + 6 + 6 = 18 and 3 × 6 = 18 in his or her notebook. Explain to your student that besides adding we can also multiply to determine the total number of something. Relate the numbers in the addition and multiplication sentences for your student as you point to the counters. Ask, *How many sets are there?* [3] *How many counters are in each set?* [6] Say, *There are 3 sets of 6.* Then explain the term **product** to your student and point out the multiplication sign. Have him or her read out loud the multiplication sentence. Ask, *What is the product of 3 × 6?* [18]

3 **ASK** Instruct your student to add a new set of 6 counters to the other sets. Ask, *How many sets of 6 are there now?* [4] Have him

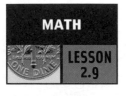
or her write the addition sentence 6 + 6 + 6 + 6 = 24 in his or her notebook. Ask, *What multiplication sentence can you write to find the number of counters?* [4 × 6 = 24] Have your student write this multiplication sentence in his or her notebook. Ask your student to make more multiplication problems using the counters.

4 **EXPAND** Explain to your student that this set of counters or buttons is an **array.** Arrays can be used to show multiplication facts. Create different arrays for your student using counters or buttons. Have him or her identify the number of rows and the number of buttons in each row that make up the total number in each group.

5 **DEMONSTRATE** Tell your student that multiplication sentences can be written across and down. Have him or her make 2 sets of 5 connecting cubes. Lay them horizontally. Then model how to write 2 × 5 horizontally on a sheet of paper. Ask, *How many sets are there?* [2] *How many cubes are in each set?* [5] *What is the product?* [10] Now turn the cubes vertically and write 2 × 5 vertically on the paper. Repeat the questions to your student. Direct your student to write 4 × 3 both horizontally and vertically in his or her notebook.

6 **APPLY** Have your student form horizontal and vertical multiplication sentences for other sets of connecting cubes.

7 **EXPAND** Explain to your student that the numbers in multiplication sentences can be written in any order, just like in addition sentences. Have him or her draw 4 sets of 2 squares. Show your student the multiplication sentence 4 × 2 = 8. Then direct him or her to draw 2 sets of 4 squares. Ask, *What multiplication sentence can we write for these sets?* [2 × 4 = 8]

8 **ASK** Now ask, *What is similar about the two multiplication sentences?* [they have the same numbers and products] *What is different?* [the 2 and 4 are in different orders] Have your student count the number of squares in both drawings. Help him or her see how the squares are arranged differently. Then have your student copy this rule in his or her notebook:

The order of numbers in a
multiplication sentence does not matter.

9 **PRACTICE** Instruct your student to draw 5 sets of 4 squares and 4 sets of 5 squares. Have him or her model the rule by writing the multiplication sentences in his or her notebook.

10 **EXPLAIN** Say to your student that the numbers 0 and 1 are special in multiplication. Explain that any number multiplied by 0 is 0, and any number multiplied by 1 equals itself. Challenge your student to use counters to model 2 × 0 and 0 × 2. Discuss why he or she is unable to model the problems. Then have your student use counters to model 1 × 6 and 6 × 1. Ask, *What is the product of both problems?* [6] *What is the product of 20 × 1?*

[20] *1,000 × 0?* [0] *How do you know?* [any number times 0 is 0 and any number times 1 is itself]

11 **REVIEW** Review the different ways in which your student can multiply. Give him or her different word problems. Start with the following: *Gary has 5 plates. There are 2 cookies on each plate. How many cookies does Gary have?* [10] Have your student solve each problem by drawing a picture, using counters, or skip counting. Then swap the numbers in the word problems and have your student repeat them.

EQUAL SETS

1 **REVIEW** Tell your student that he or she can use equal sets to explore division. Give your student 10 counters. Have him or her use the counters to find the product of 3 × 3. [9] Ask, *How many sets did you make?* [3] *How many counters were in each set?* [3]

2 **EXPLORE** Have your student continue using counters. Say, *Michelle has 3 sets of crayons. There are 3 crayons in each set. How many crayons does Michelle have?* [9]

3 **EXTEND** Now say, *Michelle shares her 9 crayons equally with Libby and Alex. How many crayons do Michelle, Libby, and Alex each get?* [3] Have your student write the name of each person on an index card. Have him or her give each "person" the correct number of crayons to solve the problem. Have your student explain how he or she solved the problem. [made equal sets]

4 **DEVELOP** Introduce remainders to your student. Explain that he or she will not always use every object when making equal sets. Give your student 9 counters. Then say, *You have 9 stickers. You want to share your stickers equally with 3 friends. Will you use all the stickers?* [no]

5 **GUIDE** Help your student solve the problem. Ask, *How many people want stickers?* [4] Have your student draw pictures to represent the 4 people. Then have him or her divide the counters equally among the 4 people. Ask, *How many sets did you make?* [4] *How many stickers are in each set?* [2] *Did you use all of the stickers?* [no] *How many are left over?* [1]

ENRICH THE EXPERIENCE

The word *share* may confuse your student. Explain to him or her that when a person shares a group of objects with others, the person sharing also gets some of the objects. This will help your student form the correct number of equal sets.

🪙 1 Left over

Exploring Multiplication and Division

6 **LINK** Have your student draw 9 flowers. Tell him or her to circle the flowers to make 3 equal sets. Then have him or her make 2 equal sets. Direct your student to copy and complete these sentences in his or her notebook:

There are _____ sets of 3 in 9.

There are _____ sets of 2 in 9.

Ask, *Can one number be divided into a different number of equal sets?* [yes] *How? Here's a hint: Think about the number in each set.* [give each set a different number]

DIVISION

1 **MODEL** Use your student's drawing of 3 equal sets. Write this division fact next to it: 9 ÷ 3 = 3. Explain what a division sign is to your student. Then read the problem out loud. Have your student repeat it. Invite him or her to write the division sentence 9 ÷ 3 = 3.

2 **EXPLAIN** Explain to your student the meanings of the numbers in the division fact. Then have him or her draw equal sets for 4 ÷ 2. Ask, *What is the answer?* [2]

3 **DISTRIBUTE** Distribute Student Learning Page 9.A to your student. Have him or her complete it for more practice with multiplication, equal sets, and division.

Branching Out

TEACHING TIP

Challenge your student with multiplication and division riddles. For example, say, *I am a number. I can be divided into 3 equal sets of 4 with no remainder. What number am I?* [12]

CHECKING IN

To assess your student's understanding of the lesson, watch your student use counters or pictures to solve additional division problems with remainders.

FOR FURTHER READING

Dazzling Division, by Lynette Long (John Wiley, 2000).

Making Multiplication Easy, by Meish Goldish (Scholastic Trade, 1999).

Time Tunes, by Marcia Miller and Martin Lee (Scholastic Trade, 1999).

Explore Multiplication and Division

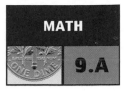

Solve each problem. Then use the answers to color the rainbow.

1.

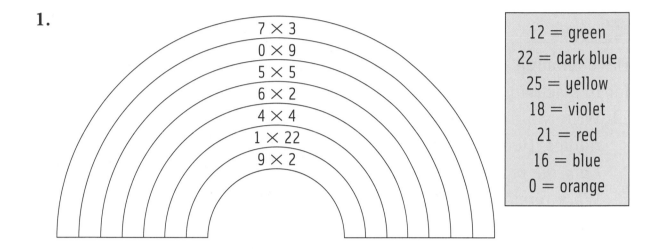

7×3
0×9
5×5
6×2
4×4
1×22
9×2

12 = green
22 = dark blue
25 = yellow
18 = violet
21 = red
16 = blue
0 = orange

Match each picture with the correct division problem. Then solve each problem.

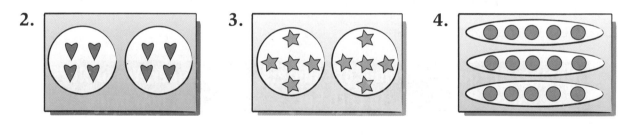

2. 3. 4.

_____ _____ _____

15 ÷ 5   10 ÷ 5   8 ÷ 4

Read the problem. Then solve.

5. Mario wants to share 27 jelly beans equally with Marta and Juan.

How many jelly beans will each person get? _____

Student Learning Page 9.A: Explore Multiplication and Division **139**

What's Next? You Decide!

Now it's your turn to choose what to do next in the lesson. Read the activities and decide which one you want to do—you may want to try them both!

Write Math Riddles

❑ **STEPS**

Have an adult check your work for this activity.

❑ Write your own multiplication riddles. Here is an example: *I am the product of 4 × 3. What number am I?* The answer is 12.

❑ Think of numbers that you want someone to guess.

❑ Write multiplication facts for each number.

❑ Then write your riddles.

Complete the Table

❑ **MATERIALS**

❑ 20 counters or buttons

❑ **STEPS**

❑ Complete the table.

❑ Use the 20 counters or buttons. The first one is done for you.

❑ Have an adult check your work.

Number of Equal Sets	Number of Counters in Each Set	Remainder: Yes or No? If yes, how many?	
1	20	No	_____
2	_____	No	_____
3	_____	Yes	2
_____	4	No	_____
8	2	_____	_____
_____	2	No	_____

Investigating Algebraic Methods

Describing patterns helps us make sense of our world.

OBJECTIVE	BACKGROUND	MATERIALS
To help your student use patterns to solve problems	Algebra involves numerical relationships. One way to recognize these relationships is to explore numerical patterns. In this lesson, your student will describe numerical patterns and use them to solve problems.	▪ Student Learning Pages 10.A–10.B ▪ 20 counters or buttons ▪ 9 connecting cubes ▪ index cards

VOCABULARY
FACT FAMILIES addition and subtraction facts that explain the relationship between addition and subtraction

Let's Begin

COUNTER PATTERNS

1 **EXPLORE** Tell your student that patterns can help him or her understand number facts. Display piles of 1, 3, and 5 counters or buttons. Have your student count each pile. Then ask him or her to describe the pattern the piles show. [increase by 2] Have him or her make the next pile with the correct number of counters for the pattern. [7]

2 **RELATE** Help your student link patterns and addition facts. Use the chart below to show the addition fact for the pattern of the first two piles. [1 + 2 = 3]

Have your student complete addition facts for the remaining piles. [5, 7] Then ask, *What number goes in the last row?* [2] Use the piles to model the subtraction fact 7 − 5 = 2. Then have your student write the remaining facts in a similar chart. [5 − 3 = 2; 3 − 1 = 2]

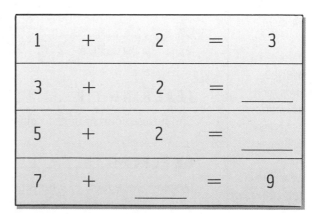

1	+	2	=	3
3	+	2	=	___
5	+	2	=	___
7	+	___	=	9

EQUAL SIDES

1 **PRESENT** Explain that your student can solve word problems by making equal sides. Display sets of 5 and 4 connecting cubes. Ask, *How many cubes are in each set?* [5, 4]

Tell your student that he or she can count on to make equal sides. Have your student count on from 4 to 5. Ask, *To make both sets equal, what should we add to the set of 4?* [1 cube] Have him or her place 1 cube by the set of 4. Write 4 + 1 = 5 on an index card. Explain that 4 + 1 is another way to say 5. Invite your student to read the addition fact out loud.

2 **APPLY** Say, *There are 5 people in Jo's family. Last year, there were 4 people in Kai's family. Then Kai's brother was born. Do Jo and Kai have the same number of people in their families today?* [yes] Have your student explain how he or she found the answer. [counted on from 4 to make equal sides]

FACT FAMILIES

1 **DISCUSS** Discuss **fact families** with your student. Have him or her write 1 + 4 = 5 and 4 + 1 = 5 in his or her notebook. Ask, *What is similar about these two facts?* [they have the same numbers] *What is different?* [the order] Repeat by having your student write 5 − 4 = 1 and 5 − 1 = 4.

2 **EXPLAIN** Explain to your student that these four facts make up a fact family. Inform your student that all fact families have addition and subtraction facts. If your student knows one fact in a family, he or she also knows the other three. Help your student write the fact family for 8 + 3 = 11 in his or her notebook. [3 + 8 = 11; 11 − 3 = 8; 11 − 8 = 3]

3 **APPLY** Say, *You know that 3 + 9 = 12. How can this fact help you solve 12 − 3?* [since the facts are related, the answer must be 9] Then distribute Student Learning Page 10.A. For math bingo on Student Learning Page 10.B, help your student make 20 index cards with addition and subtraction sentences that are missing a number needed to make equal sides. For 16 of the cards, the answer should be a number on the bingo card. For 4 of the cards, the answer should be another number.

Branching Out

TEACHING TIP

Encourage your student to check his or her work using related facts.

CHECKING IN

Display these facts to your student: 2 + 1 = 3; 3 + 1 = 4; and 4 + 1 = 5. Have him or her model them using counters.

A BRIGHT IDEA

Model equal sides of a subtraction fact. This will ready your student for fact families.

FOR FURTHER READING

Lessons for Algebraic Thinking: Grades K–2 (*Lessons for Algebraic Thinking Series*), by Leyani Von Rotz et al. (Math Solutions Series Publications, 2002).

Navigating Through Algebra in Prekindergarten–Grade 2 (*Principles and Standards for School Mathematics Navigations Series*), by Carole E. Greenes et al. (National Council of Teachers of Mathematics, 2001).

Apply Algebraic Methods

Solve. Write the missing number. Pay attention to the signs!

1. $6 = 4 + \boxed{}$

_____

2. $2 + \boxed{} = 9$

_____

3. $10 - \boxed{} = 7$

_____

4. $8 = 3 + \boxed{}$

_____

5. $5 + \boxed{} = 6$

_____

6. $4 - \boxed{} = 1$

_____

7. $9 = 1 + \boxed{}$

_____

8. $5 + \boxed{} = 10$

_____

9. $8 - \boxed{} = 4$

_____

10. $9 = 4 + \boxed{}$

_____

Read the problem. Then solve. Show your work.

11. Toby the dog digs the same number of holes every day. Yesterday, Toby dug 8 holes. Today, he dug 4. How many more holes must he dig today?

_____

What's Next? You Decide!

Now it's your turn to choose what to do next in the lesson. Read the activities and decide which one you want to do—you may want to try them both!

Play Math Bingo

MATERIALS

❏ 20 index cards with number sentences

STEPS

Ask an adult to help you prepare the cards.

❏ Lay the index cards facedown.

❏ Choose a card. Solve the number sentence to make equal sides.

❏ Look at the bingo sheet. If the number you wrote is on the sheet, circle it.

❏ When you have circled four numbers in a row, you win.

❏ Play again!

BINGO!

10	11	1	0
6	9	5	13
2	18	8	20
14	12	15	4

Make a Fact Family Tree

MATERIALS

❏ markers, crayons, or colored pencils

STEPS

❏ Write down your age.

❏ Write down the age of a parent or friend.

❏ Make fact families using the ages. For example, make one fact family using your age and any other number and one using your parent's or friend's age and any other number.

❏ In your notebook, draw a large tree with large apples and pears like shown below.

❏ Write the facts about your age in the same  type of fruit. For example, $1 + 8 = 9$. Write the facts about your parent's or friend's age in the other type of fruit.

❏ Color each type of fruit a different color.

Understanding Geometry

It's time to get things in tip-top shape!

OBJECTIVE	BACKGROUND	MATERIALS
To have your student identify plane shapes and space shapes and to compare shapes and their characteristics	Shapes are everywhere. You can see them wherever you look. Buildings and art are often based on shapes and shape patterns. Recognizing shapes can help your student identify patterns in math. In this lesson, your student will learn to identify plane shapes and space shapes and their characteristics. He or she also will learn to identify symmetry and learn about equal parts.	■ Student Learning Pages 11.A–11.B ■ 1 drinking glass ■ examples of a sphere, cylinder, cube, pyramid, cone, and rectangular prism ■ modeling clay ■ construction paper ■ 1 pair scissors

VOCABULARY

PLANE SHAPES two-dimensional shapes, such as circles and squares

SPACE SHAPES three-dimensional shapes, such as cubes and cylinders

CONGRUENT being the same size and shape

FACES the sides of a space shape (for example, a cube has six faces)

LINE OF SYMMETRY a line that divides a shape in half so that each half is the mirror image of the other

Let's Begin

PLANE SHAPES

1 **DISCUSS** Explain to your student that **plane shapes** are flat, two-dimensional shapes, such as circles and squares. Tell your student that he or she has probably been identifying circles, squares, rectangles, and triangles for many years. Having a good understanding of these plane shapes will help your student as he or she begins to explore **space shapes,** such as cubes and cylinders.

2 **SHOW** Draw a circle, a square, a rectangle, and a triangle for your student. Ask him or her to point out the shapes with three sides and four sides. [three sides: triangle; four sides: square and rectangle] Ask your student to name each shape. Give help as necessary. Now ask your student to count the corners of each shape. Ask, *What do you notice about the number of sides and corners of these shapes?* [the number is the same]

MATH

LESSON 2.11

DID YOU KNOW?

Flat shapes made of line segments are called polygons. Explain that polygons can have any number of sides. Display the polygons shown to your student and discuss.

---

3 **COMPARE** Ask, *What is the difference between a square and a rectangle?* [all the sides of a square are the same length; a rectangle has two long sides and two short sides] Trace around the bottom of a drinking glass twice so that you have two circles of the same size. Ask, *What do you notice about these two circles?* [they are the same size] Explain to your student that things that are exactly the same size and shape are **congruent.** Draw various pairs of shapes for your student. Then have him or her identify if they are congruent or not.

4 **EXPLORE** Have your student draw a triangle in his or her notebook. Ask, *Can you draw a triangle that looks different than that one?* Guide your student to draw different triangles by asking such questions as *Can you draw a wider triangle? Can you draw a taller triangle?* Now ask your student to draw a square and a rectangle. Ask, *How are these shapes the same?* [they both have four sides and four corners] Point out that these two shapes are box shaped. Ask, *Can you draw a shape with four sides that's not box shaped? Can you draw a shape with five sides, six sides, or seven sides?* Allow your student time to create these shapes.

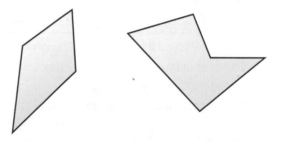

SPACE SHAPES

1 **TEACH** Explain to your student that three-dimensional shapes are called space shapes, or solid shapes. Say, *Many objects that we use every day, such as cereal boxes and basketballs, are space shapes.* Place examples of a sphere, a cylinder, a cube, a pyramid, a cone, and a rectangular prism in front of your student. Or show him or her these shapes:

Cube   Sphere   Cylinder   Cone   Rectangular prism   Pyramid

2 **EXPAND** Ask your student if he or she knows the names of any of the shapes. Help your student find the cube. Ask him or her to point out the edges and corners of the cube. Explain that space shapes also have **faces.** Faces are the sides of space shapes. They can be flat or curved. Ask, *Do you think the cube has flat or curved faces?* [flat] Have your student point out the cube's faces.

3   **EXPLORE** Ask, *Can you find the shapes that only have flat faces?* [cube, rectangular prism, pyramid] *Can you find a shape that has only a curved face?* [sphere] *Can you find the shapes that have both curved and flat faces?* [cone, cylinder] Ask, *How are space shapes different from plane shapes?* [space shapes are three-dimensional while plane shapes are two-dimensional]

4   **COMPARE** Ask your student to study each space shape and identify how many corners, edges, and faces each shape has. Give help as necessary. Help your student make a chart in his or her notebook of the number of faces, edges, and corners each space shape has. [cube: 6 faces, 12 edges, 8 corners; rectangular prism: 6 faces, 12 edges, 8 corners; pyramid: 5 faces, 8 edges, 5 corners; sphere: 1 face, 0 edges, 0 corners; cylinder: 3 faces, 2 edges, 0 corners; cone: 2 faces, 1 edge, 1 corner] Then invite your student to form each space shape using modeling clay.

5   **EXPERIMENT** Gather the space shapes your student made. Ask, *Which of these shapes do you think can roll? Do you think any of the shapes will slide if we push them across the table? Can you stack any of these shapes?* Have your student experiment with the shapes to answer the questions.

6   **IDENTIFY** Ask your student to think of other real items that are space shapes, such as an oatmeal container [cylinder], a cereal box [rectangular prism], an ice-cream cone [cone], and a globe [sphere]. Challenge your student to think of 10 items that are space shapes. Have him or her write them down in his or her notebook.

SYMMETRY

1   **TEACH** Explain to your student that a **line of symmetry** divides a shape in half so that each half is the mirror image of the other. Have your student watch as you cut a heart from a folded piece of construction paper. Open the paper so that your student can see the heart, then fold it in half again. Ask, *What do you see when I fold the heart?* [half of the heart] Open the heart again and point to the fold. Say, *Here is the fold line that divides the heart in half. Are both halves the same?* [yes] *How are they the same?* [they are the same shape and the same size, or congruent] Explain that the fold line is the line of symmetry. Have your student cut shapes from folded pieces of paper and point out the lines of symmetry.

2   **PRACTICE** Draw various shapes. Ask your student to identify which shapes have lines of symmetry and which do not. Help your student understand that a shape can have more than one line of symmetry. One example is a square, which can be divided vertically, horizontally, and diagonally. Help your student find objects or pictures in your home and in books that are symmetrical. Many vases are symmetrical, as are simple drawings of butterflies and pine trees found in picture books or

coloring books. Remind your student that when a figure is folded on a line of symmetry the two halves must match. Ask, *How can you decide if a shape has a line of symmetry?* [fold it in half and see if the two halves match]

EQUAL PARTS

1 **TEACH** Explain that being able to identify equal parts will help your student prepare to begin working with fractions. Draw several squares for your student. Draw a line dividing the first square in half. Ask, *What do you notice about this square?* [it has a line of symmetry; it is cut in half] Ask, *How many parts of the square do you see?* [2] *Are the parts equal?* [yes] Now draw lines to divide a square into three unequal parts. Ask, *How many parts is this square divided into?* [3] *Are the parts equal?* [no] *How do you know that?* [the parts aren't the same size] Continue the activity with four, five, and six parts. Ask, *Do you think all shapes can be divided into equal parts?* Have your student experiment with dividing other shapes.

2 **PRACTICE** Draw several different shapes for your student. Divide some of the shapes into equal parts and some of them into unequal parts. Have your student identify the shapes that have equal parts. Ask him or her to tell you how many equal parts the shapes have. Ask, *What are some real things that we divide into equal parts?* [a pizza, a pie, and so on] *Why might you want to divide something into equal parts?* [to share it equally]

Branching Out

TEACHING TIP

Help your student understand the term *space shape.* Tell your student that a space shape is an object, not a flat drawing. It takes up space. Ask, *Does a pencil sharpener take up space?* [yes] *Does a pyramid take up space?* [yes] *Does a sphere take up space?* [yes]

CHECKING IN

To assess your student's understanding of the lesson, ask your student to explain the difference between plane shapes and space shapes. Then have him or her show you examples of each.

FOR FURTHER READING

Discovering Shapes (*Let's Explore*), by Henry Arthur Pluckrose (Gareth Stevens, 2001).

Three Pigs, One Wolf, and Seven Magic Shapes, by Grace MacCarone and David Neuhaus (Scholastic Trade, 1998).

Work with Shapes

Draw each of these plane shapes.

1. Circle

3. Triangle

2. Square

4. Rectangle

Follow the directions.

5. Circle the pyramid.

7. Color the cone blue.

6. Put an X on the sphere.

8. Color the cube red.

Circle the shape with a line of symmetry.

9.

Student Learning Page 11.A: Work with Shapes **149**

What's Next? You Decide!

Now it's your turn to choose what to do next in the lesson. Read the activities and decide which one you want to do—you may want to try them both!

Create a Shape Picture

MATERIALS

- ❏ several sheets construction paper
- ❏ 1 pair scissors
- ❏ 1 posterboard
- ❏ glue

STEPS

- ❏ Cut many different shapes from the construction paper. Make your shapes different sizes and colors.
- ❏ Think about things you see every day. What kinds of shapes do you see in the objects?
- ❏ Use your shapes to create a picture.
- ❏ Glue the shapes onto a posterboard.
- ❏ Can you use a rectangle and a triangle to make a house? What shapes can you use to make a tree?
- ❏ Use as many different shapes as you can.

Build a Geoboard

MATERIALS

- ❏ 1 sheet graph paper with 1-inch squares
- ❏ 1 pair scissors
- ❏ 1 piece plywood
- ❏ tape
- ❏ several nails
- ❏ several rubber bands

STEPS

Have an adult help you with this activity.

- ❏ Cut a 10-by-10-unit square from the graph paper.
- ❏ Tape the graph paper to the piece of plywood.
- ❏ Use the graph paper as a pattern.
- ❏ Pound a nail into all the squares' corners on the graph paper.
- ❏ You can remove the graph paper or leave it on.
- ❏ Loop the rubber bands over the nails to make shapes.

MATH

LESSON 2.12

Learning to Measure Up

Teaching is both an art and a science. The science is the information the teacher can share with the student. The art is the teacher's ability to adapt to a student's pace and learning style.

OBJECTIVE	BACKGROUND	MATERIALS
To teach your student the customary and metric systems of length, height, weight, and capacity	In addition to grasping the foundation of geometry and science, mastering the basic concepts of measurement is an important life skill. Many students are confused by the different systems of measurement used in the world. In this lesson, your student will become more comfortable with both systems of measurement and will learn to use them for measuring length, height, weight, and capacity.	■ Student Learning Pages 12.A–12.B ■ 1 inch ruler ■ 1 yardstick ■ 1 meterstick ■ measuring cups ■ 1 object that weighs a pound, such as a package of butter or margarine ■ 1 scale ■ common household items to measure and weigh, such as paper clips, a stapler, books, pencils, pens, crayons, a drinking glass, and so on ■ 1 wire hanger ■ 2 paper cups ■ string, wire, or paper clips ■ red and blue markers, crayons, or colored pencils

VOCABULARY

METER   the basic unit of length in the metric system; equal to about 39 inches

CENTIMETER   a unit equal to a hundredth of 1 meter; equal to about 0.4 inch

GRAM   the basic unit of weight in the metric system

KILOGRAM   a unit equal to 1,000 grams, or about 2.2 pounds

CUP   a basic unit of capacity in the customary system

PINT   a customary system unit of capacity equal to 2 cups

QUART   a customary system unit of capacity equal to 2 pints or 4 cups

LITER   the basic unit of capacity in the metric system; equal to a little more than 1 quart

Let's Begin

LENGTH AND HEIGHT IN INCHES, FEET, AND YARDS

1   **REVIEW** Use a sheet of paper to review the concepts of length and height with your student. Lay down the sheet with its long

edge facing your student and ask him or her to estimate the length of the sheet. Then stand the sheet on its edge and help your student estimate its height. To reinforce the difference between length and height, ask your student to name two objects that are longer than they are tall, such as a couch. Then have him or her name two objects that are taller than they are long, such as a refrigerator.

2 **INTRODUCE** Introduce your student to two basic customary measurements: the inch and the foot. Also review the plural forms of the words. Ask, *If I add 1 inch to 1 inch, what will I have?* [2 inches] *How do we say the height of something that's more than 1 foot?* [we use feet]

3 **ESTIMATE AND MEASURE** Give your student an ordinary object that's about 1 inch in length, such as a paper clip. Ask him or her to estimate its length. Then give your student an inch ruler to measure the paper clip's actual length. Continue the activity, asking your student to estimate the lengths of ordinary objects. Then have him or her measure them.

4 **EXPAND** Have your student look at the ruler. Ask, *How many inches are in 1 foot?* [12] Have him or her indicate the starting and ending points of 1 foot on the ruler. Then give him or her the yardstick. Explain that it gets its name because it measures a unit of length called a yard. Invite your student to examine the yardstick. Then have him or her answer these questions in his or her notebook: *How many inches are in 2 feet?* [24] *How many inches are in 3 feet?* [36] *How many feet are in 1 yard?* [3] *How did you find the number of inches in 1 foot? The number of feet in 1 yard?* [counted out inches or feet] Have your student estimate the lengths and heights of different objects. Then ask him or her to measure the items and write them in his or her notebook.

LENGTH AND HEIGHT IN CENTIMETERS AND METERS

1 **EXPLAIN** Display the meterstick to your student. Introduce the terms **meter** and **centimeter.** Explain that centimeters and meters are part of the metric system of measurement. Say, *In the United States, we usually use inches, feet, and yards to measure length and height, but people in most other places in the world use the metric system.* Have your student compare the yardstick and the meterstick. Ask, *What differences do you notice?* [the meterstick is longer]

2 **EXPAND** Explain that the metric system is based on multiples of 10. There are 100 *centi*meters in a meter, just as there are 100 *cents* in a dollar. Show your student the diagram comparing inches to centimeters. Say, *You can see that 4 inches is nearly equal to 10 centimeters. Both units of measurement can help us measure lengths and heights.* Invite your student to use the

ENRICH THE EXPERIENCE

To help your student grasp the differences between inches, feet, and yards and between centimeters and meters, have him or her measure his or her own height in several different units.

meterstick to measure some of the items he or she measured with the yardstick. Ask him or her to write the measurements in his or her notebook.

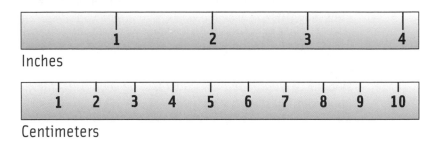

Inches

Centimeters

3 **COMPARE** Guide your student to recognize that meters, like yards, are used to measure longer or taller objects, while centimeters, like inches, are used to measure shorter objects. List or show some familiar objects and distances, such as a pair of scissors, a fork, a pen, a driveway, a door, and a swimming pool. Say, *Tell me whether you would measure the item in centimeters or meters.*

WEIGHT

1 **EXPLAIN** Review the concept of weight with your student. Explain that a pound is a common unit used to measure how heavy things are. Give him or her the object that weighs 1 pound. Say, *This weighs 1 pound.* Use the scale to determine your student's weight. Ask, *Do you weigh more than 1 pound?* Have your student use other items, such as a book, a cup, or silverware, to help him or her describe the weights as heavier than, lighter than, or about equal to 1 pound.

2 **BUILD** To explore the concept of weight measurements and comparisons, help your student build a crude balance scale using a wire clothes hanger and two containers of equal weight, such as paper cups (see the illustration). Attach the cups to each end of the hanger with string, wire, or paper clips. Have your student balance the scale on one finger to compare the weights of different items. For example, have your student see if a stapler is heavier than a pencil. Expand the activity by comparing objects to the 1-pound object. Have your student use his or her balance scale to list items that weigh less than and more than 1 pound in his or her notebook.

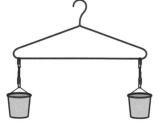

3 **INTRODUCE** Remind your student of the metric measurements for length and height. Explain that there are metric measurements for weight as well. Introduce the terms **gram** and **kilogram.** Say, *These are metric measurements. A gram is a very small unit of weight. One pound is equal to about 453 grams. A kilogram is equal to 1,000 grams. A kilogram is a little more than 2 pounds.* Repeat the activity with the balance scale, but this time have your student list objects that are heavier than, lighter than, or weigh about the same as a kilogram.

4 **REFINE** Explain to your student that pounds and kilograms are both good measures for weighing things that aren't particularly light. Say, *We can weigh ourselves in either pounds or kilograms. We can say a person weighs 55 pounds, or we can say the same person weighs about 25 kilograms. Has the person's weight changed?* [no; it's just in different measurements] Ask your student, *Would pounds or kilograms be good units for measuring the weight of a paper clip?* [no, a paper clip is too light] *What unit would be better to weigh a paper clip?* [grams]

CAPACITY

1 **INTRODUCE** Write the words **cup, pint,** and **quart** on a sheet of paper. Explain that these are the names of different measurements of liquid or other items. Have your student measure a cup of water or a dry ingredient using a 1-cup measure. Have your student repeat the activity with a 1-pint measure and a 1-quart measure. Then model for him or her how to use the 1-cup measure to fill the 1-pint measure. Ask, *How many cups are in 1 pint?* [2] Have your student use the 1-pint measure to fill the quart. Then have him or her use the 1-cup measure to fill the quart. *How many pints are in a quart?* [2] *How many cups are in a quart?* [4]

2 **EXPLAIN** Tell your student that there are also metric system units for measuring capacity. Introduce the word **liter,** explaining that it's the basic metric measure for liquid. Display the quart/liter measuring cup, showing your student the lines that mark each amount. Fill the measuring cup to the 1-liter line and invite your student to find the 1-quart line. Ask, *How does 1 liter compare to 1 quart?* [a liter is slightly more than a quart]

Branching Out

TEACHING TIP

Kilograms actually measure mass, not weight, but it is okay that this distinction is not made at this grade level.

CHECKING IN

Have your student compare objects according to length, height, weight, or capacity as appropriate. For each object, ask him or her to explain what units of measurement would best measure the item.

FOR FURTHER READING

Math and Science for Young Children, by Rosalind Charlesworth (Delmar Learning, 2002).

Math for All Seasons, by Greg Tang (Scholastic Trade, 2002).

Practice with Length and Height

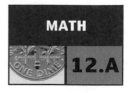
Complete the chart.

Find an object this long.	Write or draw your object.	Measure the object to check.
1. About 1 inch		About
2. About 1 foot		About
3. About 1 yard		About

Answer the questions.

4. How many centimeters are in 1 meter? _____

5. How many inches are in 1 foot? __12__

6. Are centimeters or meters better for measuring the length of

   a soccer field? __meters__

7. Which is a shorter measure, an inch or a centimeter? _____

Practice with Weight and Capacity

Circle in red the objects that are lighter than 1 pound. Circle in blue the objects that are heavier than 1 kilogram.

Complete the sentences.

1. 2 cups equal _____ pint.

2. A _____ is a measure that's slightly more than a quart.

3. A quart is equal to _____ pints.

4. 8 cups equal 1 _____.

Telling Time and Reading Calendars

The only time we have control over is this moment.
What are you doing to make the best of your time?

OBJECTIVE	BACKGROUND	MATERIALS
To teach your student to tell time and read a calendar	Most people's lives run on a schedule. The clock and the calendar help keep our lives organized. In this lesson, your student will learn how to tell time, to write and read times, and to understand a calendar.	■ Student Learning Pages 13.A–13.B ■ 1 clock ■ 1 old calendar that can be cut apart ■ 1 current calendar

Let's Begin

1 **EXPLORE TELLING TIME** Tell your student that he or she needs to be able to tell time in order to schedule activities. Show your student a clock with an hour hand and a minute hand. Talk about the hands with your student. Talk about the numbers on the face of the clock and how they stand for hours and minutes, depending on which hand is pointing to them. Point out that there are 60 minutes in an hour. Count by fives as you point to each number. Now show your student an alarm clock and explain that digital clocks are also very common. Talk about how to read a digital clock. Have your student count the number of clocks displayed in your home. Then have him or her write the total in his or her notebook.

2 **TEACH** Show 8:00 on the analog clock. Have your student identify the number the hour hand is pointing to. Do the same with the minute hand. Explain that when the minute hand points to the 12, the hour has just started, so it's 8:00. Show your student how to write 8:00 and 8 o'clock. Have your student practice reading times to the hour.

3 **REINFORCE** Now show 1:30 on the clock. Have your student identify the minute hand. Then count by fives to find the number of minutes. Say, *The minute hand is showing 30 minutes.* Point out that the hour hand is between the 1 and the 2, so it's not 2:00 yet. Say, *It's 30 minutes after one. We can also say*

A TIME-SAVER

You can purchase a clock-face rubber stamp or stickers from a teacher supply store. It could be helpful with this lesson!

one-thirty or *half-past one*. Have your student practice reading times to the half hour. Then have him or her write the times in his or her notebook in three ways—for example, 2:30, half-past two, and two-thirty.

4 **EXPAND** Show 6:20 on the clock. Have your student identify the hour [6] and then count by fives to find the minutes [20]. Ask, *What time is it?* [6:20 or 20 minutes after six] Continue by having your student practice telling time to five minutes. Introduce the terms *quarter after* and *quarter to*. Explain that 2:45 can be said as quarter to three. Have your student position the hands on the clock to show various times.

5 **DISCUSS SCHEDULES** Show your student the following schedule:

Museum Demonstrations

8:00 Dinosaur Bones	11:00 Transportation	3:00 Reptiles
10:00 Bird's Nests	1:30 Electricity	4:30 Insects

Help your student become familiar with the schedule by asking questions. Ask, *At what time does the reptile demonstration start?* [3:00] *What demonstration can you see at 11:00?* [transportation] Then ask, *How long does the demonstration on dinosaur bones last if the demonstration ends at 10:00?* [two hours] Set the clock to 8:00. Show how the hour hand has to move two hours to go from 8:00 to 10:00. Ask, *If the transportation demonstration lasts one and a half hours, when will it be over?* [12:30] Ask other questions to give your student practice.

6 **EXPLORE CALENDARS** Take an old calendar apart. Ask your student to put the months in order. Have your student find the month of his or her birthday. Ask, *What day of the week was your birthday on? What day of the week was the 14th? How many Thursdays were in this month?* Then have your student find today's date on a current calendar. Ask, *What was yesterday's date? What will the date be tomorrow? How many months after this one are left in the year?* Then ask other related questions.

FOR FURTHER READING

Telling Time (Classroom Helpers), by Vicky Shiotsu; Kathryn Wheeler, Angella Phebus, and Mary Hassinger, eds. (Frank Schaffer Publications, 2002).

Telling Time: How to Tell Time on Digital and Analog Clocks!, by Jules Older (Charlesbridge Publishing, 2000).

Branching Out

TEACHING TIP

Be sure to have your student practice positioning the hands on the clock as well as reading times. Correctly positioning the hands ensures that he or she understands the relationship between the hands and how they represent the time.

CHECKING IN

Have your student draw two clocks showing when his or her favorite television show or scheduled activity begins and ends. Ask him or her how long the activity lasts.

Practice with Time and Calendars

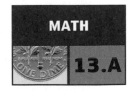
Write the time on each clock in three ways.

1. _____

2. _____ minutes after _____

3. Quarter after _____

4. _____

5. _____ minutes after _____

6. _____ minutes to _____

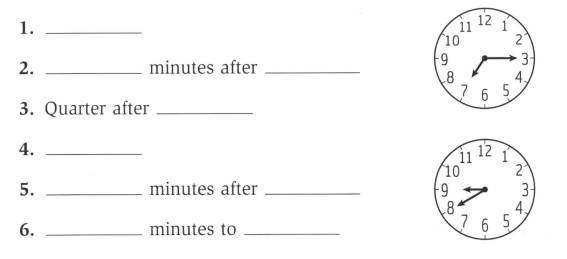

Follow the instructions or answer the questions.

Sunday	Monday	Tuesday	Wednesday	Thursday	Friday	Saturday

7. Write the current month at the top of the calendar.

8. Write the correct numbers for each day. Use a current calendar to help you.

9. How many Mondays are in this month? _____

10. What day of the week is the third? _____

11. Color the square with today's date blue.

Student Learning Page 13.A: Practice with Time and Calendars **159**

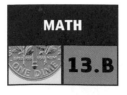

What's Next? You Decide!

Now it's your turn to choose what to do next in the lesson. Read the activities and decide which one you want to do—you may want to try them both!

Make a Schedule

MATERIALS

❑ markers, crayons, or colored pencils
❑ 1 posterboard

STEPS

Make a schedule of your day on posterboard.

❑ Think about things that you do every day.
❑ What time do you usually get up in the morning? What time do you eat breakfast?
❑ When do you do your schoolwork? When do you play?
❑ Decide which activities to put on your schedule.
❑ Draw a picture of each activity on the posterboard. Make sure you put them in order.
❑ Write the time next to each picture. Draw a clock that shows each time.
❑ Hang the schedule in your room.

Remember Special Days

MATERIALS

❑ 1 current calendar

STEPS

❑ Have an adult help you find special dates.
❑ Mark the dates of your family members' and friends' birthdays on a calendar.
❑ Mark other special days, such as holidays your family celebrates or regular activities your family enjoys.
❑ Use the calendar to remember the special days. Make cards to send to people on their special days.
❑ You can use your calendar to remember special things that happen to you, too.
❑ Mark the calendar when you lose a tooth, finish reading a good book, or learn how to jump rope backward.

Collecting and Using Data

Of all the professions, teaching shows the greatest commitment of faith in, and hope for, the future.

OBJECTIVE	BACKGROUND	MATERIALS
To teach your student to collect and use data to solve problems	Although he or she may not be aware of it, your student collects, sorts, and analyzes data almost every day. Simply sorting the people we know into relatives or friends is one way of analyzing data. Your student may be aware of numerous real-world applications for data, such as surveys or voting. In this lesson, your student will gain a greater understanding of collecting and using data.	■ Student Learning Pages 14.A–14.B ■ 7 red and 5 black checkers ■ 1 box or bag to mix counters ■ 1 die

VOCABULARY

DATA information

TALLY CHART a table that lists data

STATISTICS collected data

PROBABILITY the likelihood that something will happen

Let's Begin

1   **COLLECT DATA** Begin by asking your student to guess what letter is used most often in the names of his or her family members or friends. Say, *First, we will collect* **data.** Invite your student to think of three or four names, such as Robert, Terry, Mary, and John. Say, *These names are the data that will solve this problem.* Have your student write the names in his or her notebook. Ask him or her to count the total number of letters. [19]

2   **TALLY** Ask, *What are we trying to find?* [the letter that's used most often in the four names] Say, *We need to examine our data to answer the question. One way we can analyze the data is to make a* **tally chart.** Have your student copy the tally chart on the next page in his or her notebook. Then ask, *What letter appears most often in the names?* [r] *How many times is the letter used?* [5] *What letters are used the second most often?* [o and y each appear twice]

Letter	Tally	Total
R	⁙ℍ	5
O	‖	2
Y	‖	2
A			1
J			1

3 **EXTEND** Ask your student to guess what kind of pet is the most popular among the people he or she knows. Ask, *How many people have a dog? A cat? A fish? A bird? A hamster or guinea pig?* Encourage your student to determine the categories, but guide him or her to limit the selections to three or four. Explain that to find out what pet is the most popular, we must look at **statistics**—the collected data that will help us solve the problem. Help your student create a tally chart for the pets to answer the question.

4 **MODEL PROBABILITY** Have your student watch as you put 5 red checkers and 2 black checkers into a bag or box. Ask, *How many checkers are in the bag?* [7] *How many of the checkers are red?* [5] *If I reach into the bag without looking, which color am I more likely to choose?* [red, because there are more red checkers in the bag] Explain that there is a greater **probability** that you will pick a red checker. Probability is the likelihood that something will happen. Ask your student to express the probability of choosing a red checker using numbers. [the chance is 5 in 7] *What is the chance of selecting a black checker?* [2 in 7]

A BRIGHT IDEA

If your student is having trouble with the concept of probability, have him or her place the checker pieces into the bag or box. Use smaller numbers of pieces, such as 1 red and 3 blacks, to help him or her understand the difference between a 1-in-4 and a 3-in-4 chance.

Branching Out

TEACHING TIP

Probability can be a difficult concept for young children to understand. A kinesthetic approach can reinforce the idea. Have your student watch as you place 10 red marbles and 5 blue marbles in a bag. Then have him or her predict which color he or she will pick if he or she reaches into the bag without looking. Have your student chart the results in a tally table.

CHECKING IN

Have your student tally familiar objects to collect and analyze data, such as the ratio of spoons to forks among an ordinary set of silverware (most silverware sets include a greater number of spoons). Observe as your student completes the activity.

FOR FURTHER READING

Counting and Numbers, by Sheila Cato (Carolrhoda Books, 1998).

Math in the Kitchen, by William Amato (Children's Press, 2002).

Math Made Easy: Second Grade Workbook, by Sean McCardle (Dorling Kindersley, 2001).

Practice Collecting and Using Data

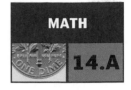

Use the tally chart to answer the questions.

Object	Tally	Total
(canoe)	‖‖ ‖‖ ‖‖ ‖‖ II	17
(car)	‖‖ ‖‖ ‖‖ ‖‖ ‖‖ IIII	29
(truck)	‖‖ ‖‖ ‖‖ I	16
(bike)	‖‖ I	6

1. How many canoes are there? _____

2. How many cars are there? _____

3. How many trucks are there? _____

4. How many bikes are there? _____

5. How many objects with engines are there? _____

6. How many objects with wheels are there? _____

7. How many objects are there all together? _____

8. Which object is most common in this data? _____

9. Which object is least common in this data? _____

10. Write your own question here: _____

_____

Practice Probability

Read the questions. Then write the answers.

1. A die has the numbers 1 to 6 on its sides. If you roll the die, what's the chance that it will show the number 2? _____

2. How many times do you think the die will show the number 2 if you roll it 60 times? _____

Roll the die 60 times. Keep track of the numbers as you roll. Use the tally chart to record the data.

Number	Tally	Total
1		
2		
3		
4		
5		
6		

3. How many times did you roll the number 2? _____

4. Does your data match your prediction? _____

5. Which number did you roll most often? _____

6. Do you think your data will change if you roll the cube 60 more times? _____

In Your Community

To reinforce the skills and concepts taught in this section,
try one or more of these activities!

All Aboard!

Reading schedules and telling time are activities that everyone must learn to do. One way to practice these is to take your student to the train station. Ask your student to find departure and arrival times, or ask him or her how much time has elapsed since a certain train has departed or arrived. Ask a ticket agent or conductor how long it takes to travel from one place to another. Because answers will continually change as the time passes, repeat the questions as necessary for more practice.

Art Museum Math

Aside from learning about art, a trip to an art museum is a good way to explore the world of geometry. Many artists use a variety of shapes in their paintings, particularly artists of the cubism movement, the art deco style of design, and the Bauhaus school of art and architecture. Observing sculptures is a great way for your student to practice visualizing space shapes. Make a list of plane and space shapes your student learned in the geometry lesson. Then take your student to an art museum or gallery. As you view each piece of art, ask your student to locate shapes that match the shapes from the list you made. Make sure your student finds at least one example of all the shapes on the list, but encourage him or her to find as many examples as possible. You can supplement this activity with a trip to the library. Locate a book of paintings and have your student locate and identify the listed shapes in the book.

Create a Math and Culinary Wizard

Having your student help with the cooking may not be the quickest way to get a meal on the table, but it does create an excellent opportunity to learn math skills. When buying groceries at the grocery store, have your student find the proper ingredients. For example, if you need three pounds of tomatoes or eight ounces of tomato paste, have your student weigh or locate the correct amount for each ingredient. When you're preparing the meal, have your student measure the correct amounts for each ingredient needed. For instance, if you need one cup of milk, your student should measure the correct amount. This activity can become a regular way for your student to review these concepts.

Shopping at the Grocery Store

The grocery store is a wonderful place for your student to practice his or her addition, subtraction, and money skills. Give your student play money and take a trip to the grocery store. As you walk through the aisles, have your student give you enough play money to pay for each item you will buy. Then have your student find how much change should be given back for each item. Make sure to bring paper and a pencil so your student can calculate figures if necessary. When you're ready to pay for your groceries, have your student use the play money to figure out how much money should be given to the cashier and how much change should be given back.

We Have Learned

Use this checklist to summarize what you and your student
have accomplished in the Math section.

☐ **Number Sense**
☐ explaining number sense using
  objects, pictures, and numbers
☐ writing about number sense using
  objects, pictures, and numbers

☐ **Patterns and Numbers**
☐ regrouping, number patterns
☐ place value, odd and even numbers,
  ordinal numbers
☐ comparing numbers, ordering numbers

☐ **Adding and Subtracting
  Two-Digit Numbers**
☐ adding tens, subtracting tens
☐ modeling addition and subtraction
☐ checking subtraction with addition

☐ **Adding and Subtracting
  Three-Digit Numbers**
☐ adding hundreds, exploring
  three-digit addition
☐ subtracting hundreds, exploring
  three-digit subtraction

☐ **Understanding Money**
☐ understanding pennies, nickels,
  dimes, quarters, and half-dollars
☐ exploring dollars and making change

☐ **Fractions**
☐ understanding and working with
  fractions
☐ using objects to represent and order
  fractions

☐ **Multiplication and Division**
☐ multiplying across and down
☐ exploring division and equal groups

☐ **Algebraic Methods**
☐ using algebraic methods to explore,
  model, and describe patterns
☐ using algebraic methods to solve
  problems

☐ **Geometry**
☐ exploring space and plane shapes
☐ corners and sides, congruent figures,
  symmetry

☐ **Measurement**
☐ length, height, weight, capacity
☐ inches, feet, yards, centimeters,
  meters
☐ pounds, grams, kilograms
☐ cups, pints, quarts, liters

☐ **Calendars and Time**
☐ understanding time and elapsed time
☐ using a calendar, reading schedules

☐ **Data Collection**
☐ understanding data collection to
  solve problems
☐ using probability and statistics to
  solve problems

We have also learned:

_____

_____

Science

Science

Key Topics

Animal and Plant Life Cycles
Pages 169–176

Animal and Plant Habitats
Pages 177–182

The Five Senses
Pages 183–188

Healthy Diet and Caring for Teeth
Pages 189–196

Natural Resources and Conservation
Pages 197–202

Earth, Sun, and Moon
Pages 203–212

Motion and Force
Pages 213–216

Sound, Light, and Heat
Pages 217–224

Researching a Science Topic
Pages 225–228

Investigating Animal Life Cycles

Animal life cycles are different and alike in many ways.

OBJECTIVE	BACKGROUND	MATERIALS
To help your student learn about the changes that occur when a young animal grows into an adult	All young animals eventually grow up to look similar to their parents. But animal life cycles are different from one another. In this lesson, your student will explore examples of animal life cycles and learn about different animal young and their parents.	■ Student Learning Pages 1.A–1.B ■ 8 index cards with pictures: caterpillar/butterfly, puppy/dog, newborn bird/adult bird, human infant/human adult ■ various family photos ■ 1 copy Student Learning Page 1.A ■ several mealworms (from pet store) ■ 1 large glass jar with a cover that lets in air ■ 1 hand lens ■ 1–2 children's books about animal life cycles ■ 1 photo of a group of people

VOCABULARY

LIFE CYCLE a pattern of growth that repeats again and again

LARVA the stage in the life cycle of an insect after it hatches from an egg

PUPA the stage in the life cycle of an insect before it becomes an adult

VARIATIONS the differences between animals

Let's Begin

1 **EXPLAIN** Point out that all adult animals and people were once babies. Explain that when a baby animal grows into an adult and then has a baby of its own, a **life cycle** has occurred. Show your student the index cards with pictures of animal young and adults. Ask him or her to match each young animal with its corresponding adult animal.

2 **DISCOVER** Explain to your student that an animal's life cycle begins when it is born and continues as the animal grows into an adult. The life cycle is repeated when the adult has young of its own. Find at least four photos of yourself or of another adult who your student knows well. Select one photo as an infant or a toddler, one at your student's age, one as a teenager, and one as

SCIENCE

LESSON
3.1

ENRICH THE EXPERIENCE

Go to the library with your student and select several children's books that discuss animal life cycles. Reference the *For Further Reading* section for book ideas. Ask your student to spend time reading on his or her own to learn more.

Puppies are ready to leave their mother's care when they are about eight weeks old.

FOR FURTHER READING

Animal Life Cycles: Growing Up in the Wild, by Tony Hare (Facts on File, Inc., 2001).

The Life Cycle of a Chicken (*Life Cycles*), by Lisa Trumbauer and Gail Saunders-Smith, ed. (Pebble Books, 2002).

What Is a Life Cycle? (*Science of Living Things*), by Bobbie Kalman and Jacqueline Langille (Crabtree Publishing,1998).

an adult. Present the photos to your student and have him or her place them in order from youngest to oldest. Have your student take some time to think about how people grow.

3 **EXPLORE** Some animals, such as bears, dogs, and humans, are born looking like miniature versions of their parents. These baby animals become adults simply by growing bigger. Other animals are born looking very different from their parents. These animals' bodies go through big changes between birth and adulthood. Explain to your student that some baby animals, such as baby insects, birds, fish, and reptiles, hatch out of eggs. Frogs are one example. Frogs hatch from eggs as tadpoles and later grow legs and become adult frogs. Help your student research the life cycle of frogs and then complete Student Learning Page 1.A.

4 **DISCOVER** Explain that insects, such as butterflies, have life cycles that include a **larva** stage and a **pupa** stage. The larva is the stage in an insect's life cycle that occurs after it hatches from an egg. A caterpillar is the larva stage of a butterfly. Insects eat a lot and grow fast during their larva stage. Explain that the pupa stage in an insect's life cycle occurs right before it becomes an adult. A pupa does not move. It stays protected in one place for several weeks while it changes into an adult. One insect life cycle that is easy to observe is the darkling beetle, which begins as a mealworm. Purchase a few mealworms at a pet store. Keep them in a cool, covered container and feed them fresh apple slices. Have your student observe their transformation with a hand lens. The mealworms will mature into adult beetles in four to eight weeks. You can return them to the pet store when done.

5 **IDENTIFY** Point out that within a group of the same kind of animals, each individual looks different. Tell your student that these differences are called **variations.** Hair color and the shape of ears are two examples of things that can vary on a person's face. Show your student the picture of the litter of puppies. Ask, *How can you tell the puppies apart?* [color, ear size, and so on]

Branching Out

TEACHING TIP

Show your student a picture of himself or herself as an infant and as a toddler. Then show a recent picture of your student. Ask your student to draw a picture of himself or herself as an adult.

CHECKING IN

You can assess your student's understanding of animal life cycles by having him or her draw the life cycle of a butterfly or other insect and of a dog or other mammal.

Order a Frog's Life Cycle

Cut out the pictures of a frog's life stages. (Make sure you are done with page 1.B.) Glue the pictures in the correct order of the life cycle.

A Frog's Life Cycle

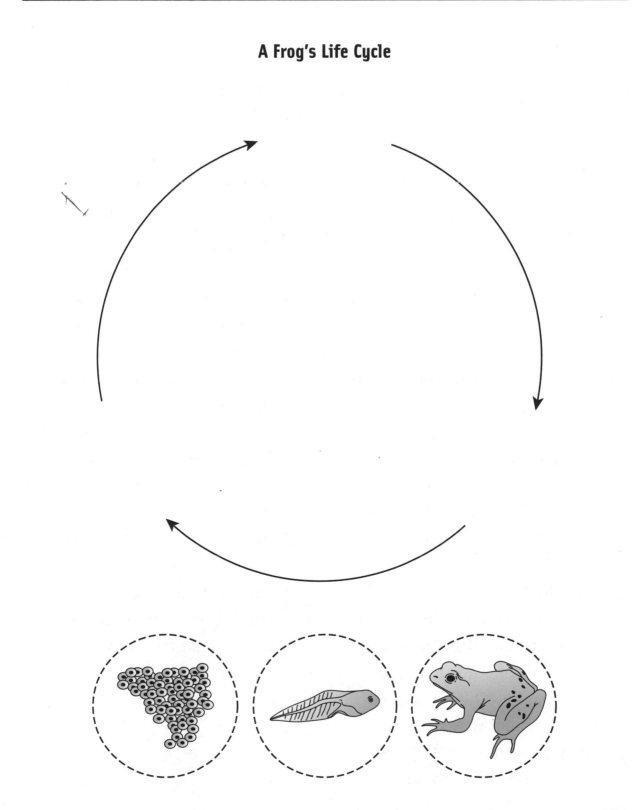

What's Next? You Decide!

Now it's your turn to choose what to do next in the lesson. Read the activities and decide which one you want to do—you may want to try them both!

Show Babies and Parents

MATERIALS

❑ 1 large posterboard
❑ 1 pair scissors
❑ glue
❑ crayons or markers
❑ old nature magazines

STEPS

❑ On one side of the posterboard, write "Same." On the other side, write "Different."

❑ Look in magazines for animals that look the same as babies and adults. Cut out pictures of five adult animals.

❑ Glue the pictures onto the "Same" side of the posterboard. Leave room next to each picture for a drawing.

❑ Now look for pictures of animals that look different as babies and adults. Cut out five adult pictures and glue them to the "Different" side of the posterboard.

❑ Next to each animal, draw what it looks like as a baby.

Act Out a Life Cycle

MATERIALS

❑ 1 blanket, box, basket, or other props

STEPS

❑ Choose an animal that begins its life cycle as an egg, such as a bird, snake, or turtle.

❑ Act out the animal's life cycle for your family and friends.

❑ Use props such as a blanket, box, or basket to help you become the egg.

❑ Act out the way the animal breaks out of the shell. Show how it moves and what it does as a baby.

❑ Act out the rest of its life cycle to an adult.

❑ Act out more than one life cycle. Can your audience guess what animal you are?

Discovering Plant Life Cycles

Seeds, spores, cones, and fruits are little miracles in each plant life cycle.

OBJECTIVE	BACKGROUND	MATERIALS
To show your student how different kinds of green plants make new plants	We depend on green plants for our food and for the oxygen we breathe. Learning about the different ways plants make more plants can help your child appreciate the variety in the natural world. In this lesson, your student will learn that plants are divided into two groups—flowering plants and spore-bearing plants.	■ Student Learning Pages 2.A–2.B ■ 1 simple flower with large parts, such as a day lily, tulip, violet, or iris ■ 1 hand lens ■ common household fruits, vegetables, and seeds ■ glue ■ 8–10 small seeds (radish, grass, or birdseed) ■ paper towels ■ 1 plastic bag ■ 1 fern plant or leaf with spores

VOCABULARY

FLOWERS the parts of plants from which seeds or fruits develop

SEEDS baby plants surrounded by stored food and a tough outer coating

POLLEN tiny, yellow male cells of a flowering plant

SPORES single cells that seedless plants use to make new plants

Let's Begin

1 **GUIDE** Collect one or more simple flowers with easy-to-see parts. Good choices are day lilies, tulips, violets, or irises. Sometimes florists will give you flowers that cannot be sold at no cost. You could also take your student on a flower hunt and collect weed flowers for this activity. Ask, *Why do you think plants have flowers?* [flowers help the plant make seeds, fruits, and more plants] If your student doesn't suggest this idea on his or her own, explain that **flowers** are plant parts that help the adult plant make **seeds** and start new plant life. Carefully remove a few outer petals from a flower. Have your student look inside the flower with a hand lens. Distribute Student Learning Page 2.A. Look at the diagram of the flower together. Compare the real flower with the picture.

DID YOU KNOW?

In simple flowers, both the male and female parts are on each plant. Other flowering plants have the male and female parts on differ-ent flowers or on differ-ent plants. Some flowers are made up of clusters of many tiny flowers.

SCIENCE
LESSON 3.2

✚ ENRICH THE EXPERIENCE

Have your student write two or three sentences in his or her notebook about how he or she feels about flowers and why flowers are important for life and enjoyment.

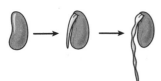

The sprouting process

📖 FOR FURTHER READING

Oh Say Can You Seed?: All About Flowering Plants, by Bonnie Worth and Aristides Ruiz, ill. (Random House, Inc., 2001).

A Tree Is a Plant, by Clyde Robert Bulla (HarperCollins Children's Books, 2001).

What Is a Plant?, by Bobbie Kalman (Crabtree Publishing, 2000).

2 **DISCUSS** Point out that flower parts grow in rings. Show your student the long male flower parts and the female part in the center of the real flower. Shake some yellow **pollen** from the male flower parts onto a piece of white paper. Have your student look at the pollen with the hand lens. Explain that before a seed can grow, a tiny grain of pollen must go into the female part of the plant. Insects such as bees carry pollen from one flower to another. A fleshy fruit or pod grows around the seed to protect it. Ask, *Why do you think flowers are so colorful?* [the colors help attract insects] Then have your student complete Student Learning Page 2.A by drawing and labeling the flower you worked with and answering the questions.

3 **OBSERVE** Tell your student that you are now going to grow some new plants from seeds. Moisten several layers of paper towels with water and lay them flat in a clear plastic bag. Have your student sprinkle the seeds onto the toweling. Make sure they are not crowded together. Observe their growth over several days. Have your student make a series of drawings showing how the seedlings change each day. Point out how the roots grow right into the paper just as they would in soil to anchor the plants. Ask, *Did all the seeds sprout?* [probably not, as not all seeds grow into plants] Have your student write at least three sentences about what he or she learned while watching the seeds sprout.

4 **REVEAL** Tell your student that not all green plants grow from flowers. Explain that the moss that grows on rocks and trees don't have seeds. Show your student a fern plant or leaf. Explain that ferns have roots, stems, and leaves, but they make new plants with **spores** instead of seeds. Point out the brown spots on the underside of the fern leaves. Explain that they are filled with hundreds of tiny spores. Emphasize that spores are much simpler than seeds. They don't contain either a baby plant or food. Ask, *How are spores like seeds?* [they help the parent plant make new plants]

Branching Out

TEACHING TIP

Help your student learn to identify plant parts, such as the roots, stems, and leaves, by pulling up a weed plant, complete with its roots.

CHECKING IN

To assess your student's understanding of the lesson, have him or her explain the different ways plants make new plants. Then ask your student to point out the parts on a fresh flower.

Draw a Flower

Look at a real flower. Compare it with the picture.

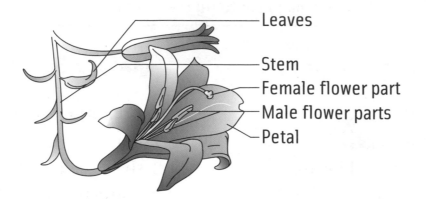

Leaves

Stem

Female flower part

Male flower parts

Petal

1. On a sheet of paper, draw a picture of your flower. Label its parts.

2. How are the real flower and the flower in the picture different?

_____

_____

_____

_____

_____

3. How are the real flower and the flower in the picture the same?

_____

_____

_____

_____

_____

_____

What's Next? You Decide!

Now it's your turn to choose what to do next in the lesson. Read the activities and decide which one you want to do—you may want to try them both!

Collect Seed Travelers

MATERIALS

- ❏ 2–3 plastic bags
- ❏ 1 dandelion seed head
- ❏ 2–3 maple seeds
- ❏ 1 pinecone
- ❏ 2–3 cranberries
- ❏ 1 hand lens
- ❏ 1 bowl water

STEPS

Seeds travel with the help of wind, water, animals, and insects.

- ❏ Go outside with an adult. Collect wild dandelions, maple tree seeds, pinecones, cranberries, or any other wild seeds in your area.
- ❏ Put the seeds that you found in plastic bags. Return home.
- ❏ Look at the seeds and the pinecone with the hand lens. Do any of the seeds have stickers that cling to clothes?
- ❏ Blow on the dandelion seed head. Toss maple seeds into the air. Try floating the cranberries in water.

Make a Spore Print

MATERIALS

- ❏ 2 mushrooms
- ❏ 1 sheet light or dark construction paper
- ❏ 1 glass bowl
- ❏ 1 hand lens

STEPS

- ❏ Ask an adult to help you get a few mushrooms with caps from the store.
- ❏ Break off the stem. Rest the mushroom cap underside-down on a sheet of construction paper.
- ❏ If the mushroom is dark in color, use light paper. If it's light, use dark paper.
- ❏ Cover the mushroom caps and paper with a bowl and leave them overnight.
- ❏ Wash your hands after handling the mus~
- ❏ The next d~
  design
  with the

Exploring Plants and Animals

Every plant or animal has special ways of keeping itself alive and safe.

OBJECTIVE	BACKGROUND	MATERIALS
To give your student an understanding of the variety of plants and animals in different habitats and some of the ways they protect themselves	Earth is filled with a great diversity of plant and animal life. This diversity helps plants and animals survive in their habitats. In this lesson, your student will learn about plant and animal habitats and different ways plants and animals protect themselves to stay alive. Your student will also learn about some of the ways plants and animals depend on each other.	■ Student Learning Pages 3.A–3.B ■ 1 photograph of a tropical rain forest ■ 5–7 photographs of other land and/or water habitats, such as a desert, meadow, deciduous forest, coniferous forest, African grassland, alpine tundra, freshwater marsh, pond, and rocky seashore from library books or the Internet ■ 1 sheet green construction paper ■ 1 apple or pear ■ 1 knife ■ 1 flower with a lot of pollen, such as a lily ■ 1 copy Venn Diagram, page 353 ■ several books and magazines with pictures of animals and plants ■ crayons or markers

VOCABULARY

TROPICAL RAIN FOREST a habitat that gets a lot of rain and that has more different kinds of plants and animals than any other habitat

HABITAT the place where a plant or an animal lives

DEFENSES ways that plants and animals keep from being eaten

MIMICRY the imitation when animals make themselves look like other animals for protection

POLLEN GRAINS tiny, dust-like material in flowers that's needed for making seeds

Let's Begin

PLANTS AND ANIMALS

1 **OBSERVE** Show your student a picture of a **tropical rain forest.** Ask, *What do you see?* [lots of different plants] Tell your student that many different plants grow in a tropical rain forest. Explain that many different animals live there too. Ask, *Why do you think you don't see many animals in the picture?*

SCIENCE
LESSON
3.3

2 **COMPARE** Show your student several pictures of other environments. Explain that each picture shows a different **habitat.** Invite him or her to discuss how the pictures are different. Point out that a desert is very dry, while a tropical rain forest is very wet. A rocky seashore is constantly washed by saltwater, and a mountaintop is cold and windy with lots of snow. A marsh contains freshwater that stands still. A meadow is moist, and an African grassland is dry. An evergreen forest grows in colder places, colder than where forests of trees that lose their leaves grow. Point out that the plants and animals that live in each of these places are different. Ask your student to think of one or two animals that might live in each of these habitats.

3 **READ** Go to the library with your student and look for children's books about different habitats like the tropical rain forest or the desert. Have your student do some reading on his or her own. Ask your student to share what he or she learned.

4 **EXPAND** Lay out the habitat pictures in front of your student. Ask, *What is the same about all of these places?* [they're all places where plants and animals live together] Ask, *What kinds of plants and animals live in our neighborhood?* Take your student on a walk around the neighborhood. Challenge him or her to point out different habitats, such as an open field, a small grove of trees, and a pond. Discuss how they are similar and how they are different. Invite your student to suggest what plants or animals might live in each habitat and why they could or couldn't live in other habitats.

5 **EXPLAIN** Tell your student that plants and animals have various kinds of **defenses** to protect themselves. Explain that the color of a plant or an animal can protect it. Have your student tear off a small piece of green construction paper and place it on top of a larger one. Ask, *In what way does this show how a green bug can protect itself when it sits on a green leaf?* [it's hard to see the small piece of green paper, and it's hard to see a green bug on a green leaf]

6 **CONTINUE** Explain that the size of a plant or an animal also can protect it. Ask, *How do you think that being big can protect an animal?* [it makes it hard for smaller animals to hurt it] *How do you think that being small can protect an animal?* [it makes it easy to hide from other animals] Explain that the shape of a plant or an animal can protect it as well. Tell your student that some animals take the shape of plants to trick other animals. Have your student go to http://www.pansphoto.com. Have him or her click on "Insects" and then on "Camouflage." He or she can click on each picture to see some insects that use color or shape to hide themselves.

7 **EXPLAIN** Tell your students that sometimes animals use **mimicry** to stay safe. One kind of caterpillar looks like a snake.

Some butterflies have large spots on their wings that look like the eyes of big animals. A type of harmless butterfly uses mimicry by making itself look like a poisonous butterfly. Ask, *How do you think looking like a more dangerous animal helps keep an animal safe?* [other animals are more likely to stay away from it]

SCIENCE LESSON 3.3

8 **EXPAND** Tell your student that plants and animals also have special body features that help them get food from their habitats. For example, butterflies have a special straw-like tube on their bodies that helps them reach deep into a flower for food, like drinking juice out of a straw. Octopi are another example. An octopus has suckers on its arms that it uses to grab fish and crabs to eat. Distribute Student Learning Page 3.A. Have your student complete the exercises. Discuss how each animal's body parts help it find food or protect itself.

ENRICH THE EXPERIENCE

Your student can visit the site http://www.fieldmuseum.org and search for "butterfly mimicry" to see pictures of butterflies that use color and mimicry to protect themselves.

9 **EXPLAIN** Tell your student that plants and animals rely on each other. One example is how plants need birds and insects to land in their flowers and carry tiny **pollen grains** from one flower to the next. This makes it possible for seeds to form and new plants to grow. Explain that some animals carry seeds away from the parent plant. A dog or a fox may brush up against sticky burrs that have tiny hooks at the ends. The burrs get stuck in the fur. Later, the seeds drop off and sprout and grow in a new place. Explain that the seeds are more likely to grow if they are not right underneath the parent plant. Ask, *Why is it important to realize that animals and plants in every habitat help each other?* [because then we can learn to respect and take better care of our habitat]

A BRIGHT IDEA

Show your student the flower with pollen. Have your student test how the pollen sticks to his or her fingers. Discuss how birds and insects carry pollen from one plant to another.

10 **SHOW** Cut an apple or a pear in half and point out the seeds inside it. Explain that seeds have a tough outer coating and that if they aren't chewed up they can pass through an animal's body and still grow into a plant. Have your student consider how a bear or a coyote that eats an apple carries the apple seeds to a new place where they can grow into a new tree.

11 **DESCRIBE** Explain to your student that some animals live in groups. Prairie dogs are a type of squirrel that lives in the ground in large groups. They dig burrows and form large underground towns. Some prairie dogs work as guards and stand watch. If they hear something that means danger, they call out to the others. Invite your student to discuss what he or she knows about animals that live in groups. Have him or her suggest some advantages of living in a group. [sharing jobs, warning each other of danger, helping each other find food, helping each other take care of young animals]

12 **EXPAND** Explain that another animal that lives in a group is the ant. Ants build tunnels underground where they live and work. Ants go out in search of food to bring back home to share with the other ants. A special queen ant lays eggs and other ants take care of the eggs. Honeybees live in groups, too. They live in

hives made of wax. Some honeybees go to flowers to find food. They bring the food back to the hive to share with the other bees. A queen bee lays eggs. Other honeybees stay in the hive to care for the young. Ask, *How do people in families help each other?* [they share work, food, and a home, and take care of babies and children together]

13 **WRITE** Ask your student to think about how his or her family works together and helps each other. Have your student write at least three sentences in a notebook about how he or she feels about this.

14 **DISTRIBUTE** Give your student a copy of the Venn Diagram found on page 353. Have him or her label one circle "Ants" and the other "Honeybees." Have your student complete the Venn Diagram by writing down the comparisons between the two animals and how they live.

Branching Out

TEACHING TIP

Have your student look through books and magazines for pictures of animals and plants. For each one, invite him or her to try to identify a body part, color, shape, or other factor that helps keep the plant or animal safe or helps it find food.

FOR FURTHER READING

Crinkleroot's Guide to Knowing Animal Habitats, by Jim Arnosky (Aladdin Library, 2000).

Hide and Seek (National Geographic Action Book), by Toni Eugene (National Geographic, 1999).

Pond Animals (Animals in Their Habitats), by Francine Galko (Heinemann Library, 2002).

Tropical Rain Forest, by Donald M. Silver (McGraw-Hill Trade, 1998).

CHECKING IN

To assess your student's understanding of the lesson, have him or her draw an imaginary animal and include ways for the animal to stay safe. These may be special body parts or ways of living, or they may have to do with the color, size, or shape of the animal. Tell your student to draw the habitat of the animal as well. Ask your student to explain the type of habitat his or her animal lives in and how its special parts help it to stay alive.

Connect the Dots

Connect the dots. Then name the body part. Write how it helps the animal find food or stay safe.

1. Body part: _____

2. How it helps: _____

_____

_____

_____

_____

_____

3. Body part: _____

4. How it helps: _____

_____

_____

_____

5. Body part: _____

6. How it helps: _____

_____

_____

_____

What's Next? You Decide!

Now it's your turn to choose what to do next in the lesson. Read the activities and decide which one you want to do—you may want to try them both!

Check the Temperature

MATERIALS

- ❏ 2 plastic plant pots
- ❏ potting soil
- ❏ 1 spoon
- ❏ 2 thermometers

STEPS

Some animals that live in the desert stay under the ground when it's hot. Find out why.

- ❏ Fill two pots with soil.
- ❏ Dig a hole in one pot. Put one thermometer in the hole. Pack the soil around it.
- ❏ Put the other thermometer on top of the soil in the second pot. Cover the end with a little soil.
- ❏ Wait five minutes and then check the temperature in each pot. Write the temperatures on a sheet of paper.
- ❏ Put the pots in the sun. Wait about one hour. Check the temperature in each pot. What happened?

Watch the Birds

MATERIALS

- ❏ 1 large pinecone
- ❏ 1 plastic knife
- ❏ $\frac{1}{2}$ cup peanut butter
- ❏ 1 paper towel
- ❏ $\frac{1}{2}$ cup birdseed
- ❏ 12-inch piece string
- ❏ 1 pair binoculars (optional)

STEPS

Make a bird feeder. Watch how birds use their body parts to get food and stay safe.

- ❏ Tie the string to the top of the pinecone.
- ❏ Use the knife to put peanut butter into the spaces of the pinecone.
- ❏ Spread the birdseed on the paper towel. Roll the pinecone in the seeds. Press the seeds into the peanut butter.
- ❏ Hang the feeder from a bush or tree outside where you can see it from a window.
- ❏ Watch birds at the feeder.

SCIENCE

LESSON
3.4

Understanding Your Senses

The sense organs are the body's link to the outside world.

OBJECTIVE	BACKGROUND	MATERIALS
To show your student how his or her senses and brain work together	The five senses of sight, hearing, taste, touch, and smell allow people to take in information about the world around them. The brain helps interpret the messages from these sense organs. In this lesson, your student will learn about the five sense organs, how the senses work, and how people can use their senses to keep themselves safe.	■ Student Learning Pages 4.A–4.B ■ 1 clipboard with drawing paper ■ 1 piece string, 6 feet long ■ 1 hand lens ■ 1 copy Writing Lines, page 355 ■ 4 plastic cups ■ 1 small round balloon ■ 1 rubber band ■ 8–10 rice grains ■ 1 metal saucepan and spoon ■ 1 teaspoon each salt, sugar, and lemon juice ■ 1 cup grapefruit juice ■ 4 cotton swabs ■ 4 crayons or markers ■ apple, pear, potato, and onion pieces ■ 1 blindfold and nose clip ■ 1 large box

VOCABULARY

SENSES the ability to see, hear, touch, taste, and smell

ORGANS parts of the body that do specific jobs, such as seeing or breathing

WAVES energy that moves like the ripples in a pond; light and sound travel in waves

VIBRATIONS back and forth motions

EARDRUM a flap of skin inside the ear that passes on sound vibrations

TASTE BUDS bumps on the tongue that help us sense basic flavors

Let's Begin

1 **DISCUSS** Explain to your student that you will be talking about the five **senses.** Ask your student to list them. [sight, hearing, taste, touch, and smell] Point out that people depend on special **organs,** or body parts, to find out what is happening around them. Our eyes, ears, skin, noses, mouths, and tongues are our major sense organs. They tell us that a knife is sharp and fire is hot. They allow us to look at a rainbow, smell and taste a fancy dessert, hear music, and feel a soft breeze. They help us react to

danger and find our way home. Ask, *How would not having one of your senses change your life?* [communication would be different, there would be more risk of getting hurt, wouldn't be able to enjoy certain things]

2 **EXPLORE** Take a brief trip outdoors with your student. Carry along a clipboard, some drawing paper, a hand lens, and a snack. Give your student a hand lens, and assign him or her a small patch of ground. Use the loop of string to mark the area. Ask your student to explore the space with each of the five senses. Ask him or her to choose one object and draw an enlarged view through the lens. Next, have your student close his or her eyes and listen to the sounds. Have your student sniff the air and ground for odors. Let your student explore the textures in the space with his or her hands. Give your student the snack to taste. Have your student draw or write a brief description on the drawing paper each time he or she uses a sense.

3 **GUIDE** Point out that we use specific words to describe the experiences of our senses. Invite your student to think about his or her observations during the field trip. Give your student a copy of the Writing Lines, found on page 355. Ask your student to list different sensory words that he or she associates with each of the senses. For example, for the sense of touch your student might describe the texture of a rock as rough or smooth; for the sense of sight he or she might list shapes and colors of leaves. Then have your student write one sensory word for each sense in a sentence.

4 **EXPERIMENT** Tell your student that sense organs contain many small parts that we can't see. These parts sense substances, as in smell and taste, or **waves** of energy, as in hearing, sight, and touch. Then they send signals to the brain. To discover how eyes work together with the brain, put a plastic cup on a table. Crumple up a small wad of paper. Have your student step back from the table. Ask him or her to try to drop the wad into the cup while covering each eye in turn. On the third try, tell him or her to leave both eyes uncovered. Compare your student's results on the three trials. Ask, *Why is it harder to aim the paper wad with only one eye?* [your brain needs the pictures coming from both eyes to find the cup]

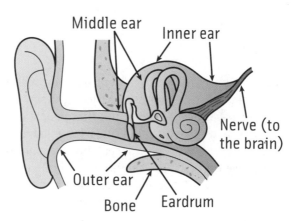

5 **REVEAL** Show your student the drawing of the ear. Explain that sounds are caused by the back and forth motion of matter called **vibrations.** Vibrations travel in waves. Point out that the outside part of the ear sticks out a little bit to help catch sound waves. When sound enters the ear, it travels into the long ear canal until it comes to the **eardrum,** which is a flap of skin that looks like a drum. The eardrum starts to vibrate. The vibration is passed into the tiny bones in the middle ear. Then the liquid and hair in the inner ear begin to vibrate, and the little hairs send the sound signals to the brain. Ask, *Why is it important to be careful when cleaning your ears and to never stick anything into your ear?* [because it could damage the eardrum and harm your ability to hear]

6 **MODEL** Model for your student how sound waves are passed from one part of the ear to another. Take a small round balloon and cut off the spout. Stretch the balloon over the opening of a small plastic cup. Secure it tightly with a rubber band. Invite your student to tap the thin skin to see how tight it is. Explain that the small drum is a model of your eardrum. Drop a few grains of rice on top of the balloon. Tell your student to watch the rice grains carefully. Take a metal saucepan. Hold it right above the eardrum model and strike it with a metal spoon. Ask, *What happens to the rice grains?* [they start to dance around on top of the drum]

7 **GUIDE** Stick out your tongue. Invite your student to look closely at its surface with the hand lens. Explain that the tiny bumps are called **taste buds.** They help us sense four basic tastes: salty, sweet, sour, and bitter. Distribute Student Learning Page 4.A.

8 **TEST** Together with your student mix one teaspoon of salt, one teaspoon of sugar (sweet), and one teaspoon of lemon juice (sour) with some water in three different cups. Pour some grapefruit juice (bitter) into a fourth cup. Have your student label and color code the cups and the key on Student Learning Page 4.A. Help your student use a cotton swab to test each liquid on different areas of his or her tongue. Ask, *Which part has the most taste buds for salt?* [most people taste salt on the sides near the back] Have your student rinse his or her mouth with water and repeat the process for each liquid. Have him or her color the tongue diagram with the corresponding taste colors to make a taste map of his or her tongue.

9 **EXPERIMENT** Explain to your student that our brain combines taste mixtures with the smells of different foods. Show him or her how taste and smell work together. Cut up pieces of apple, pear, potato, and onion. Put them in separate cups. Have your student wear a blindfold and nose clip. Give your student the first three foods, sipping water between taste tests. Your student will probably have a hard time sensing what he or she is eating. Then hold a piece of onion under your student's nose while he

---

!

A BRIGHT IDEA

Have your student experiment with catching sound waves in his or her ear. Stand across the room from your student and speak softly while he or she tries to hear you. Then have your student cup a hand beside each ear. Speak again in the same volume. Ask, *Which time was it easier to hear?* [the second time, because cupping the hands helped catch the sound waves]

ENRICH THE EXPERIENCE

Have your student write three sentences that tell the story of how sound waves travel to the ear and make the eardrum vibrate.

or she tries apple, pear, or potato again. Ask, *What does it taste like now?* [onion] Repeat the tests without the nose clip. Your student shouldn't have any trouble telling the foods apart. Ask, *Why do you have trouble tasting when you have a cold?* [when your nose is blocked, you cannot smell the foods]

10 **EXPLORE** Explain to your student that the sense of touch helps us respond to heat, cold, pressure, and pain. Point out that the other four senses (sight, hearing, smell, and taste) are found in specific body parts. But the sense of touch is found all over your skin. Ask your student to consider how his or her sense of touch varies in different body parts. To find out, try this activity. Collect a variety of familiar objects. Use small balls, blocks, chalk, crayons, pencils, stones, erasers, and so on. Put the objects inside a box. Ask your student to wear the blindfold and try to identify the objects using just his or her hands. Have your student repeat the exercise with his or her feet. Compare your student's success rates in the two trials. Ask, *Which body part is more sensitive to touch?* [hands]

11 **DISCUSS** Explain to your student that all living things, even tiny one-celled creatures, use senses to learn about their surroundings and escape dangers. They move toward sources of food or away from heat. Ask your student to think of some ways our senses can warn us that trouble is coming. For example, sight lets us see a stoplight and hearing lets us hear a train coming. Point out that the sense of touch is part of the body's early warning system. It helps us avoid things that are too hot, too cold, or painful. Ask, *How does your sense of smell protect you?* [by smelling smoke, rotten food, and so on] Ask your student to draw pictures of three ways that we use our senses to protect ourselves.

Branching Out

FOR FURTHER READING

The Five Senses, by Sally Hewitt (Children's Press, 1998).

Fun with My 5 Senses: Activities to Build Learning Readiness, by School Library Journal with Jill Frankel Hauser and Loretta Trezzo Braren, ill. (Williamson Publishing Co., 1998).

The Magic School Bus Explores the Senses, by Joanna Cole (Scholastic Press, 1999).

TEACHING TIPS

☐ To give your student more experience with the different senses, make sound or smell containers out of film canisters. Fill the containers with cotton balls soaked in various scents or small objects that make interesting sounds. Let your student try to figure out what's inside.

☐ Our senses are wonderful things! Take turns with your student sharing how you each feel about the senses and which one you appreciate the most. Then ask your student to take a few minutes to write down how he or she feels about having five senses.

CHECKING IN

To assess your student's understanding of the five senses, hand him or her a familiar object such as an apple, a sheet of paper, or a toy. Tell your student to describe it using as many senses as possible.

Make a Taste Map

Ask an adult to help you fill plastic cups with salty water, lemon juice and water, sugary water, and grapefruit juice. Label and color the cups and the taste color key. Test each liquid on your tongue using a cotton swab. Then color a map of your taste buds on the picture of the tongue.

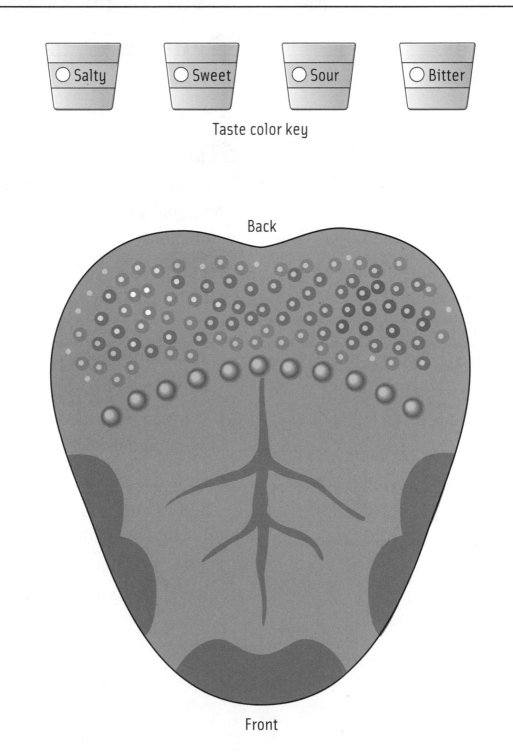

○ Salty   ○ Sweet   ○ Sour   ○ Bitter

Taste color key

Back

Front

What's Next? You Decide!

Now it's your turn to choose what to do next in the lesson. Read the activities and decide which one you want to do—you may want to try them both!

See a Hole in Your Hand

MATERIALS

❑ 1 cardboard tube, 1 foot long

STEPS

You can sometimes trick your brain into seeing things that aren't there.

❑ Keep both eyes open.

❑ Hold the cardboard tube in your right hand.

❑ Put it up to your right eye so you can see through it.

❑ Put your left palm next to the end of the tube facing your face.

❑ Slowly slide your palm toward you along the side of the tube.

❑ Can you see the hole in your left hand?

Understand Balance

MATERIALS

❑ 1 glass

❑ 1 spoon

STEPS

Your ear is not just for hearing. The liquid in your ear also helps you balance.

❑ Fill the glass halfway with water.

❑ Stir the water with the spoon. Take the spoon out and watch how the water keeps spinning.

❑ With an adult close by, try spinning around in a circle.

❑ How do you feel when you stop? How long does it take for the feeling to go away?

❑ Why do you think you feel dizzy after you stop spinning?

Maintaining a Healthy Diet

We eat because food tastes good and we're hungry, but we're hungry because our body is telling us it needs nutrients!

OBJECTIVE	BACKGROUND	MATERIALS
To teach your student how to maintain a healthy diet	Keeping the body healthy is an important task for everyone, and having a healthy, balanced diet is one way to do this. In this lesson, your student will use the food guide pyramid as the basis for learning how to choose healthy foods.	■ Student Learning Pages 5.A–5.B ■ 1 posterboard ■ crayons or markers ■ several children's books about food and health ■ food magazines or flyers ■ 1 pair scissors ■ glue ■ 4–5 paper plates ■ several newspapers

VOCABULARY

DIET the foods a person eats on a regular basis

FOOD GUIDE PYRAMID a diagram that shows how much of each food group a person should eat each day

ENERGY the ability to do work

NUTRIENTS substances in food that the body needs to stay healthy

Let's Begin

1 INTRODUCE Explain to your student that the foods a person eats make up his or her **diet.** Ask your student to make a written list of some of the foods he or she eats regularly. Explain that every food belongs to a food group. Point out that one of the food groups is the vegetable group. Invite your student to identify foods from his or her diet that belong to the vegetable group.

2 DISTRIBUTE Distribute Student Learning Page 5.A. Explain that the **food guide pyramid** is a guide to a balanced diet. A balanced diet is one that gives the body all the nutrition it needs. Have your student find the food group for each food on his or her list from Step 1. Then have your student list his or her favorite foods and draw his or her own food guide pyramid on posterboard showing the foods he or she likes to eat in each food group.

3 EXPLAIN Explain to your student that one important way the body uses food is for **energy.** The body needs energy for

A BRIGHT IDEA

Have your student create a riddle about his or her favorite fruit or vegetable. One example is: I am orange. I am long. I grow underground. What am I? [a carrot]

ENRICH THE EXPERIENCE

Go to the library with your student and check out several children's books on foods and eating healthy. Have your student choose one of the books to read. Give your student enough time to complete the book. Then have him or her describe what he or she learned from the reading.

FOR FURTHER READING

The Food Pyramid (*What Should I Eat*), by Amanda Rondeau (Sandcastle, 2002).

Good Enough to Eat: A Kid's Guide to Food and Nutrition, by Lizzy Rockwell (HarperCollins Children's Books, 1999).

Oh the Things You Can Do That Are Good for You!: All About Staying Healthy, by Tish Rabe and Aristides Ruiz, ill. (Random House Children's Books, 2001).

You Are What You Eat (*Rookie Read-About Health*), by Sharon Gordon (Children's Press, 2002).

everything it does, even sleeping. Ask, *What are some ways you use energy?* [sports, studying, talking, and so on] Explain that after food is swallowed, the body breaks it down into smaller and smaller particles. When the particles are small enough, they are absorbed into the blood. The blood carries these **nutrients** to all parts of the body. The body then uses them for energy as well as for growth and repair. Ask, *What happens if you don't eat enough food?* [your body doesn't have enough nutrients to give you a lot of energy]

4   **EXPAND** Explain that different foods contain different nutrients. Ask, *Which foods does the food guide pyramid say to eat sparingly?* [fats, oils, and sweets] Explain that these foods don't have a lot of nutrients, so a balanced diet includes only a small amount of these foods.

5   **RELATE** Tell your student that one very important nutrient is not on the food guide pyramid. Ask, *What do you think it might be?* [water] Explain that every living thing needs water and that a person's body is mostly made of water. The body uses water for breaking down food, carrying nutrients around the body, removing wastes, cooling the body when it's hot, providing the body with energy, and many other things. These activities use up the water in the body, so we need to replace it. Some foods, such as fruits, contain water, but the best way to give the body the water it needs is to drink liquids such as milk, juices, and, of course, water. Explain that it's recommended for adults to drink six to eight glasses of water every day. Ask, *How many glasses of water or other liquids have you had today?*

6   **MENTION** Mention that newspaper articles about eating healthy are written all the time. Have your student look through a few recent newspapers and find articles about healthy eating. Then discuss.

Branching Out

TEACHING TIP

Provide your student with bite-sized pieces of foods from all the different groups, such as oyster crackers, cooked macaroni, raisins, apple slices, cheese, milk, turkey bits, and broccoli. Have your student eat a sample of each food and identify where it belongs on the food pyramid.

CHECKING IN

Give your student food magazines or flyers and have him or her cut out pictures of food and drinks and sort them by food groups. Then have your student use the pictures to create a menu for one day that will include the correct number of servings from each food group as well as enough water. Have your student glue the pictures for each meal or snack on a separate paper plate.

Make Your Own Food Guide Pyramid

Look at the food guide pyramid. Write your favorite foods. Then draw your own pyramid using the foods you like to eat on a separate sheet of paper.

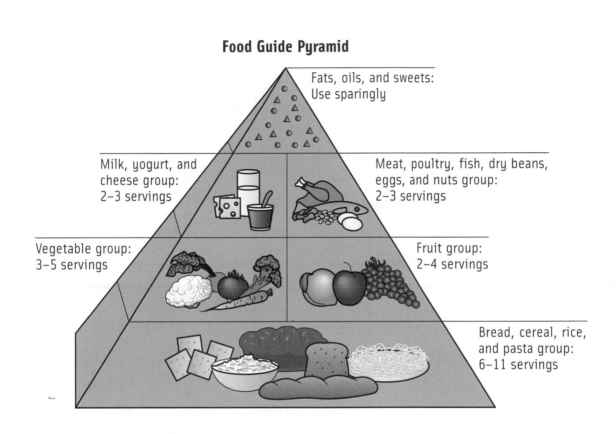

Food Guide Pyramid

Fats, oils, and sweets: Use sparingly

Milk, yogurt, and cheese group: 2–3 servings

Meat, poultry, fish, dry beans, eggs, and nuts group: 2–3 servings

Vegetable group: 3–5 servings

Fruit group: 2–4 servings

Bread, cereal, rice, and pasta group: 6–11 servings

1. Favorite fruit: _____

2. Favorite bread/cereal: _____

3. Favorite vegetable: _____

What's Next? You Decide!

Now it's your turn to choose what to do next in the lesson. Read the activities and decide which one you want to do—you may want to try them both!

Put Ants on a Log

MATERIALS

- ❏ 1 celery stick cut into 3 pieces
- ❏ 1 plate
- ❏ 1 butter knife
- ❏ peanut butter
- ❏ raisins

STEPS

Ask an adult to help you make a healthy, yummy snack.

- ❏ Put the celery pieces on a plate.
- ❏ Fill each piece of celery with peanut butter.
- ❏ Press raisins into the peanut butter.
- ❏ Name the food groups that are in your snack.
- ❏ Enjoy!

Break It Up

MATERIALS

- ❏ 2 sugar cubes or bouillon cubes
- ❏ 1 paper towel
- ❏ 1 spoon
- ❏ 2 clear cups

STEPS

See what happens to food in your body.

- ❏ Put two sugar cubes or bouillon cubes on a paper towel. Use a spoon to break one of the cubes into small pieces.
- ❏ Fill the cups halfway with water.
- ❏ Put the whole cube in one cup. Put the broken cube in the other cup. Stir the water. What happens?

Caring for Your Teeth

Keep that set of chompers clean!

OBJECTIVE	BACKGROUND	MATERIALS
To teach your student about the different kinds of teeth and how to care for them	Your student uses his or her teeth for chewing food and speaking clearly. Keeping teeth healthy is the only way to have them last a lifetime. In this lesson, your student will learn the functions of the various kinds of teeth and how to keep teeth clean and healthy.	■ Student Learning Pages 6.A–6.B ■ 2 apples ■ 1 mirror ■ 2 toothbrushes ■ 2 lengths dental floss, 1–2 feet long ■ 10 index cards

VOCABULARY

BABY TEETH the first set of teeth

ADULT TEETH the second set of teeth, also known as permanent teeth

FLOSS a special type of string for cleaning between the teeth

TOOTH DECAY the rotting of teeth, usually caused by improper care

CAVITY a hole in a tooth caused by tooth decay

X RAYS special pictures that show the insides of teeth, including any holes

FILLING the material put into a cavity to fill the hole

Let's Begin

1 **INTRODUCE** Ask your student, *Why do we need our teeth?* [for chewing food] Discuss the foods your student wouldn't have been able to eat for breakfast without teeth for chewing. Point out that teeth are also needed for speech. The tongue and teeth work together when *this, that,* and other *th* words are spoken. Ask your student to say the word *teeth* while paying attention to the position of his or her teeth and tongue.

2 **OBSERVE** Ask, *What happens to your teeth at about age six or seven?* [they start to fall out] Explain that **baby teeth** fall out and are replaced by **adult teeth.** These adult teeth need to last the rest of a person's life. Distribute Student Learning Page 6.A. Have your student identify the baby and adult teeth in the first picture. Ask, *Why do baby teeth get pushed out?* [adult teeth begin to grow up under the baby teeth and push them out]

DID YOU KNOW?

A child has 20 baby teeth. An adult has 32 adult teeth.

3 **EXPAND** Tell your student that there are three kinds of teeth. Give your student an apple and have him or her take a bite out of it. Then ask your student to tell which teeth he or she used to bite the apple and how they were used. Explain that the front teeth are biting teeth. The sharp teeth next to them are used for tearing meat. The flat teeth in the back grind food. Have your student identify the three kinds of teeth in the second picture and then complete the rest of Student Learning Page 6.A.

4 **EXPLAIN** Explain to your student that it's important to take good care of one's teeth by brushing them at least twice a day, and, if possible, after every meal. It's also important to use **floss** to remove food from between teeth. Point out that brushing and flossing help prevent **tooth decay.** Sugar is one cause of tooth decay. When sugar or other food stays on the teeth, germs in the mouth combine with it to form a substance that sticks to the teeth. Over time, the germs can create a **cavity.** Ask, *What is one reason adults tell children not to eat too many sweets?* [to help keep their teeth healthy]

5 **EXPAND** Explain that the correct way to brush one's teeth is to brush: (1) down on the top teeth; (2) up on the bottom teeth; (3) in circles across the teeth; (4) the inside of the teeth; and (5) over the flat chewing surfaces. Then explain how to floss: (1) wrap floss around the fingers; (2) put it between two teeth; and (3) move it back and forth gently from the top down to the gums. Together with your student model and practice brushing and flossing in front of a mirror.

6 **CONCLUDE** Explain that another important way to keep teeth healthy is to go to the dentist regularly. The dentist cleans the teeth and takes **X rays** to look for cavities. The dentist puts a **filling** in any cavities that are found. Invite your student to share his or her experiences at the dentist.

ENRICH THE EXPERIENCE

Have your student complete a short writing exercise about the first time he or she lost a baby tooth. Ask your student to write a short paragraph that describes things such as how old he or she was, what it felt like, what happened to the baby tooth, and anything else he or she wants to write about.

FOR FURTHER READING

Danny Goes to the Dentist, by Robert Robinson (Peter Bedrick Books, 2002).

Make Your Way for Tooth Decay, by Bobbi Katz (Scholastic Paperbacks, 2002).

Open Wide: Tooth School Inside, by Laura Keller (Henry Holt and Company, 2000).

Branching Out

TEACHING TIP

Show your student an apple to represent a tooth. Poke a hole in the apple and explain that the hole is like a cavity. Discuss why cavities can form. Have your student predict what will happen to the cavity in the apple after some time has passed. Leave the apple on display. Each day have your student make observations. After about a week, discuss what has happened. Discuss how your student can prevent cavities from forming.

CHECKING IN

Write "tearing tooth" on two index cards, "chewing tooth" on four index cards, and "biting tooth" on four index cards. Challenge your student to put the cards in the correct order.

Check Out Your Teeth

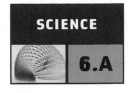
Look at the pictures. Draw lines to label the teeth.

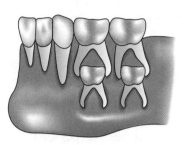

Baby teeth

Adult teeth

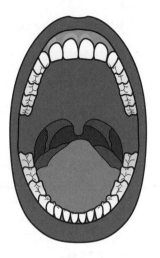

Biting teeth

Tearing teeth

Grinding teeth

Count your teeth. Use a mirror to help you.

1. How many baby teeth have you lost? _____

2. How many adult teeth do you have? _____

3. How many tearing teeth do you have? _____

4. How many grinding teeth do you have? _____

5. How many biting teeth do you have? _____

What's Next? You Decide!

Now it's your turn to choose what to do next in the lesson. Read the activities and decide which one you want to do— you may want to try them both!

Observe an Egg

MATERIALS

- ❑ 1 hard-boiled egg
- ❑ 1 jar with lid
- ❑ vinegar

STEPS

Both your teeth and an egg have a hard shell to protect them. Use an egg to see what happens when teeth decay.

- ❑ Feel the shell of an egg. How does it feel?
- ❑ Fill the jar with vinegar. Put the egg in the jar. Put the lid on the jar. What do you think will happen to the egg?
- ❑ Wait two days. Gently take the egg out of the jar. How has it changed? How is this like tooth decay? How can you stop tooth decay?

Make a Set of Teeth

MATERIALS

- ❑ 2 strips card stock, 1 by 5 inches
- ❑ 8 dry navy beans
- ❑ 12 dry lima beans
- ❑ 1 pink crayon or marker
- ❑ glue
- ❑ 1 hole puncher
- ❑ 2 pieces string, 6 inches long

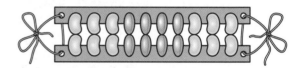

STEPS

- ❑ Color the paper pink.
- ❑ Use the large beans to show grinding teeth. Use the small beans for tearing and biting teeth. Glue the beans to the paper in the right order.
- ❑ When the glue is dry, punch holes in the ends of both strips of paper.
- ❑ Put the strips together so the teeth face each other. Tie a string through the holes.

Learning About Earth's Natural Resources

Natural resources may be all around us, but they won't last forever!

OBJECTIVE	BACKGROUND	MATERIALS
To help your student identify Earth's natural resources and learn how to conserve them	Earth's natural resources are what support plant and animal life. The way we use natural resources today affects the future. In this lesson, your student will identify natural resources, learn how to conserve them, and gain an understanding of how pollution changes the environment.	■ Student Learning Pages 7.A–7.B ■ 1 photo of Earth from space ■ 1 book ■ 1 drinking glass ■ 1 cooking pot or pan ■ 1 clean glass or plastic container ■ 1 small bag peat moss ■ several magazines and newspapers

VOCABULARY

NATURAL RESOURCES the materials that come from Earth that plants and animals need

FOSSIL FUELS natural resources such as coal and oil that take millions of years to form

ENVIRONMENT everything that's around us

POLLUTION the release of harmful materials into the environment

CONSERVATION the protection and careful use of Earth's natural resources

REDUCE to use something less

REUSE to use something more than once

LANDFILL an area of land where garbage is spread out in layers and allowed to break down

RECYCLE to take something that has already been used and use it in a different way

Let's Begin

1 **INTRODUCE** Tell your student that Earth provides the materials that animals and plants need to live. These materials are called **natural resources.** Explain that natural resources include air, soil, and water. Show your student a photograph of Earth taken from space. Ask, *What natural resource gives Earth its blue color?* [water] Then ask him or her to give examples of ways that he or she uses water. [drinking, bathing, cooking]

2 **DISCOVER** Explain to your student that natural resources are used to make many useful items. People use trees to make

paper and build houses. Rocks are used to make things such as cement and metal. Show your student three objects—a book, a drinking glass, and a cooking pot or pan. Ask your student if he or she knows what kinds of natural resources were used to make each item. [the book was made from the wood of trees, the glass was made from sand, the pan was made from the metal in rocks]

3 **REVEAL** Explain to your student that **fossil fuels** are a type of natural resource that come from the remains of plants and animals that lived millions of years ago. Coal is a natural resource that comes from plants. Explain to your student that when ancient trees died, parts of the trees were buried deep in the soil. Over time, heat and pressure turned the plant parts into coal. Show your student a bag of peat moss. Explain that the peat moss is one of the final stages in the process of coal formation.

? DID YOU KNOW?

The first oil well in the United States was located in Titusville, Pennsylvania. On August 27, 1859, Edwin L. Drake struck oil at 69.5 feet beneath the land's surface.

4 **EXPLAIN** Explain to your student that fossil fuels, such as coal, natural gas, and oil, are used to produce different kinds of energy. For example, natural gas and oil are used as sources of power and heat for homes. Have your student turn on a light switch. Ask, *Where do you think the energy that makes the light turn on comes from?* [from electricity that's generated from fossil fuels] Remind your student that it takes many years for fossil fuels to form. Ask your student why it's important to use fossil fuels wisely and not waste energy. [since it takes so long for fossil fuels to form, we can eventually run out of them]

5 **DISCUSS** Explain to your student that the process of getting natural resources out of Earth affects the **environment.** Our environment is everything that's around us. Fossil fuels are buried deep below the surface of Earth and have to be dug out using machines and drills. Have your student imagine what the land around a coal mine might look like. Ask, *How does the digging affect the plants and animals there? What happens to the environment?* [it changes the environment into a place where plants and animals can't live anymore]

+ ENRICH THE EXPERIENCE

Have your student do independent reading about conservation and natural resources. Ask your student to choose a topic from the lesson that he or she is interested in and write down one or two questions about the topic. Together, look for books at the library that your student can read to learn more and find the answers to his or her questions.

6 **EXPLAIN** Tell your student that **pollution** occurs when the environment is harmed in some way. Air, water, and soil can all be affected by pollution. Smoke from chimneys and exhaust from cars cause air pollution. Chemicals from factories and garbage dumped in lakes or near rivers create water pollution. Explain that although humans can adapt and survive when the environment is polluted, plants and animals can't adapt as easily. Pollution can be dangerous to plants and animals. Ask, *Can you think of ways that pollution could affect animals such as fish and ducks?* [if the water where they live becomes polluted, they might be poisoned or not be able to find food]

7 **REVEAL** Explain to your student that by practicing **conservation,** people can help save Earth's natural resources.

When we practice conservation, we use natural resources without wasting them and without polluting the environment. Point out that resources used at home, such as water and electricity, can be conserved. Ask, *How could you conserve water and electricity at home?* [turn off the lights when you leave the room, use water sparingly]

8 **IDENTIFY** Tell your student that one way we can practice conservation is to **reduce** our use of things. Explain that when we reduce, we use something less. For example, we can conserve the energy that gives us heat or cools our home by adjusting the thermostat at night and at times we aren't home. We can reduce the use of products made from trees, such as paper towels, by using cloth napkins during meals or cloth rags for cleaning spills. Have your student try this exercise. Fill a gallon container with fresh water. Whenever your student needs water during the day, he or she can only use the water from the container. At the end of the day ask, *Was one gallon of water enough? Did you have to conserve your water use?*

9 **RELATE** Another way we can conserve our resources is to **reuse** things. When we reuse something, we use it more than once. Explain to your student that garbage and trash is taken to a **landfill** by garbage trucks. Tell him or her that at a landfill, bulldozers spread out the garbage and cover it with soil. Over time, the garbage breaks down and becomes part of the soil. Ask your student to consider how reusing things can help decrease the amount of garbage that is dumped into landfills. Have him or her think of examples of household items that can be reused. [plastic and paper grocery bags, writing paper, plastic water bottles]

10 **EXPAND** Explain that a third way we can conserve our resources is to **recycle** things. To recycle means to take something that has already been used and use it for something else. Show your student a used glass or plastic container, such as a spaghetti sauce jar, olive jar, juice container, or peanut butter container. Point out that these containers can be used again as pencil holders, filled with sand and used as paperweights, or painted and used as vases for flowers. Ask, *What other things can be recycled? How?* [newspaper can be recycled by using it to pack boxes or line pet cages, milk containers can be cut and used as scoops for potting soil, and so on]

11 **EXPLAIN** Point out that many communities have recycling programs. These programs collect used glass, metal cans, and paper and deliver them to a recycling company. Then the materials are broken down and made into new glass, metal, and paper products. Show your student the symbol for recycling. Ask, *Do you recognize this symbol? Where have you seen it before?* [on product packaging, community recycling bin]

Learning About Earth's Natural Resources   **199**

FOR FURTHER READING

Earth Day: Keeping Our Planet Clean (*Finding Out About Holidays*), by Elaine Landau (Enslow Publishers, Inc., 2002).

The Water Hole, by Graeme Base (Abrams Books for Young Readers, 2001).

Waste, Recycling and Re-Use (*Protecting Our Planet*), by Steve Parker (Raintree/Steck Vaughn, 1998).

What If We Run Out of Fossil Fuels? (*What If?*), by Kimberly M. Miller (Children's Press, 2002).

12 **REVEAL** Explain that in some communities recycling bins are distributed to every house. People put all their used glass, metal cans, and paper into the bins instead of the garbage. Special trucks come to each house to pick up the bins every week. This reduces the amount of garbage that goes into landfills. Neighborhoods that don't pick up recyclables at each house sometimes have a recycling drop-off center. People in these neighborhoods can bring their recycling material to the drop-off center. Ask, *Does your neighborhood have a recycling program? How can you play your part in recycling?* [make sure that all used glass, cans, and paper go into the recycling container instead of the garbage]

13 **EXAMINE** Have your student look through a few recent magazines or newspapers for articles on natural resources and recycling. Ask him or her to write about what he or she learned and how he or she feels about it.

14 **INSTRUCT** Distribute Student Learning Page 7.A. Have your student write a sentence about how each picture relates to the conservation of natural resources.

Branching Out

TEACHING TIP

Ask your student to reduce, reuse, or recycle all items he or she uses in one day. Have him or her write down all the items that he or she successfully reduces, reuses, and recycles, and how he or she did it. Ask which items were the most difficult and which were the easiest to conserve.

CHECKING IN

To assess your student's understanding of the lesson, show him or her a lightbulb. Ask your student to explain how a lightbulb and fossil fuels work together. Then have your student explain how water pollution can affect the environment and why it's important to conserve the natural resources in the environment.

Know How to Conserve

Look at the pictures. Write a sentence about how each picture is related to conservation.

1. _____

_____

_____

_____

_____

_____

WE RECYCLE

2. _____

_____

_____

_____

_____

_____

3. _____

_____

_____

_____

_____

_____

What's Next? You Decide!

Now it's your turn to choose what to do next in the lesson. Read the activities and decide which one you want to do—you may want to try them both!

Make a Reduce, Reuse, Recycle Handout

MATERIALS

❑ crayons or markers

❑ 1 sheet construction paper

STEPS

Create a flyer about conservation.

❑ Fold the sheet of construction paper in half.

❑ On the front half of the paper, write "Reduce, Reuse, Recycle" in large letters.

❑ On the inside halves of the paper, draw pictures that show ways that people can reduce, reuse, and recycle.

❑ Color and decorate your flyer. Share it with your family and friends.

Write a Conservation Song

MATERIALS

❑ 1 audiocassette recorder

❑ 1 audiocassette tape

STEPS

Record a song about natural resources.

❑ Write a short rhyming poem about natural resources (such as air, rocks, water, and trees) and why they are important to us.

❑ Include ways to conserve natural resources in your poem.

❑ Use a tune that you know or make one up and turn your poem into a song.

❑ Record your song with the recorder and play it for your family.

Understanding Changes on Earth's Surface

Earth's surface is always changing.

OBJECTIVE	BACKGROUND	MATERIALS
To help your student understand the gradual but constant changes that occur on Earth's surface	Rocks, minerals, and other features of Earth are being destroyed and created all the time. In this lesson, your student will learn about the processes of soil and fossil formation and how weathering and erosion change rocks and minerals.	■ Student Learning Pages 8.A–8.B ■ 1 hand lens ■ 4–5 different kinds of rocks ■ 1 handful sand ■ samples of different soil ■ 1 metal spoon ■ 1 paper cup and plate

VOCABULARY

MINERALS nonliving substances that are usually found in the ground

ROCK a combination of one or more minerals

WEATHERING the breaking up of rocks by wind and water

SOIL a combination of weathered rock and plant material

EROSION the movement of rocks and soil by water or wind

FOSSILS the remains of prehistoric plants or animals that have been preserved in the layers of Earth's surface

Let's Begin

1 **INTRODUCE** Explain what **minerals** are to your student. Tell him or her that a mineral is a nonliving substance that's usually found in the ground. Point out that one or more minerals combine to form a **rock.** Have your student examine an assortment of different rocks with a hand lens. Ask your student to describe each rock by color, shape, size, and texture.

2 **REVEAL** Explain to your student that rocks change over time for many reasons. One reason that rocks change is **weathering.** Tell your student that weathering occurs when wind and water wear away at the surface of rocks and break them into smaller pieces. An example of weathering is when waves crash onto a sea cliff and wear down the rocks. Show your student a small handful of sand. Point out that over a long period of time weathering breaks down rocks into smaller and smaller pieces.

3   **EXPLAIN** Show your student several samples of **soil.** Explain that soil is a combination of weathered rock and dead plants and animals. Soil also holds air and water. Point out to your student that different soils can have different colors and textures (and even different smells) depending on the things that make them up. Mention that new soil is always forming but that it takes a long time to form. Some soil is very sandy and dry, while other kinds of soil are moist and soft. Ask, *What kind of soil do you think is best for growing plants?* [moist, soft soil]

4   **RELATE** Explain to your student that once rock has been weathered into small enough pieces, a force called **erosion** can move it from one place to another. When wind blows, it carries away tiny bits of rock. Water can also cause erosion in the form of rain, streams, and rivers. Show your student several photos of rock that show examples of weathering such as in canyons or mountain cliffs. Your student can see photos of the rock formations at Bryce Canyon, Utah, at http://www.nps.gov/brca.

5   **EXPAND** Tell your student that **fossils** are the preserved remains of prehistoric animals or plants. Explain to him or her that one way fossils form is when the bones and teeth of dead animals are replaced with minerals. Look at the diagram for an example of how a fossil is formed. First, a fish dies and falls to the ocean floor. Over time, the soft parts of the fish break down, leaving only the bones and teeth. The remains of the fish become buried by layers of soil. After millions of years, the fish remains have been changed to rock. Erosion then uncovers the fossilized remains.

How Fossils Form

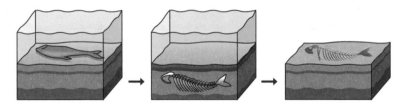

Branching Out

TEACHING TIP

With your student, mix together a batch of his or her favorite cookies. As you work, point out that minerals are the ingredients that make up rocks. When the cookie dough is mixed together, form and bake the cookies. How many of the original ingredients can your student still identify?

CHECKING IN

You can assess your student's understanding of this lesson by asking him or her to explain how soil, sand, and fossils are formed. Encourage your student to draw pictures to explain his or her ideas.

Identify Erosion and Weathering

Look at the pictures. Circle *erosion* or *weathering* for each picture. Write a sentence about each one. Then draw the steps of fossil formation.

1.

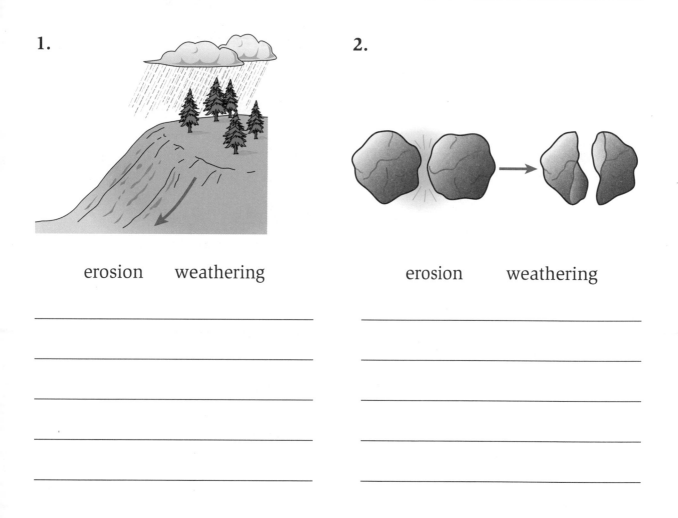

erosion   weathering

_____

_____

_____

_____

2.

erosion   weathering

_____

_____

_____

_____

What's Next? You Decide!

Now it's your turn to choose what to do next in the lesson. Read the activities and decide which one you want to do—you may want to try them both!

Make a Rock Garden

MATERIALS

- ❏ 1 shallow pan or container
- ❏ sand
- ❏ assorted rocks
- ❏ small plastic figures or marbles

STEPS

Use rocks to create your own rock garden!

- ❏ Fill the container with the sand. Pat it down gently.
- ❏ Arrange the rocks in the sand. Be creative. You can arrange them according to size, shape, and color, or you can mix them up.
- ❏ Add a few plastic figures or marbles to decorate your garden.

Make a Soil Chart

MATERIALS

- ❏ 3 soil samples
- ❏ 1 small posterboard
- ❏ glue
- ❏ 1 hand lens

STEPS

- ❏ Ask an adult to help you collect soil from three different places.
- ❏ Divide the posterboard into three sections. In the first section, spread some glue over an area and sprinkle one of the soil samples over the glue. Shake off any soil that did not stick to the glue.
- ❏ Write down where you found it.
- ❏ Do the same for the other soil in the other sections.
- ❏ Then use the hand lens to look at the soil more closely. Write what you see.

SCIENCE

LESSON
3.9

Exploring Earth and the Moon

The cyclical motions of the planets create the cycles of day and night, of the seasons, and of the phases of the moon.

OBJECTIVE	BACKGROUND	MATERIALS
To teach your student about the motions of Earth, the moon, and the sun	The cyclical rhythms we experience on Earth are part of the larger cyclical rhythms of the solar system. In this lesson, your student will learn about why we have day and night, the moon's phases, and the annual cycle of seasons.	<ul><li>Student Learning Pages 9.A–9.B</li><li>1 foam ball</li><li>1 dowel rod</li><li>1 pushpin</li><li>1 flashlight</li><li>1 roll masking tape</li><li>1 roll aluminum foil</li><li>1 lamp without a shade</li><li>1 quarter and 1 penny</li><li>1 globe</li><li>1 package modeling clay</li><li>1 thermometer</li><li>8 index cards</li></ul>

VOCABULARY

ROTATE to spin around

SHADOW a dark area created when an object blocks light

AXIS an invisible line through the center of a planet around which it spins

REVOLVES moves around another object

ORBIT an egg-shaped path on which planets or moons travel around another object

REFLECTS bounces off of a surface

PHASES the regular changes in appearance of a planet or moon

SEASONS the four divisions of the year, marked by different weather conditions

Let's Begin

1 **MODEL** Explain to your student that if you could watch Earth from space you would see it **rotate,** or spin around, once every 24 hours. Earth's rotation is what creates day and night. While the half of Earth facing the sun has daylight, the other half facing away has night. Model how Earth's rotation causes day

and night. Push a dowel rod into the foam ball to make a handle. Tell your student to imagine that the ball is Earth. Insert a pushpin into the ball and say that it represents your student's hometown. Dim the lights. Use a flashlight to represent the sun. Have your student hold the lit flashlight while you rotate the ball. Watch as the light and **shadow** move across the ball. When the pushpin is in the light ask, *Is it day or night in your town right now?* [day] Continue turning the model. Have him or her point out when the pushpin goes into the shadow, or night.

2 **ROLE PLAY** Ask your student to describe how the sun moves across the sky. [each day the sun comes up in the east, travels across the sky, and sets in the west] Point out that although the sun seems to move, it's really Earth that moves in relation to the sun. The effect is caused by our changing viewpoint as Earth rotates. Ask your student to suppose that he or she is Earth. Have your student stand up facing west. Have him or her turn around slowly counterclockwise until he or she is facing east. While turning, have your student watch what happens to the things in the room. Ask, *In what direction do objects in the room appear to be moving?* [they seem to be moving in the opposite direction]

3 **REVEAL** Explain to your student that Earth's rotation takes place around an invisible line called an **axis.** Earth's axis is not straight up and down but is tilted at an angle. This tilt is what causes Earth's seasons. Explain to your student that Earth does more than spin around in space. Tell him or her that Earth also **revolves,** or moves, around the sun. The path that Earth follows when it revolves around the sun is called its **orbit.** Point out the egg-shaped orbit in the drawing. One complete orbit, or revolution, of Earth around the sun takes about 365 days. Ask, *What do we call this time period?* [a year]

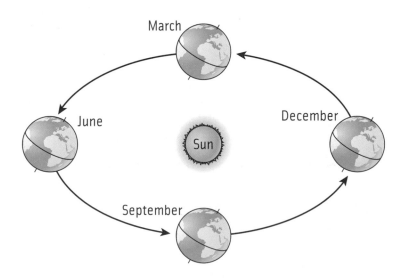

4 **MODEL** Ask, *What is the brightest object in the sky besides the sun?* [the moon] Point out that the moon doesn't produce any light of its own. The moon shines when sunlight **reflects,** or bounces, off its surface rocks. To show how this occurs, tape a

---

> ,
> **TAKE A BREAK**
> You and your student can learn more about our home planet as well as the sun at http://kids.msfc.nasa.gov/earth.

square piece of aluminum foil to a wall. Have your student hold another square of foil to the side. Dim the room lights. Shine a flashlight beam on the second piece of foil at an angle so the light reflects onto the foil that's taped to the wall. Ask, *How is the light from the foil like the moon's light?* [it's reflected from another light source]

5 **GUIDE** Explain that just as Earth revolves around the sun, the moon revolves around Earth. It does so once every 29 days. As it revolves, the moon appears to change its shape, growing from a small crescent to a full disk and then shrinking again. Explain to your student that these changes in shape are called **phases.** Then distribute Student Learning Page 9.A. Discuss the diagram with your student.

6 **MODEL** Use the foam ball again to model how moon phases occur. Tell your student to imagine that the ball is the moon and his or her own body is the rotating Earth. Place a lamp in the center of the room. Dim the lights. Have your student stand next to the lamp and turn around counterclockwise while holding the ball at arm's length. The ball's lit and shadowed parts will change just like the moon phases. Have your student compare what he or she notices to the phases in the drawing. Then have your student complete Student Learning Page 9.A.

7 **DEMONSTRATE** Tell your student that as the moon circles Earth, it always presents the same face, or side, toward Earth. This is because the moon takes about the same amount of time to rotate on its axis as it takes to orbit Earth. To model this, put a quarter heads-side up on a table to represent Earth. Lay a penny alongside the quarter to represent the moon. Make sure that Lincoln's profile is facing the quarter. Have your student move the penny around the quarter one full circle, while making sure that Lincoln's profile is facing the quarter. To do so, your student will have to rotate the penny. Ask, *How many complete rotations did the penny make?* [one]

8 **DISCUSS** Ask your student to name the four **seasons** of the year. [spring, summer, autumn, winter] Point out that each of these seasons lasts about three months every year. Point out the equator on the globe. Show how Earth is tilted on its axis. Tell your student that places near the equator are warm all year round because they receive the same amount of sunlight throughout the year. Seasons change in places north and south of the equator because Earth is tilted. This causes the intensity of the sun's light to change as Earth revolves around the sun. Ask, *What do you notice about the changes in the seasons?* [winter is cold and days are short; summer is hot and days are long; autumn and spring are in between] Discuss with your student the differences in the seasons in the area where he or she lives.

9 **MODEL** Use the modeling clay and the flashlight to show what causes these seasonal differences. Mold the clay into a ball to

DID YOU KNOW?

The Italian scientist Galileo Galilei was among the first people to observe the moon through a telescope in 1609.

represent Earth. Insert a pencil through the middle of the clay ball. Draw a line around the center of the ball for the equator. Return to the drawing showing Earth's orbit. Point out the angle at which Earth's axis is tilted. Find the position in the drawing that represents the month of June. Hold your model at the same angle. Have your student hold the flashlight six inches from the model. Ask, *What part of Earth is lit?* [the northern, or upper, part] *What season is it in that part of the world?* [summer] Repeat for the position that represents December when the southern part is lit and it's winter in the north.

10 **EXPERIMENT** Point out that the model shows why there is more daylight during summer months. But this is only part of the story. Explain that the angle at which light strikes Earth also affects temperatures. Hold the flashlight four inches above one side of a sheet of paper. Have your student trace the outline of the circle of light with a pencil. Label this circle "Summer." On the other side of the paper, hold the flashlight at the same height but tilt it at a 45 degree angle. Have your student trace the oval of light and label it "Winter." Put a thermometer inside the circle for summer. Hold the flashlight four inches above the thermometer for three minutes. Repeat with the circle for winter, this time holding the flashlight at an angle. Ask, *Did the temperature rise more in winter or summer?* [summer]

Branching Out

TEACHING TIP

Help your student make a lunar phase flipbook to keep track of the phases of the moon. Together draw each phase of the moon in the same place on eight separate index cards. Flip through the cards and watch the moon change.

CHECKING IN

FOR FURTHER READING

The Moon, by Tim Furniss (Raintree Steck-Vaughn, 2001).

Our Earth and the Solar System, by Ken Graun (Ken Press, 2001).

The Science of the Sky, by Jonathan Bocknek (Gareth Stevens Publishing, 2000).

To assess your student's understanding of the lesson, give your student a lump of clay, a pencil, and a flashlight. Ask him or her to use the materials to model and explain how the motions of Earth create day and night and the seasons.

Know the Phases of the Moon

Use the chart to draw what the moon looks like from Earth in five phases. Shade the part of the moon that is dark. Leave the bright part of the moon white. Then answer the questions.

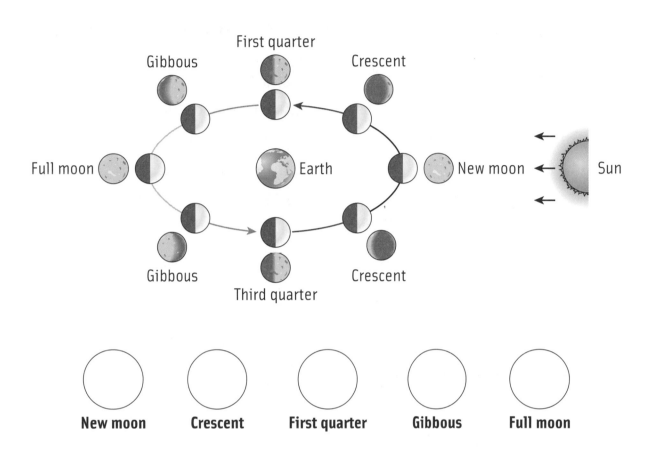

New moon **Crescent** **First quarter** **Gibbous** **Full moon**

1. Does the moon really change its shape each day? Explain.

_____

_____

_____

2. How long is it from one full moon until you see the full moon again?

_____

_____

_____

What's Next? You Decide!

Now it's your turn to choose what to do next in the lesson. Read the activities and decide which one you want to do—you may want to try them both!

Follow the Shadow

▓ MATERIALS

❑ 1 long stick

❑ 3–5 rocks or other weights

❑ 1 clock

▓ STEPS

Before there were clocks, people kept track of time by watching shadows. Ask an adult to help you try this activity on a sunny day.

❑ Push the long stick deep into the ground. Mark the end of the stick's shadow with a rock.

❑ Write the time on a sheet of paper and put it under the rock.

❑ One hour later, mark the new position of the shadow with another rock and note the time.

❑ Repeat a few more times. How does the shadow change throughout the day?

Create Moon Craters

▓ MATERIALS

❑ 1 large box lid

❑ newspaper

❑ 1–2 cups flour

❑ $\frac{1}{4}$ cup cocoa

❑ 1 ruler

❑ 3–4 marbles or small rocks

▓ STEPS

The craters on the moon's surface were formed when meteors hit the moon.

❑ Spread newspapers under the box lid.

❑ Put a one-inch layer of flour in the lid. Smooth the surface with the ruler.

❑ Sprinkle a thin layer of cocoa over the flour.

❑ Drop different sized marbles or small rocks into the flour from the same height. Look at the craters that form.

❑ Gently lift out the marbles or rocks. Notice what happens to the layers of cocoa and flour.

Getting into Motion

Moving is essential to living.

OBJECTIVE	BACKGROUND	MATERIALS
To give your student an introduction to how forces cause motion	Every time something moves, forces are at work. Pushing and pulling forces cause motion in your student's life every minute. In this lesson, your student will learn about motion and the forces that cause it. Your student will also learn about speed and direction and how friction changes them.	■ Student Learning Pages 10.A–10.B ■ 1 wooden or plastic block ■ 2 balls, 1 heavy and 1 light ■ 2 toy cars ■ pictures of objects being pushed or pulled

VOCABULARY

MOTION   the movement of an object from one place to another

FORCE   a push or pull on an object

GRAVITY   the force that pulls all objects toward Earth

DIRECTION   the line along which something moves

FRICTION   the force created when two objects rub against each other

Let's Begin

1   **INTRODUCE** Place a wooden or plastic block on a table and ask your student to push it. Have him or her tell what happens to the block. Then have your student pull the block and describe what happens. Explain to your student that he or she has demonstrated **motion** with the block. Tell him or her that pushing and pulling objects causes motion. Every push or pull is a **force.** A parent pushing a child on a swing is exerting a force. Invite your student to give other examples of motion and to try to identify the force involved.

2   **EXPAND** Have your student hold the block above the table and then let go of it. Ask, *What happened?* [a force acted on the block to cause it to move downward] Explain that the force that acted on the block was **gravity.** Gravity is a force that pulls all objects toward Earth. Have your student jump up in the air. Explain that without gravity he or she would go flying off into space. Whenever an object is lifted, the force pushing or pulling it must fight against gravity. Ask your student to give other

DID YOU KNOW?

Gravity pulls all objects in the universe toward each other. The larger an object is, the greater the pull. Earth has more gravitational pull than the moon, and the sun has more pull than Earth.

examples of how gravity pulls objects toward Earth. Ask, *Why can't you lift up a car?* [the force of gravity pulling the car toward Earth is greater than the force you can create upward]

3 **DEMONSTRATE** Have your student roll a ball across the floor, first slowly and then more quickly. Explain that how fast or slow an object moves is called its speed. Speed describes the amount of time it takes an object to move from place to place. Ask, *What did you have to do to make the ball roll faster?* [push it harder] Now give your student two balls, one heavy and one light. Have him or her push them. Ask, *Which one is harder to push?* [the heavy one] Ask, *Which one is easier to roll fast?* [the light one] Explain that the speed of a moving object is affected by its weight, the force acting on it, and the length of time the force acts on it. Ask, *How can you find the speed of an object?* [measure how long it takes it to move from one place to another]

4 **EXPAND** Have your student roll the ball again. While it's still rolling, bump the ball to change its **direction.** Have your student describe what happened to the ball. Explain that the ball changed its direction because you exerted another force on it by pushing it. Forces cause traveling objects to change directions and to speed up or slow down. Have your student use the ball to experiment with forces to show changing speeds and directions.

5 **EXPLAIN** Have your student roll the ball in an area with no obstructions so the ball can stop on its own. Ask, *What must be happening to the ball to make it stop?* [a force must be acting on it] Explain that the force acting on the ball to make it stop is called **friction.** Friction results when two objects rub against each other. Ask, *What was the ball rubbing against?* [the floor] Ask your student what it's like to walk on ice. Explain that smooth objects produce less friction than rough objects, so they are more slippery. Ask, *How does friction help us walk?* [it keeps our feet on the floor and keeps us from slipping and falling]

Branching Out

FOR FURTHER READING

Forces and Motion (*My World of Science*), by Angela Royston (Heinemann Library, 2001).

Learn About the Way Things Move, by Heidi Gold-Dworkin (McGraw-Hill Trade, 2000).

TEACHING TIP

Have your student race two toy cars. Ask him or her to experiment with ways to make one car go faster than the other. Have your student push the cars across various surfaces, such as a wooden floor and a carpeted floor.

CHECKING IN

To assess your student's understanding of the lesson, provide your student with pictures showing an object being pushed or pulled. Have your student describe the motion and identify the type of force being exerted.

Match the Body Parts

Draw a line between the objects and the body parts that move them. Write "push," "pull," or "both" on the line.

1. _____

2. _____

3. _____

4. _____

5. _____

6. _____

What's Next? You Decide!

Now it's your turn to choose what to do next in the lesson. Read the activities and decide which one you want to do—you may want to try them both!

Watch It Flow

MATERIALS

- ❏ 1 tablespoon honey
- ❏ 1 plate
- ❏ 1 magazine

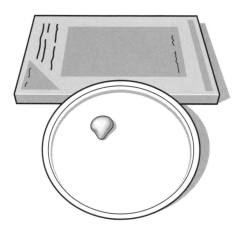

STEPS

Some things move very slowly.

- ❏ Put a spoonful of honey on the plate.
- ❏ Raise one side of the plate with the magazine. Can you see the honey moving?
- ❏ Leave the plate for an hour. Check the honey again. How much did it move?

Race Your Cars

MATERIALS

- ❏ 2 books
- ❏ 1 piece wood or heavy cardboard, about 6 by 24 inches
- ❏ 2 similar toy cars
- ❏ tape
- ❏ 3 large metal washers

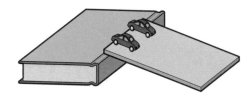

STEPS

- ❏ Prop up the end of the wooden board or cardboard with a book to make a ramp.
- ❏ Put the cars at the top of the ramp. Let them go. Notice the speed of the cars and how far they go.
- ❏ Now put two books under the board. Race the cars down the ramp again. Does the speed of the cars change?
- ❏ Tape the washers to one car. Race the cars again. Which one wins? Why?

Learning About Sound

Sounds are all around us.

OBJECTIVE	BACKGROUND	MATERIALS
To explore what sound energy is, how it is produced, and why we hear different sounds	Sound is a kind of energy that is produced by vibrations. The kind of sound we hear depends on the speed and strength of its vibrations. In this lesson, your student will discover how sound energy is produced and why sounds sound the way they do.	■ Student Learning Pages 11.A–11.B ■ 1 rubber band ■ 2 empty soup cans with a hole in the closed end ■ 1 length string, 10 feet long ■ assorted kitchen bowls, pans, and utensils

VOCABULARY

SOUND a kind of energy that we can hear
VIBRATIONS back and forth motions
SOUND WAVES the way sound travels through air
VOLUME how loud or quiet a sound is
PITCH how high or low a sound is

Let's Begin

1 **INTRODUCE** Go outside with your student and have him or her stand very still and be quiet. After two minutes, ask your student to name the sounds that he or she heard. Repeat the exercise. This time, instruct your student to listen to and remember as many sounds as possible. Explain to your student that **sound** is a kind of energy that we can hear. Explain that sound is produced when **vibrations** happen. A vibration is a quick, repeating back and forth movement. To demonstrate, have your student hold one end of a rubber band while you hold the other end. Pluck one side of the rubber band. Ask your student to listen to and observe what happens. [the rubber band vibrates and a sound is produced]

2 **DISCOVER** When objects vibrate, they produce **sound waves** that travel through the air. Explain to your student that we do not hear sound until the sound waves reach our ears. Demonstrate how sound waves travel from their source to our ear by using two soup cans connected by a length of string. Have your student hold one of the soup cans against his or her ear. Stretch the

A BRIGHT IDEA

The next time the stereo is playing, have your student place his or her hand on one of the speakers. Ask, *Can you feel the vibration of the music?* Then have your student place one hand in front of his or her mouth and say, "Ohhhhhh." Ask, *Can you feel the sound vibrating against your palm?*

string taut. Speak softly into the other can. Ask your student, *Can you hear me?* If he or she can't, check that the string is taut.

3 **EXPLORE** Ask your student for examples of sounds that are loud and sounds that are quiet. Tell your student that the **volume** of a sound is how loud or quiet it is. The larger the sound wave, the more volume a sound has and the louder it will be. The smaller the sound wave, the less volume a sound has and the quieter it will be. Ask your student to use his or her voice or hands to make a sound that's loud. Then ask him or her to make a sound that's quiet. Ask, *What was different?* [the loud sound takes more energy; the quiet sound takes less energy]

4 **IDENTIFY** Explain that sounds can be described as high or low. This is called a sound's **pitch.** Tell your student that sound waves that vibrate slowly make low sounds. Sound waves that vibrate quickly make high sounds. Ask, *Which do you think has a higher pitch, the sound of a mouse squeaking or a dog barking?* [a mouse squeaking] Point out that small animals often make high-pitched sounds while large animals usually make low-pitched sounds. Then have your student write three sentences describing things that make low-pitched sounds and the sounds they make and three sentences describing things that make high-pitched sounds and the sounds they make.

5 **DISTRIBUTE** Distribute Student Learning Page 11.A and have your student complete the page.

Branching Out

TEACHING TIP

Use an assortment of kitchen pans, bowls, and utensils to make different kinds of sound with your student. Discuss which sounds have high or low pitches and which are loud or quiet. Experiment with making different kinds of sound using the same utensil.

CHECKING IN

You can assess your student's understanding of the lesson by asking him or her to use household items to make the following kinds of sounds: high volume, low volume, high pitched, and low pitched.

A BRIGHT IDEA

Your student might enjoy learning more about how the human ear works. Take a trip to the library or use the Internet to help your student find information about the human ear and how it functions. Then have him or her use the information to write a paragraph about the ear. You can find more information about nonfiction writing in Lesson 1.10.

FOR FURTHER READING

Hearing Sounds (*It's Science*), by Sally Hewitt (Children's Press, 1999).

Sound (*Step-By-Step Science*), by Helena Ramsay (Children's Press, 1998).

Sound and Hearing (*My World of Science*), by Angela Royston (Heinemann Library, 2001).

Classify Animal Sounds

Imitate the animal sounds listed in the chart. Circle the pitch and volume of the sound. Then answer the questions.

Animal Sound	Pitch		Volume	
1. Purring kitten	high	low	high	low
2. Howling wolf	high	low	high	low
3. Hissing snake	high	low	high	low
4. Roaring lion	high	low	high	low
5. Singing bird	high	low	high	low
6. Large barking dog	high	low	high	low

7. What is sound? _____

_____

_____

8. What causes sound? _____

_____

_____

9. What is one of your favorite sounds? How is this sound made?

_____

_____

_____

What's Next? You Decide!

Now it's your turn to choose what to do next in the lesson. Read the activities and decide which one you want to do—you may want to try them both!

Make an Instrument

MATERIALS

- ❏ 1 shoebox with cover
- ❏ 1 pair scissors
- ❏ 3–4 large rubber bands of different thickness

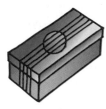

STEPS

- ❏ Draw a circle in the center of the top of the shoebox cover. The circle should be at least half the width of the shoebox.
- ❏ Cut out the circle.
- ❏ Wrap each rubber band around the length of the shoebox so that they run over the hole in the cover. Your shoebox should look a little bit like a guitar.
- ❏ Pluck each of the rubber bands and listen. Do they sound different? Pluck them all at the same time. How does that sound?

Record Jungle Sounds

MATERIALS

- ❏ 1 audiocassette recorder
- ❏ 1 audiocassette tape

STEPS

Use an audiocassette recorder to record a story about the sounds you might hear in a jungle. Use your voice or other instruments to make the different sounds.

- ❏ Begin the story with the sentence, "As I was walking through the jungle one day, I heard. . . ."
- ❏ Imagine what kinds of sounds you would hear in a jungle. What kinds of animal sounds would you hear? Would they be loud or quiet, high pitched or low pitched?
- ❏ Add other sounds, too. Would branches crack as you walked along the jungle floor? Would leaves rustle from the wind? Would it be raining?

Investigating Light and Heat

Without light we couldn't see, and without heat we would freeze!

OBJECTIVE	BACKGROUND	MATERIALS
To teach your student about sources of light and heat	Light and heat are two forms of energy that are critical to life on Earth. The sun is a major source of both, but light and heat come from other sources as well. In this lesson, your student will learn about sources of light and heat and find out how shadows are formed.	■ Student Learning Pages 12.A–12.B ■ black, white, and colored construction paper ■ 1 clear empty glass ■ 1 clear glass filled with lemonade ■ 1 piece clear plastic ■ 1 cereal box ■ 1 flashlight ■ 1 copy Venn Diagram, page 353

VOCABULARY

LIGHT the energy that produces brightness and makes it possible to see things
REFLECT to bounce off
ABSORB to soak up
HEAT the energy that's felt as warmth or hotness

Let's Begin

1 **PREVIEW** Invite your student to look around the room and make note of what he or she sees. Then darken the room by turning off lights and closing shades. If possible do this in a room without windows. Ask your student to describe what happened and how it affects what he or she can see.

2 **EXPLAIN** Tell your student that **light** makes it possible to see. Some things make their own light and are easy to see. Discuss with your student things that make their own light, including the sun, electric lights, and candles. Most things can only be seen when light shines on them. Explain that objects **reflect** some light and **absorb** some light. When an object absorbs light, it warms up. Dark colors absorb more light than light colors. White objects reflect almost all light and black objects absorb almost all light. Set out various colors of construction paper. Have your student place them in order from the one that reflects the most light to the one that absorbs the most light.

3 **DEMONSTRATE** Place a clear empty glass, a clear glass filled with lemonade, a piece of clear plastic, and a cereal box in front of a blank wall. Darken the room. Shine a flashlight onto the objects. Have your student describe how much light passes through each one onto the wall. Point out that when the light doesn't pass through an object, a shadow forms. Three things are needed to form a shadow: a light source, an object, and something on which to see the shadow. Have your student point out objects around the room that create shadows and identify the light sources. Then distribute Student Learning Page 12.A and have your student complete the page. After your student has completed the activity, have him or her write a paragraph describing the formation of a shadow.

4 **EXPLORE** Ask your student how he or she feels when standing in the sun on a warm day. Explain that the sun produces not only light but **heat.** Explain that the sun contains fuel that's always burning and that this creates heat. Ask, *What are some other ways that burning fuel creates heat?* [logs burning in a fire; oil, coal, or gas burning in a furnace; gasoline burning in a car] Explain that oil, coal, and gas can be burned to create electricity, which can then be used to heat homes and buildings. Have your student search his or her home for sources of heat. Have him or her identify the sources that use electricity to produce heat.

5 **EXPAND** Tell your student that some people heat their homes without using wood, oil, coal, or gas. Instead, they use the heat from the sun. These houses have special black panels on the roof that absorb the sun's light, which is changed to heat and stored. The stored heat can then be used to heat water or the air inside the house. Ask, *In what locations would this type of heating be most useful?* [places where the sun shines a lot]

FOR FURTHER READING

Hot and Cold (*It's Science*), by Sally Hewitt (Children's Press, 2000).

Hot and Cold (*My World of Science*), by Angela Royston (Heinemann Library, 2001).

Light and Shadow (*Yellow Umbrella Books: Science*), by Susan Ring (Pebble Books, 2003).

What Is a Shadow? (*How? What? Why?*), by Jackie Holderness (Copper Beech Books, 2002).

Branching Out

TEACHING TIP

Demonstrate the three things needed to make a shadow. In a darkened room, shine a flashlight on a wall. Ask, *What is missing that's needed to form a shadow?* [an object] Have your student move between the light and the wall to form a shadow. Then turn off the light. Ask, *Why isn't a shadow formed now?* [there's no light source]

CHECKING IN

To assess your student's understanding of the lesson, provide him or her with a copy of the Venn Diagram found on page 353. Have your student fill in the diagram for light sources and heat sources.

Investigate Light and Heat

Draw a line from each object to its shadow.

Student Learning Page 12.A: Investigate Light and Heat   **223**

What's Next? You Decide!

Now it's your turn to choose what to do next in the lesson. Read the activities and decide which one you want to do—you may want to try them both!

Feel the Heat

MATERIALS

- ❏ 2 clear plastic cups with lids
- ❏ 1 sheet black construction paper
- ❏ 1 pair scissors
- ❏ tape

STEPS

- ❏ Fill the cups with cool water. Put on the lids.
- ❏ Use tape to cover one cup with black construction paper. Cut the paper as needed.
- ❏ Put the cups in bright sunlight.
- ❏ After one hour, remove the black paper and test the water in the cups with your finger. Which one is warmer? Why?

Make a Shadow Play

MATERIALS

- ❏ 4–6 index cards
- ❏ 1 pair scissors
- ❏ markers, crayons, or colored pencils
- ❏ 4–6 wooden sticks
- ❏ tape
- ❏ 1 lamp
- ❏ 1 blank wall or curtain

STEPS

Use shadows to perform a play. Tell a story that has animals and people in it.

- ❏ Draw a person or an animal on at least four index cards. Cut them out.
- ❏ Tape each figure to a stick.
- ❏ Darken the room. Shine a light onto a blank wall or curtain.
- ❏ Hold the pictures between the light and the wall. Make a shadow play!

Researching a Science Topic

Fact finding is fun!

OBJECTIVE	BACKGROUND	MATERIALS
To show your student how to research a science topic	Researching a science topic requires interest in an idea and skill with evaluating information for accuracy and reliability. In this lesson, your student will learn what steps to take when researching a science topic.	■ Student Learning Pages 13.A–13.B ■ 1 small houseplant ■ 1 copy Writing Lines, page 355

VOCABULARY

RESEARCH to collect information about a chosen topic

FACT an objective, proven statement

SOURCES places where information can be found

EVALUATE to decide if something is acceptable

Let's Begin

1 **EXPLAIN** Ask your student what he or she thinks of when you say the word **research.** Tell your student that research is the process of collecting information about a given topic. Explain that people can learn and make new discoveries by researching topics that interest them. Have your student list three things he or she is interested in knowing more about.

2 **THINK** Explain to your student that research usually begins with a question about a topic. Show your student a houseplant. Help your student think about some questions he or she could ask about the plant. For example, one could ask, *How much sunlight does the plant need to live?* Have your student write questions in his or her notebook.

3 **EXPLORE** Explain to your student that a **fact** is an objective, proven statement. When conducting research on an idea or a topic, a scientist gathers together facts and information from reliable **sources.** Examples of sources include original experiments or experiences, books and encyclopedias, Web sites, experts, museums, documentaries, and so on. Ask, *Can you think of two reliable sources of information about houseplants?* [a gardener, a book on houseplants]

(?)

DID YOU KNOW?

The ancient Greek philosopher Thales is considered to be the father of Greek science and the first person to use scientific reasoning. Thales used astronomical records to predict an eclipse in 585 B.C.

4 **EXPLAIN** Point out that when doing research it's important to gather information from several different sources and it's important to **evaluate** information before accepting it as fact. Explain that encyclopedias are considered reliable sources since the information in them is researched by a group of people and double checked for accuracy. Show your student the fact card on grizzly bears. Ask, *Which source do you think is more reliable? Why?* [the encyclopedia, because most often the facts in encyclopedias are checked] Then distribute Student Learning Page 13.A.

Topic:	Grizzly Bears
Question:	How fast can a grizzly bear run?
Fact:	50 miles per hour
Source:	"Grizzly Attacks" by Forest Hunter
Fact:	30 miles per hour
Source:	World Encyclopedia

5 **DISCUSS AND DISTRIBUTE** Discuss with your student the topics that he or she has learned about in all of the previous science lessons. Ask him or her to choose a topic that he or she would like to learn more about. Then take your student to the nonfiction section in the library and encourage him or her to use the skills learned in this lesson to find books to research this topic. Then distribute a copy of the Writing Lines found on page 355. Have your student write a few paragraphs about the topic that he or she selected.

Branching Out

FOR FURTHER READING

Mummies and Pyramids (*Magic Tree House Research Guide*), by Will Osborne and Mary Pope Osborne (Random House, 2001).

Space (*Magic Tree House Research Guide*), by Will Osborne and Mary Pope Osborne (Random House, 2002).

TEACHING TIP

Show your student an encyclopedia. Have your student go through the pages and look at the information and illustrations presented. Discuss some of the different topics he or she finds most interesting.

CHECKING IN

You can assess your student's understanding of the lesson by having him or her research a topic he or she listed in Step 1. Have your student develop a question and an idea, identify possible sources, perform the research, evaluate the facts and information, then present an oral report.

Identify Reliable Sources

Draw a circle around the best source for researching each pictured topic.

1. *Weather Facts,* by the National Weather Service

   The Weather in Our Town, by Ernest Watt

3. *What Do Gorillas Do?,* by Dr. Donald Lawrence of the San Diego Zoo

   Let's Go on a Safari!, by Hamilton Brown

2. *Our Whale-Watching Vacation,* by Dan Seal

   Whales of the World, by Dr. Philip Kent

4. *What I Think the Sun Is Like,* by Natalie Corman

   Everything You've Always Wanted to Know About the Sun, by Dr. Sharon Day and Dr. Nancy Light

What's Next? You Decide!

Now it's your turn to choose what to do next in the lesson. Read the activities and decide which one you want to do— you may want to try them both!

Make a Research Tape

MATERIALS

❑ 1 audiocassette recorder

❑ 1 audiocassette tape

❑ 3 index cards

STEPS

❑ Choose a science topic that interests you.

❑ Suppose you're a scientist researching a topic.

❑ Make a list of three questions about your topic. Write the questions on index cards.

❑ Use an encyclopedia to research the answers to the questions. Write the answers on the backs of the cards.

❑ Record a presentation of your research. Begin by saying, "Hello, my name is _____, and I'm here to describe my latest research on _____."

❑ Describe each step of your research, the sources you used, and what you learned.

Be a Photo Researcher

MATERIALS

❑ 1 camera

❑ 1 posterboard

❑ markers, crayons, or colored pencils

❑ tape

STEPS

❑ Choose an interesting science topic that you can research using photographs.

❑ Think of a question and an idea about your topic.

❑ Use a camera to take different photos that show facts about your idea. Ask an adult to help you get the photos developed.

❑ Write your question at the top of a posterboard.

❑ Tape the photos on the posterboard. Write a sentence that describes a fact that each photo shows.

❑ Share your research with your family.

In Your Community

To reinforce the skills and concepts taught in this section,
try one or more of these activities!

Green Thumb

Take your student on a tour of a local greenhouse. Most greenhouses have a large variety of plants to study, along with staff who are qualified and knowledgeable about many different kinds of plants. If possible, arrange to have an employee walk through the greenhouse with you and your student to provide information and to answer any questions your student may have. At the end of your visit, allow your student to purchase some seeds or a plant. Ask a greenhouse employee to provide your student with specific instructions and care tips so your student can cultivate a green thumb at home.

Rock Exploration

Visit your library and find a book that describes the local geological history and types of rocks that exist in the area where you live. If there is a college or university nearby, contact the geology department to ask about additional information. Make a list of the things you're likely to find and where they might be located. Then take a field trip with your student to various locations to explore what you've researched. Together locate and identify the various rocks and rock layers that are prevalent in your community. Riverbeds and streambeds are great places to look for interesting rocks.

Your Local Music Shop

Musical instruments make fun examples of how sounds are produced and heard. Contact your local musical instrument shop and arrange a tour and an interview with one of their technicians or instructors. For example, most guitar stores have qualified technicians who can explain to your student how sounds are produced and amplified, how and why sounds can be altered, and various other sound related information. Make sure your student has prepared a list of questions before your visit to maximize the benefit.

An Appointment with the Dentist

Why not go to an expert to teach your student about the importance of caring for your teeth? If possible call your family dentist and arrange an interview and a tour of the facilities. Your dentist can explain to your student the importance, kinds, and function of teeth. Furthermore, your student can learn proper brushing and flossing techniques and how dentistry techniques help keep teeth healthy. Your dentist also may be able to show your student examples of X rays and what may happen if teeth aren't cared for.

Where Your Garbage Goes

Most garbage we throw away is put into landfills. Have your student help you find out what landfill your garbage is taken to. If possible, plan a visit to see what the landfill looks like and how it's maintained. Follow up your landfill visit with a trip to a local recycling center.

Animals and Their Young in Person

Look in the classified section of the newspaper under "Pets" for announcements about new litters of puppies or kittens. Call and ask if you and your student could visit the new mother and her young. Have your student observe the differences and similarities among the members of the litter and between the mother and the babies. Alternative places to find out about new litters include a veterinary clinic, a zoo nursery, and a local dairy farm or feed store.

We Have Learned

Use this checklist to summarize what you and your student have accomplished in the Science section.

❑ **Plants and Animals**
❑ life cycles of flowering and flowerless plants
❑ similarities and differences in animal life cycles
❑ habitats, protection, interdependence

❑ **Planet Earth**
❑ Earth's natural resources
❑ how people change the environment, conservation

❑ **Earth's Surface**
❑ rocks, minerals, soil
❑ weathering and erosion
❑ fossils

❑ **Sun, Moon, and Earth**
❑ day, night, and Earth's rotation
❑ Earth's orbit and seasons
❑ phases of the moon

❑ **Forces and Motion**
❑ pushes, pulls, gravity
❑ speed, direction, friction

❑ **Sound**
❑ vibrations, sound waves
❑ volume, pitch

❑ **Light and Heat**
❑ light and seeing
❑ heat, fuel, electricity

❑ **Senses**
❑ five senses, their organs, and how they inform
❑ senses and safety

❑ **Teeth**
❑ kinds of teeth
❑ brushing, flossing, causes of tooth decay
❑ the dentist, X rays, fillings

❑ **Diet and Health**
❑ food guide pyramid, eating a balanced diet
❑ food and energy
❑ why the body needs and uses water

❑ **Science Research**
❑ developing an idea
❑ evaluating information from a variety of sources

We have also learned:

_____

_____

_____

_____

_____

_____

Social Studies

Social Studies

Key Topics

Maps and Charts
Pages 233–236

Different Communities
Pages 237–248

Natural Resources, Goods, and Services
Pages 249–260

Our Government
Pages 261–268

Early Americans
Pages 269–284

Immigration
Pages 285–288

Landmarks and Symbols
Pages 289–292

Communication in the World
Pages 293–296

Researching a Social Studies Topic
Pages 297–300

SOCIAL STUDIES
LESSON 4.1

Discovering Maps and Charts

Maps and charts help us learn information from a different perspective.

OBJECTIVE	BACKGROUND	MATERIALS
To teach your student how to use maps, time lines, tables, graphs, and diagrams	Maps and charts are often used with text to support and extend information. There are different types of maps, including globes, history maps, city maps, and grid maps. Different types of charts include time lines, tables, graphs, and diagrams. Knowing how to read these graphics is a useful skill. In this lesson, your student will learn how different maps and charts organize information.	■ Student Learning Pages 1.A–1.B ■ 1 globe ■ 1 children's atlas ■ sticky notes ■ 1 copy Venn Diagram, page 353 ■ markers, colored pencils, or crayons ■ 1 newspaper

Let's Begin

1 **INTRODUCE** Explain to your student that in this lesson he or she is going to learn more about maps as well as charts, such as time lines, tables, graphs, and diagrams. Tell your student that maps and charts help us to better understand what we read. Ask your student to give examples of information that a map or chart might show.

2 **INSTRUCT** Distribute Student Learning Page 1.A. Tell your student that a time line shows when events happened, such as the events of a person's life. Invite your student to complete the time line with important events in his or her life. Help your student identify some of the events.

3 **DISCUSS** Tell your student that tables can be used to organize information in rows and columns. Show your student the table on Student Learning Page 1.A. Help your student interpret the table so he or she can answer the questions. Invite your student to complete the table by drawing pictures of the pets listed.

4 **ANALYZE** Direct your student's attention to the bar graph on Student Learning Page 1.A. Point out that bar graphs show different amounts of something. Have your student answer the

questions about the bar graph. Invite him or her to use different colors to fill in the bars. Then ask your student to write in a notebook about how charts can be helpful.

5 **POINT OUT** Show your student a map from a children's atlas. Help your student locate continents. Tell your student that continents are very large areas of land. Point out the seven continents: North America, South America, Asia, Europe, Australia, Africa, and Antarctica. Then help your student find important bodies of water. Show the same continents and bodies of water on a globe. Challenge your student to tell how a map and a globe are similar and different.

6 **EXPLAIN** Tell your student that many maps have a symbol called a compass rose. Point out a map with a compass rose in your children's atlas. Encourage your student to look closely at the compass rose. Tell him or her what *N, S, E,* and *W* stand for. Show how these directions correspond to the information on a map and how they might help someone travel.

7 **DISCUSS** Explain that maps called history maps show how places change over time. Show your student a history map from the Internet or from a children's atlas. For example, you might find a map that shows how the Louisiana Purchase or western expansion changed the United States. Encourage your student to tell what a history map shows. Then share a map of your city. Have your student identify where he or she lives. Have your student draw pictures of important places on sticky notes and place them on the city map.

8 **DESCRIBE** Show your student the grid map on Student Learning Page 1.A. Point out that a grid map has letters and numbers. Have your student answer the questions to practice identifying coordinates on this type of map. Then have your student look through a newspaper for maps and charts.

DID YOU KNOW?

Long ago mapmakers gave the compass rose its name because they thought the compass points looked like flower petals.

Branching Out

FOR FURTHER READING

The Blackbirch Kids Almanac of Geography, by Alice Siegel and Margo McLoone (Blackbirch Press, 2000).

Facts on File Children's Atlas, by David and Jill Wright (Facts on File, 2000).

TEACHING TIP

Tell your student that a diagram is another type of chart. Point out the Venn Diagram on page 353. Use a copy of the diagram to practice comparing and contrasting two things your student knows about.

CHECKING IN

To assess your student's understanding of the lesson, give him or her clues about maps and different charts. For example, *What shows lakes, rivers, mountains, and other types of land?*

Use Maps and Charts

Follow the directions. Then color the map and chart.

---

1. Complete the time line with events from your life.

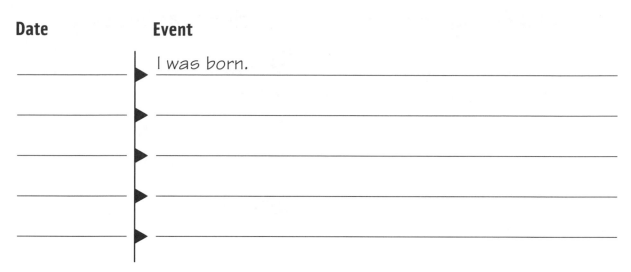

Date	Event
_____	I was born.
_____	
_____	
_____	
_____	

2. What is the most popular pet in Maintown? Least popular?

_____

3. What place is at point A1 on the map? _____

4. At which point is the playground? _____

Most Popular Pets in Maintown

Pet	Number	Picture
Cat	81	
Dog	63	
Bird	45	
Fish	39	

Map of Maintown

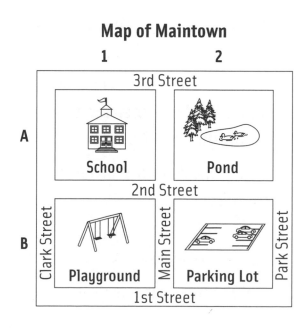

What's Next? You Decide!

Now it's your turn to choose what to do next in the lesson. Read the activities and decide which one you want to do— you may want to try them both!

Make a Compass Rose

MATERIALS

❑ 1 map with a compass rose

❑ 1 large sheet cardboard

❑ 1 large plate and 1 small plate for tracing

❑ markers, colored pencils, or crayons

❑ 1 ruler

STEPS

❑ Look at the map with the compass rose. Locate north, south, east, and west.

❑ Trace a circle on the cardboard with the large plate.

❑ Cut out the circle. Draw a small circle in the middle using the small plate.

❑ Draw eight points around the circle.

❑ Draw lines to north, south, east, and west.

❑ Color your compass rose.

Hunt for Treasure

MATERIALS

❑ 1 box

❑ 1 book, 1 treat, or 1 small toy

❑ 1 large sheet paper

STEPS

Plan a treasure hunt for a group of friends!

❑ Find or make a box for a treasure chest.

❑ Place a book, treat, or small toy in the chest.

❑ Hide your treasure chest.

❑ Draw a treasure map.

❑ Label the starting point on the map. Show the route.

❑ Place an X where the treasure is.

❑ Ask your friends to use the map to find the treasure.

❑ See how well your friends follow the map!

Understanding and Comparing Communities

*The diversity of our communities adds flavor
to the melting pot of America.*

OBJECTIVE	BACKGROUND	MATERIALS
To help your student understand how communities are similar and different	Although communities have many things in common, they can also be very different from one another. These differences make each community special. In this lesson, your student will learn about the features that make up a community. Your student will also identify how communities are similar and different.	■ Student Learning Pages 2.A–2.B ■ 1 copy Venn Diagram, page 353 ■ 1 U.S. map ■ 1 newspaper ■ 1 magazine

VOCABULARY

LAWS rules that people must follow

DIVERSITY a mixture of many cultures and traditions

HISTORY what has happened in the past

URBAN having to do with a city

SUBURBS areas just outside of cities

RURAL having to do with an area that is spread out, such as a countryside

Let's Begin

1 **INTRODUCE** Begin this lesson by asking your student, *Do you know the special name we use for the area in which we live?* Guide him or her by giving a hint, such as *It begins with the letter N.* Then prompt your student to say, *neighborhood.* Continue by saying, *A community is made up of a group of neighborhoods. Can you think of some different things that make up your community?* [schools, stores, post offices, homes, apartments, churches, hospitals, police stations, and so on]

2 **DISCUSS** Explain that a community is made up of people who must follow official rules, or **laws.** These laws help the community function in an orderly and fair way. For example, drivers must stop at stop signs before they continue across intersections. Ask, *What do you think would happen if a*

community didn't have stop signs? [there would be a lot more accidents] Invite your student to brainstorm three other laws people in a community must follow. Discuss what might happen if those laws didn't exist. Then ask your student to write a short story describing the importance of laws in a community and have a discussion with him or her about its content.

3 **COMPARE** Explain to your student that most communities have a lot in common. However, communities can also be very different, or diverse. When a community has a lot of **diversity,** it's made up of various cultures and traditions. Some people might speak Spanish, while others might speak Chinese. Some neighborhoods might have a lot of Italian restaurants, while others might specialize in Asian restaurants. As an example, point out that the neighborhoods of New York City have a lot of diversity. Together with your student use the Internet or resource books to learn more about the diverse neighborhoods of New York City, such as Chinatown or Little Italy. Or invite your student to research the communities of another city in which he or she is interested.

4 **EXTEND** Explain that communities change over time because people change, technology advances, and cities grow. Two hundred years ago people in a community might have traveled by horse-drawn carriages and buggies, while in the same community today people might travel by cars and buses. By looking at pictures of the past, we can learn about a community's **history.** Show your student the pictures below and say, *Let's look at two pictures of New York City. One is from 100 years ago and the other is from the present. Let's compare how the city is the same and different.* Hand out a copy of the Venn Diagram found on page 353. Have your student label one circle "New York: Past" and one circle "New York: Present." Ask your student to share his or her ideas about the community during the two eras. Help your student complete the Venn Diagram with his or her responses.

New York City

Past   **Present**

How has New York City changed?

5 **INTRODUCE** Inform your student that some communities are in **urban** areas. Urban areas are also called cities. Cities are busy places with many people, homes, and businesses. Tourists often like to visit cities around the world to see interesting museums, parks, and different types of buildings. Urban areas are often crowded with cars, buses, and buildings that are close together. Point out that there are a lot of fun things to do in a city, such as go to plays, concerts, restaurants, and movies. Ask, *Can you tell me about a city you have visited? What did you do there? What did you like? What didn't you like?*

6 **EXPLAIN** Tell your student that some areas just outside the city are called **suburbs.** Suburbs are towns that have many homes and businesses but are smaller than cities. Tell your student that suburbs in the United States have grown quickly over the past 50 years. Some people like to live in suburbs because there is more space than in a city, but residents can still take advantage of conveniences such as nearby stores. Many people who live in suburbs often work in nearby cities. If your student lives in a suburb, ask him or her to describe it. Or invite your student to describe another suburb he or she knows about.

7 **EXPAND** Tell your student that other people choose to live in **rural** areas, where homes and neighborhoods are very far apart. Some people who live in rural areas have farms where they plant crops and raise animals. There is little traffic in rural areas, and stores and places of entertainment are usually farther apart. Invite your student to complete Student Learning Page 2.A.

8 **REVEAL** Explain that communities have different locations. Some communities are near the ocean. Children who grow up in these places can visit the beach and marinas very often. Some communities are located in areas where it's warm all year round, such as Florida, southern California, and Hawaii. Children who live in these places can swim and play sports outside even in January! Other communities are found in places that receive a lot of snow and are close to mountains. Children who grow up in areas such as Colorado, parts of California, and West Virginia have more opportunities to learn how to snowboard and ski. Say, *Imagine what it would be like to live in Hawaii (or another place). Draw a picture of yourself in this place. What might it be like to live there?*

9 **DISCUSS** Point out that despite the differences between communities, there are also similarities. For example, every community has families and people of all ages who live there. Each community has laws that people must follow. Together with your student discuss the similarities that people share no matter where they live, and the laws they must follow. [children like to play; people like to be safe; people like to do things for fun; people work and eat; the emergency number is 911 in any American community]

ENRICH THE EXPERIENCE

Check with your local chamber of commerce or look for them on the Web to find printed material regarding activities that your community has to offer. Guide your student to read the material and then have him or her explain how the activities offered reflect the characteristics of the community.

10   **INFORM** Tell your student that the land and resources of an area can affect the activities of the people who live there. For example, fishing is an important industry in areas that are near large bodies of water. Lumbering is an important industry in areas where there are many trees and forests. Invite your student to name some types of land and resources that he or she would like to live near. Ask, *Would you want to live near water where it's warm or by mountains where it snows a lot?* Look at a U.S. map with your student. Help your student locate an area that he or she finds interesting.

11   **SHARE AND CONNECT** Have your student look in your local newspaper for an article that tells something about your community. Help him or her read the article. Then have your student write a paragraph about how he or she feels about what he or she has just read.

12   **READ AND EXPAND** Together with your student find a children's magazine, such as *Ranger Rick,* that has a story about another community. Have him or her read the article. Then have your student tell you how his or her community is similar and different to the one he or she just read about. Discuss.

Branching Out

TEACHING TIP

It's always a good idea to have visual representations of what your student is learning, even if they are family photos. Chances are that your student has visited an urban, suburban, and rural area. Perhaps pictures were taken at a farm or at the top of the Empire State Building. By connecting the lesson to your student's experiences, he or she will become interested. If you don't have family photos, picture books of different kinds of communities are a great way to enhance the lesson.

FOR FURTHER READING

Colonial Home, by Bobbie Kalman (Crabtree Publishing, 2000).

I Live at a Military Post, by Stasia Ward Kehoe (Rosen Publishing Group, 1999).

I Live in a Town, by Stasia Ward Kehoe (PowerKids Press, 1999).

CHECKING IN

Make sure your student understands that all communities are similar in some ways but different in others. Every community has its good things and not-so-good things. Making a community collage would be a great way to assess your student's understanding of the lesson. Have your student decorate one half of the poster with images that represent what your community has in common with other communities. On the other half of the poster, have your student use images that represent what makes your community unique.

Guess Where You Are!

Read the clues. Figure out if you are in an urban, suburban, or rural area. Then write the area by each clue.

1. You look out your window and see a farm. It's very quiet in this community. Where are you?

   _____

2. There are many cars and buses on the street. The buildings are close together. Some of them reach high into the sky. Where are you?

   _____

3. Your dad just came home from working in a big city. Your family lives in a town near the city. There are many houses on your block. Where are you?

   _____

Draw a picture showing which type of community you like the most.

What's Next? You Decide!

Now it's your turn to choose what to do next in the lesson. Read the activities and decide which one you want to do— you may want to try them both!

Find the Signs

MATERIALS

- ❏ several sheets construction paper
- ❏ 1 camera (optional)
- ❏ glue
- ❏ crayons, markers, or colored pencils

STEPS

Go on a hunt with your parents to see how many signs you can find in your community.

- ❏ Take a picture of each sign with the camera or draw it on paper.
- ❏ Glue each picture or drawing on a sheet of construction paper. Then write a caption for each sign telling how it helps us follow the law or stay safe.
- ❏ Find any other signs that are in your community and learn why they are there!

Make a Model of Your Neighborhood

MATERIALS

- ❏ fabric
- ❏ blocks
- ❏ craft sticks
- ❏ clay
- ❏ aluminum foil

STEPS

How well do you know your neighborhood? Show everyone by making a model of it!

- ❏ You can draw your model on paper if you wish.
- ❏ You can also make it three dimensional by using materials such as fabric, blocks, craft sticks, clay, or aluminum foil. Use any other materials you like.
- ❏ Try to make your model look as real as you can!

Exploring Communities in the World

It's important to always remember that we are members of a world community.

OBJECTIVE	BACKGROUND	MATERIALS
To help your student learn how his or her community relates to the larger world	We are members of many different communities. We are part of our smaller neighborhood communities just as we are part of the larger world community. In this lesson, your student will learn that his or her community is part of a larger world community. He or she will also discover more about continents and explore how to use a globe.	<ul><li>Student Learning Pages 3.A–3.B</li><li>1 North America map</li><li>1 globe</li><li>1 world map</li><li>1 copy Venn Diagram, page 353</li><li>markers, crayons, or colored pencils</li><li>1 sheet construction paper</li><li>1 solar system picture</li><li>1 newspaper or magazine</li></ul>

VOCABULARY

GLOBE a round, or spherical, model of Earth that indicates different characteristics

EQUATOR an imaginary line that goes around Earth and divides it in half

CONTINENT one of the seven large areas of land on Earth

BORDER a boundary line that separates two political entities

OCEAN a large body of saltwater

PLANET one of the nine large bodies that revolve around the sun

SOLAR SYSTEM the sun, the nine planets, and the other heavenly bodies that move around the sun

POLLUTION harmful materials that are in the environment

Let's Begin

1   **INTRODUCE** Use the map of North America to introduce your student to how his or her community relates to larger communities. Tell your student that his or her neighborhood is part of a city or town. Locate your city or town on the map. Show your student that his or her city or town is part of a state. Ask, *Which is bigger, a state or a city/town?* [state] Then explain to your student that his or her state is part of a country, the United States. On a sheet of paper, draw five concentric circles like the ones pictured here. In the innermost circle have your student write "Me." On the rest of the circles have your student

write "My Neighborhood," the name of his or her city or town, the name of his or her state, and the name of his or her country. Ask your student to think of more circles that could be added to the drawing.

2 IDENTIFY Explain that a **globe** is a round ball with a map of the world on it. Identify the United States on the globe. Then show your student the **equator.** Explain that the equator is an imaginary line that goes around Earth and divides it in half. Allow your student to trace the equator with his or her finger all the way around the globe. Help your student identify some countries north of the equator (such as the United States, Spain, and Italy) and south of the equator (such as Brazil, Australia, and Argentina). Provide your student with a map of the world and help him or her find the equator on the map. Ask, *What is the same about a map and a globe?* [they both show what the world looks like] *What is different about a map and a globe?* [a map is flat and a globe is round]

3 LABEL Have your student look at the United States on the globe. Show your student the two countries that are right next to the United States: Mexico and Canada. Tell your student that together the United States, Mexico, Canada, and the countries that make up Central America make a **continent.** A continent is one of seven large bodies of land on Earth. Tell your student that Earth has seven continents: North America, South America, Europe, Africa, Australia, Asia, and Antarctica. Identify all seven continents on the globe with your student. Provide your student with Student Learning Page 3.A. Invite him or her to use markers, crayons, or colored pencils to label the seven continents on the blank map of the world. He or she may also color each of the continents a different color.

4 DISCUSS Tell your student that each of the seven continents is special and unique. Point out the continents and tell your student many interesting facts about each of them. You can tell your student that Africa is the second largest continent and contains more countries than any other continent. Asia includes many diverse countries, such as China, Vietnam, and India, with different ethnic groups, religions, and languages. The South Pole is located in Antarctica. And, on the continent of Australia, people say hello by saying "g'day" and call kangaroos "roos," friends "cobbers," and candy "lolly." Challenge your student to use the library or the Internet to find one or two interesting facts about Europe and South America.

5 COMPARE Challenge your student to show you the United States and North America on the globe. Ask, *Which is smaller, the United States or North America?* [the United States] *Which is bigger, the United States or North America?* [North America] Emphasize that countries are usually smaller than continents. On the globe, point out Botswana in the southern part of Africa. Explain that Botswana is a country that's part of the continent of Africa and is smaller than Africa. Find Venezuela and South America on the map. Ask, *Which is bigger, Venezuela or South America?* [South America] *Which one is a country?* [Venezuela] *Which one is a continent?* [South America]

6 **IDENTIFY** Together with your student look at the map of North America and point to Mexico and Canada again. Tell your student that Mexico and Canada share a **border** with the United States. A border is a boundary line that separates two political entities. Allow your student to use his or her finger to trace the borders the United States shares with Canada and Mexico. Help your student identify some of the states along the borders with Canada and Mexico.

7 **CREATE AND COLOR** Tell your student that people in Mexico speak Spanish and that in Canada many people speak both French and English. Then practice saying the word *hello* in Spanish (*hola*) and in French (*bonjour*) with your student. Provide your student with one sheet of construction paper to create a sign titled "North American Hello." He or she can write "United States: hello," "Mexico: hola," and "Canada: bonjour or hello" on the sign. Then invite him or her to hang the sign in a place where his or her family members can read it.

8 **LABEL** Remind your student that he or she has learned the names of the seven continents of land on Earth. Ask, *What else do you see on the globe?* [bodies of water] Explain that an **ocean** is a large body of saltwater. Tell your student that there are four oceans: the Atlantic, Pacific, Indian, and Arctic Oceans. Help your student identify the four oceans on the globe. Ask, *Which oceans touch the United States?* [the Atlantic and Pacific Oceans]

9 **WRITE** Discuss with your student what he or she has learned about globes in this lesson. Then distribute a copy of the Venn Diagram found on page 353. Have your student label one circle "Globe," one circle "Map," and the area where the circles overlap "Both." Ask your student to write individual characteristics of maps and globes under their appropriate headings and to write shared characteristics under "Both." Then have your student write in his or her notebook whether he or she thinks a globe or a map is more helpful along with an explanation.

10 **ILLUSTRATE** Look at the globe with your student and ask, *Is there more land or water on the surface of Earth?* [water] Tell your student that water covers more than 70 percent of Earth's surface and that there's a lot going on under these waters. More than 1 million known species of plants and animals live in the ocean, and scientists think that there are millions more that haven't been discovered yet. Fish, sharks, octopi, dolphins, starfish, eels, lobsters, and jellyfish are just some of the animals that live in the ocean. Emphasize to your student that the ocean is very important to life on Earth because it's the home of so many animals and plants. Explain that we can help protect the

DID YOU KNOW?

The oceans contain 97 percent of Earth's water and make up 71 percent of Earth's surface. The Pacific Ocean—the largest ocean—covers about 64,186,300 square miles of Earth.

ocean by conserving water, keeping garbage out of the ocean, and taking part in beach cleanups. Invite your student to draw a picture of some of the animals that live in the ocean.

11 **NAME** Remind your student that a globe is a small model of Earth. Tell your student that the seven continents and the four oceans are all part of Earth. Earth is our home **planet.** A planet is a large body that revolves around the sun. There are nine planets in our **solar system.** Our solar system includes the sun, the nine planets, and all the other bodies (such as moons and comets) that revolve around the sun. Show your student a picture of the solar system. Then name the planets in our solar system with him or her: Mercury, Venus, Earth, Mars, Jupiter, Saturn, Uranus, Neptune, and Pluto.

12 **RELATE** Tell your student that what we do affects the whole world. Many plants and animals need special attention. We need to protect our planet from **pollution.** Pollution is damage to the land and ocean by waste and garbage. Some ways we can protect our world include recycling cans, glass bottles, and newspapers; turning off the lights when we aren't using them; picking up litter; walking or riding our bikes instead of driving cars; using less paper by drawing or writing on both sides of a piece of paper; and giving our toys to someone instead of throwing them away. Invite your student to choose one thing to do today to help protect the environment.

13 **EXPAND** Have your student look through a newspaper or magazine that you have in the house. Challenge him or her to look through it for articles about different countries. Then have him or her discuss with you what he or she has learned.

Branching Out

FOR FURTHER READING

Around the World Art and Activities: Visiting the 7 Continents Through Craft Fun, by Judy Press (Williamson Publishing, 2000).

Eyewitness: Ocean, by Miranda Macquitty (DK Publishing, 2000).

How We Learned the Earth Is Round, by Patricia Lauber (HarperCollins Juvenile Books, 2003).

TEACHING TIP

Use a piece of mail sent to your house to illustrate the idea of different communities to your student. Show your student the address on the envelope indicating his or her house, town, and state. He or she belongs to a neighborhood community, a town community, and a state community.

CHECKING IN

To assess your student's understanding of the lesson, provide your student with the globe. Ask him or her to show you the seven continents and the four oceans.

Discover the World's Continents and Oceans

SOCIAL STUDIES

3.A

Label the seven continents and the four oceans on the map.
Then color the map.

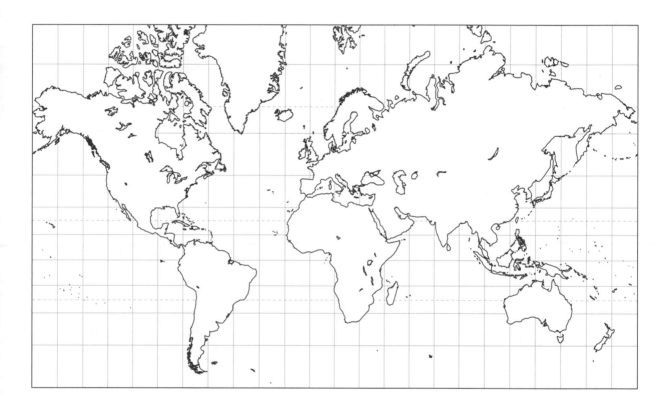

What's Next? You Decide!

Now it's your turn to choose what to do next in the lesson. Read the activities and decide which one you want to do—you may want to try them both!

Write a Letter

MATERIALS

❑ markers or colored pencils

STEPS

What if a child from a different continent wanted to know more about North America? What would you tell him or her?

❑ Write a letter telling what's special about North America. You can write about:

- the names of the countries in North America

- the languages of North America

- the oceans that are close to North America

- the other continents that are close to North America

- what you like about living in North America

❑ Then add a picture that shows something about North America.

Use the Globe

MATERIALS

❑ 1 globe

STEPS

Play this game with a partner to learn more about our world community.

❑ Find a country, continent, or ocean on the globe. Don't tell your partner what it is.

❑ Describe the place on the globe. Tell about nearby countries or bodies of water. If you choose a continent, tell what countries are there. Share anything else you know about this place.

❑ Tell your partner to guess this place by pointing on the globe.

❑ Take turns with your partner and learn more about our world!

SOCIAL STUDIES

LESSON 4.4

Caring for Earth

Earth has given us many gifts, and we must care for it in return.

OBJECTIVE	BACKGROUND	MATERIALS
To teach your student about Earth's resources and how to care for them	Earth has many natural resources that people use to meet their needs. To make sure that these resources are available in the future, people must conserve and replenish them. In this lesson, your student will learn about Earth's resources and the importance of conserving them.	■ Student Learning Pages 4.A–4.D ■ 1 grocery store ad ■ 1 national newspaper

VOCABULARY

NATURAL RESOURCES the materials that come from Earth that plants and animals need
CROPS plants that are grown in large quantities for food
CONSERVATION the protection and careful use of Earth's natural resources
REPLENISHING replacing something that has been used
RECYCLING reusing something that has already been used in a different way

Let's Begin

1 **PREVIEW** Tell your student that Earth is full of **natural resources.** Explain that natural resources are materials from Earth that people, animals, and plants use. Provide an example, such as water. Then challenge your student to name another natural resource. Together with your student brainstorm other natural resources. Some your student should know about include soil, air, trees and other plants, sunlight, and minerals (including oil). Ask your student to choose a natural resource and tell how people use it. Then look through a national newspaper and identify stories dealing with natural resources. Read the stories aloud to your student and discuss the content.

2 **EXPLAIN** Tell your student that people use natural resources every day. For example, people use water, soil, and sunlight to grow **crops** of vegetables or fruit. Tell your student that a crop is a plant that is grown in large quantities for food. Ask, *Can you name some crops that people eat?* [wheat, corn, potatoes, beans, apples, and so on]

ENRICH THE EXPERIENCE

Show your student a grocery store ad. Invite him or her to pick out pictures of fresh produce and identify the food.

3 **APPLY** Distribute Student Learning Page 4.A. Tell your student that he or she is going to learn more about products that come from certain crops. Then read the directions to your student. Be sure he or she understands the activity.

4 **DESCRIBE** Explain that animals also use natural resources. Farmers use crops and their by-products to feed their animals. In turn, people use these animals to meet their needs. For example, sheep provide wool and cows provide milk. Have your student make a list of how animals use natural resources. [water for drinking and bathing, the sun for light and warmth, grass for grazing]

5 **MODEL** Tell your student that because we depend so much on natural resources, it's very important to care for them. Explain that **conservation** means saving resources by using them carefully. Name some ways we can conserve resources. For example, we can use less of the resources used to make electricity by turning off the lights when they aren't needed. Ask your student to brainstorm ways to save natural resources.

6 **PRACTICE** Tell your student that many people work to save natural resources. Some of these people try to get others to do the same. Then distribute Student Learning Page 4.B.

7 **EXPAND** Tell your student that we can make natural resources last by **replenishing,** or replacing, them. One way to replenish trees is to plant new ones. Point out that soil that has eroded, or worn away, can be replenished as well. Tell your student that people can also save resources by **recycling,** or reusing, them. People can recycle paper, cans, plastic, glass, and so on. Explain some ways that people can recycle things they use at home. Then distribute Student Learning Page 4.C.

FOR FURTHER READING

Creating by Recycling, by Anna Limos and Laia Sadurni (Blackbirch Press, 2000).

How to Save the Planet, by Barbara Taylor (Oxford University Press, 2001).

Recycling, by Rhonda Lucas Donald (Children's Press, 2001).

Branching Out

TEACHING TIP

You may recycle one or more kinds of items at home. If so, show your student how you recycle. Point out the items you recycle and the natural resources they come from. Then explain how you dispose of the items so that they may be reused as something else.

CHECKING IN

To assess your student's understanding of the lesson, show him or her various pictures of nature scenes. Ask your student to identify different natural resources he or she sees in the pictures. Then invite your student to name some ways the resources are used.

Match the Product with the Crop

Look at the four bushels of crops. Read the name of the crop for each bushel. Then look at the products listed in the box. Write the name of two products we get from each crop on the correct bushels.

| pancakes | popcorn | cornmeal | soup |
| apple juice | bread | french fries | apple pie |

1. _____
2. _____

Corn

5. _____
6. _____

Wheat

3. _____
4. _____

Potatoes

7. _____
8. _____

Apples

SOCIAL STUDIES

4.B

Make a Conservation Button

Color and decorate the button. Cut it out and wear it to remind others to conserve natural resources every day. (Make sure you are done with page 4.C!) Then write three ways that you and your family can conserve natural resources.

Conserve!

Join the Recycling Team

Look at the objects. Draw a line to match each object to the correct recycling basket. The first one has been done for you. Now see how you can recycle these items in your home. If you already are recycling these, think of other objects you can recycle.

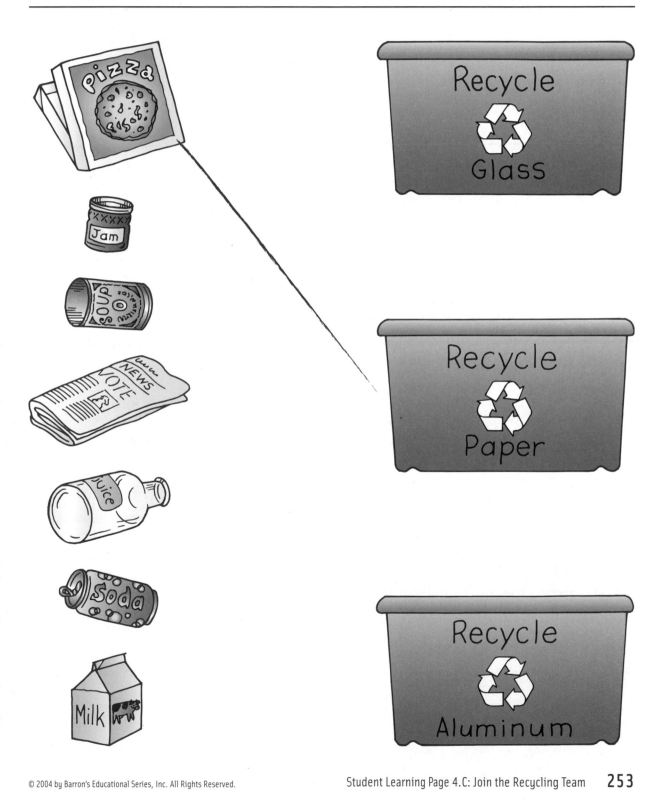

What's Next? You Decide!

Now it's your turn to choose what to do next in the lesson. Read the activities and decide which one you want to do—you may want to try them both!

Write a Song

MATERIALS

❑ several books about natural resources

❑ 1 audiocassette recorder (optional)

❑ 1 audiocassette tape (optional)

STEPS

Write a song about Earth's natural resources.

❑ Brainstorm how you feel about Earth's resources.

❑ Think about ways to tell others to conserve resources.

❑ Write a song about natural resources to show your ideas. Use music from a nursery rhyme if you like.

❑ Practice singing your song. If you can, record the song. Ask an adult to help you do this.

❑ Share the song with your friends and family!

Plant Your Own Tomato Crop

MATERIALS

❑ several tomato seeds

❑ 1 bag soil

❑ 1 planting pot

❑ 1 watering can

STEPS

❑ Ask an adult to help you find some tomato seeds.

❑ Place the seeds on a paper towel with a little water.

❑ Watch the seeds sprout.

❑ Put some soil in the pot.

❑ Put two to three seeds on the soil. Cover them with a little more soil.

❑ Put the pot in a warm, sunny spot.

❑ Water the plant. Then watch it grow!

Discovering How We Work Together

By teaching the meaning of community, you teach your student a lifetime of serving others.

OBJECTIVE	BACKGROUND	MATERIALS
To show your student how different members of a community work together	Many different people throughout your community, and throughout the country, work to provide needed goods and services to others. Through these jobs people earn incomes. In this lesson, your student will learn about goods, services, and incomes.	<ul><li>Student Learning Pages 5.A–5.B</li><li>markers, crayons, or colored pencils</li></ul>

VOCABULARY

GOODS things that are sold

SERVICES jobs where a person does something for others

TAXES money that people must pay to support the government

PRODUCE to make something

CONSUME to buy something

INCOME the money that a person earns from work

BANK a place where people keep their money

SAVINGS ACCOUNTS bank accounts that people save their money in

INTEREST the money that is added by the bank to a person's savings account

TRADE the business of buying and selling goods

TRANSPORTATION the way something is moved from place to place

BARTERING trading goods and services for other goods and services without using money

Let's Begin

1 **INTRODUCE** Ask your student to name some things his or her family has spent money on recently. Explain that we use our money to buy **goods** and **services.** Goods are things that are made and sold. Services are jobs where a person does something for someone else. Tell your student that food, toys, and clothes are all goods we buy. When we get our hair cut or go to the doctor, we spend money on a service. We give our money to the barber and the doctor to pay for the services they give us. Ask, *What are some goods and services our family uses?*

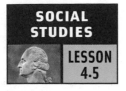

2 **REMIND** Tell your student that there are many people in his or her community who have service jobs that are very important. Ask, *What does a dentist do?* [fix people's teeth] Explain that a dentist is one person who provides a very important service to others. A dentist cares for other people by making sure their teeth are healthy. Tell your student that a car mechanic is another person who provides an important service. He or she fixes other people's cars so they can travel from place to place. Challenge your student to name three other people in his or her community who provide important services to others.

3 **ASK** Tell your student that there are some people who have service jobs in the government. For example, a police officer works to keep people in the community safe and is paid by the government. A mail delivery person provides another type of service. He or she is responsible for delivering mail to the community. Tell your student that a firefighter also has a service job in the government. Ask, *Why are firefighters important to a community?* [they help keep community members safe from fires] Have your student choose a service job that he or she finds interesting and locate a book at your local library that describes it. Then guide your student to read the book and discuss what he or she has learned.

4 **EXPAND** Explain that the money used to pay people such as firefighters, mail carriers, and mayors comes from **taxes.** Taxes are money that people pay the government. Everyone in the United States pays taxes. The government uses tax money for many different things, including fixing roads, paying teachers, and building libraries. Ask, *What money is used to pay the president of the United States?* [tax money]

5 **WRITE AND DRAW** Provide your student with Student Learning Page 5.A. Brainstorm with your student five to ten different service jobs. Have your student choose three of these jobs. Challenge him or her to draw a person doing each of these jobs in the boxes. On the lines below each box, tell your student to label the drawing and write one sentence about how that job helps others in the community. You may need to help your student with his or her spelling.

6 **EXPLAIN** Inform your student that people **produce** and **consume** goods. Producing goods means making something, and consuming goods means buying something. People who produce goods are known as producers and people who consume goods are known as consumers. Ask, *Is a person who's shopping at a grocery store a consumer or a producer? Why?* [a consumer, because he or she is buying food] Then have a discussion with your student about examples of producers and consumers that can be found in your community.

7 **RELATE** Explain to your student that many goods he or she uses every day are produced in factories. For example, pencils are made in factories. First, trees are cut into logs that are sent to a factory. At the factory the logs are cut into big blocks and then cut again into smaller blocks called slats. The slats are waxed and stained. A machine is used to cut grooves into the slats of wood. These grooves are where the gray writing part of a pencil will go. This gray writing part is called the writing core. The writing core is made from a mixture of clay and a material called graphite. The writing core is placed in between two grooved slats and glued together like a sandwich. The slats are then sanded and painted. Help your student retell the steps in the production of a pencil.

Many people work together to produce pencils.

8 **DISCUSS** Remind your student that people receive an **income** from their jobs. An income is money people earn. People use the income from their jobs in a number of different ways. People use it to pay bills. People use it to pay for the apartment or house where they live, for the food they eat, and for the clothes they wear. Invite your student to brainstorm some other things people might use their income for.

9 **DEFINE** Tell your student that people often try to save some of their income. When people save part of their income, they usually put the money in a **bank.** A bank is a place where people save money. Tell your student that people put the money they are saving in **savings accounts.** People like to keep their money at the bank because it's a safe place where their money is protected. Also, when people keep their money in a savings account, the money earns **interest.** Interest is the money a bank adds to a person's savings account. Ask, *Where could you keep money you want to save?* [a bank]

'

TAKE A BREAK

Take your student to your bank with you. Show him or her how to fill out a deposit slip. Tell your student that you're putting money in your savings account.

10 **CHALLENGE** Explain to your student that **trade** is the business of buying and selling goods. Countries are connected through trade. For example, the United States trades with other countries, selling goods produced here and buying goods produced in other countries. The United States is a major producer of corn and wheat, so we sell these goods to other countries. But there are many goods made in other countries that the United States needs and wants. We buy goods such as oil, coffee, and cocoa beans from other countries. Remind your student that the money people use to buy things in other countries looks different from the money used in the United States. Challenge your student to use the library or Internet to see what money looks like in other countries.

11 **NAME** Explain that goods travel to different countries on ships, trains, airplanes, and trucks. These are all forms of **transportation.** Transportation is the way things or people get from place to place. Ask, *What are some other types of transportation that take people from place to place?* [buses, bicycles, cars]

12 **EXPLAIN** Tell your student that in the past people didn't use money to pay for goods and services. Instead, they directly traded goods and services for other goods and services. This system is called **bartering.** For example, if an apple farmer wanted a new pair of boots, he or she might have given a basket of apples to a storeowner in exchange for boots. Then the farmer would have the boots he or she wanted and the storeowner would have apples to eat. Ask your student to imagine the life of a fisherman who lived long ago and what he might need and want. Ask, *What would a fisherman barter to get the things he needed to live?* [fish he caught]

13 **IMAGINE** Have your student think of something he or she would like to have and what good or service he or she would be willing to trade for it. Discuss. Then share with him or her any examples of your family bartering for goods or services. For example, perhaps a friend might fix your vehicle in exchange for you helping him or her install a light.

Branching Out

TEACHING TIP

While you're out in the community, point out people who have service jobs. When you see someone such as a police officer, mail carrier, barber, or librarian, remind your student that he or she has a service job. You can also remind your student how these people help others in your community.

CHECKING IN

To assess your student's understanding of the lesson, have your student make two columns on a piece of paper. One column should be titled "Goods" and the other column should be titled "Services." Read the following list to your student and have him or her write each item in the correct column: apples, police, pencil, doctor, nurse, watch, barber, and computer.

FOR FURTHER READING

Jobs People Do, by Christopher Maynard (DK Publishing, 2001).

Money Sense for Kids, by Hollis Page Harman (Barron's Educational Publishing, 1999).

Paying Taxes: A True Book, by Sarah DeCapua (Children's Press, 2002).

Write and Draw About Different Jobs

Draw a picture of a person doing a different job in each box. Write who each person is on the first line under the box. Write a sentence about how each person helps the community on the other lines.

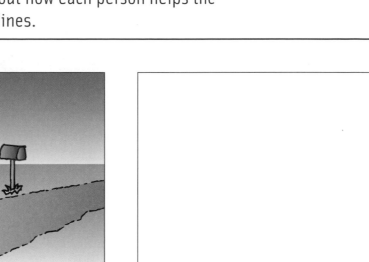

Job: mail carrier

A mail carrier brings letters

to people's homes.

Job: _____

_____

_____

Job: _____

_____

_____

Job: _____

_____

_____

What's Next? You Decide!

Now it's your turn to choose what to do next in the lesson. Read the activities and decide which one you want to do—you may want to try them both!

Make Your Own Money

MATERIALS

❑ 3–5 sheets construction paper
❑ markers, crayons, or colored pencils
❑ 1 pair scissors

STEPS

Make your own money with your favorite colors.

❑ Use scissors to cut your money out of construction paper. The money can be different shapes, such as triangles and stars. Be creative!
❑ Draw pictures and write words and numbers on your money.
❑ Try to make your money look colorful and fun!

Play Bank

MATERIALS

❑ 3 sheets green construction paper
❑ 1 black marker
❑ 1 calculator
❑ 1 chair
❑ 1 desk or table

STEPS

❑ Cut three sheets of green construction paper into small rectangles.
❑ Use the black marker to draw a dollar sign on each rectangle.
❑ Now invite a friend or family member to play bank with you!
❑ Take turns being the banker and the customer.
❑ The banker can sit in a chair at a desk or table with the calculator.
❑ The customer can bring his or her money to the bank.
❑ Practice using the terms *deposit* and *savings account*. The customer can deposit his or her money into a savings account.

Understanding Our Local and State Governments

Who's in charge of your town and state? Let's find out!

OBJECTIVE	BACKGROUND	MATERIALS
To help your student understand the roles and responsibilities of local and state governments	Local and state governments play an important part in the management of our entire country. In this lesson, your student will learn about the structure of local and state governments. He or she will also learn about the people who lead these governments.	■ Student Learning Pages 6.A–6.B ■ 10 index cards ■ 1 state map ■ 1 current newspaper or magazine

VOCABULARY
GOVERNMENT people who lead and guide a town, city, state, or country **MAYOR** the person who leads a city or town **CITY COUNCIL** a group of people who work with the mayor to make decisions **CITIZENS** members of a city, town, state, or country **GOVERNOR** the person who leads a state

Let's Begin

1 **DISCUSS** Introduce the lesson by asking your student who is responsible for leading and guiding his or her family. Then invite your student to share how his or her parents or guardians take care of the family.

2 **EXTEND** Explain further that the members of a community also need people to lead and guide them. The residents of a community choose people who they trust to be in **government.** Define *government* as "people who lead and guide a town, city, state, or country." People in government work to make laws, keep people safe, offer services, and solve problems. Ask, *Do you know what we call the leader of a town or city?* [the **mayor**]

3 **EXPAND AND RESEARCH** Correct or confirm that the leader of a town or city is called a mayor. This person leads a group called the **city council.** The mayor and the members of the city council are chosen by **citizens.** Explain that a citizen is a member of a

town, city, state, or country. Inform your student that if citizens have an idea for improving the community, they can share it with the mayor and the city council. If the city council members think the idea would help the community, they can put the idea into action. Ask your student to name some things that members of a community often want to improve. [schools, safety, parks] Then have your student draft a letter to the mayor or city council identifying something that needs to be improved along with an explanation why.

4 **EXPLAIN AND IDENTIFY** Explain that citizens also choose a person called a **governor** to lead their state. The governor works in the capitol building in a city called the state capital. The governor and other leaders of the state meet in the capitol building to make laws for the state. The governor also decides how to use money to pay for such services as schools, parks, roads, health services, housing, and state police. Look at a map of your state with your student. Point out the capital city and the symbol that identifies it. [possible answers: a star, a circle] Say, *Look at the map of your state. What is the capital city?* [answers will vary] Then direct your student to your town or city on the map. Discuss other features of the map.

5 **APPLY** Distribute Student Learning Page 6.A and review the directions with your student. Invite him or her to apply the information in the lesson by completing the page. Then ask your student to write in his or her notebook about how leaders in the community and state are like leaders in his or her family.

6 **EXPLORE** Help your student look through a current newspaper or magazine for stories about your local or state government. Discuss with your student the importance of the story and then discuss your student's feelings about it.

TAKE A BREAK

Take a field trip to your city hall. Show your student the mayor's office and other departments that offer various services. You may even want to take your student to an open city council meeting!

Branching Out

TEACHING TIP

Be sure your student knows the names of his or her mayor and governor. Help your student make real-world connections by pointing out newspaper articles or television news coverage about these local and state leaders.

CHECKING IN

To assess your student's understanding of the lesson, write the vocabulary words on index cards and the definitions on other index cards. Have your student match the cards.

FOR FURTHER READING

Local Government (*Kid's Guide*), by Ernestine Gieseckle (Heinemann Library, 2000).

Your Government (*Pacemaker Book*), Ted Sileira (Lake Publishing Company, 1999).

Match the Government Words

Look at each picture. Match each picture with a word from
the box. Write the words on the lines under the pictures.

| citizens | state capitol | mayor | governor |

I lead and guide the people in my state.

I lead and guide the people in my town.

1. _____ 2. _____

State leaders work here.

3. _____

We choose the leaders of our city and state.

4. _____

What's Next? You Decide!

Now it's your turn to choose what to do next in the lesson. Read the activities and decide which one you want to do—you may want to try them both!

Write a Letter

■ MATERIALS

❑ 1 envelope

❑ 1 postage stamp

■ STEPS

❑ Write your mayor a letter. Tell him or her what you think about your town or city. You could thank him or her for something you like about your town or city. Or you could give your mayor an idea for making your town or city better.

❑ Write the date and your name and address at the top of your letter.

❑ Find the address where your mayor works. Ask an adult to help you.

❑ Write your mayor's address in the middle of the envelope. Write your name and address in the top left corner of the envelope.

❑ Put a postage stamp on the envelope and mail the letter.

Organize a Kids' City Council

■ MATERIALS

❑ several sheets construction paper

❑ markers, crayons, or colored pencils

■ STEPS

Put together a kids' city council. Ask your friends and family members to help you.

❑ Get together with other kids you know. Suppose that you are members of a kids' city council.

❑ Meet with your city council. Talk about how you can make your community a better place. For example, you can help pick up garbage or you can be kind to your neighbors. Think of other ideas.

❑ Write each idea on a sheet of construction paper. Then draw a picture for each idea.

Celebrating Freedom

Our federal government works to keep America the home of the free.

OBJECTIVE	BACKGROUND	MATERIALS
To help your student learn about the federal government, voting, and freedom	In the United States, all people have the right to freedom. One way we celebrate this freedom is by voting for the representatives of our federal government. In this lesson, your student will explore the ways Americans express their freedom. He or she will also learn more about voting and the federal government.	<ul><li>Student Learning Pages 7.A–7.B</li><li>1 U.S. map</li><li>1 quarter</li><li>1 penny</li><li>1 photo White House</li><li>1 photo U.S. Capitol</li></ul>

VOCABULARY

FEDERAL GOVERNMENT the government for the entire United States

CONGRESS the part of the government that makes laws

ELECTED chosen by voting

VOTE to make a choice on a form called a ballot

SYMBOL something that stands for something else

Let's Begin

1 **INTRODUCE** Explain to your student that our **federal government** is the government for the entire United States. It includes the president and **Congress.** Ask, *Who is the leader of the entire United States?* [the president]

2 **TELL** Tell your student that the president lives and works in Washington, D.C. Show your student the location of Washington, D.C., on a map of the United States. The building where the president lives and works is called the White House. Part of the president's job is to meet with the leaders of other countries. The president also signs laws. The president is **elected,** or chosen by the citizens of the United States who **vote.** Explain that when people vote, they make a choice on a form called a ballot. All people who are citizens of the United States and who are 18 years old or older are allowed to vote for their government leaders. Ask your student to share his or her ideas on why it's important to vote.

? DID YOU KNOW?

Share with your student that there are 132 rooms, 35 bathrooms, and 6 levels in the White House! The White House has also been called the President's House and the Executive Mansion.

3   **CHALLENGE** Tell your student that Congress is the part of government that makes laws for the country. People who live in every state elect their own representatives to work in Congress. The building where leaders of Congress meet is called the U.S. Capitol. This building is also in Washington, D.C. The job of Congress is to write and vote on the laws for all the states in the United States. Have your student use the Internet to find the name of a leader in Congress who's from his or her state.

4   **DEFINE** Tell your student that in the United States we have the right to freedom, or the right to make our own choices. Some of our freedoms include the right to vote, the right to practice any religion, and the right to speak our opinions. Challenge your student to name some other things that Americans have the freedom to do.

5   **TELL** Tell your student that a **symbol** is something that stands for something else. In America, we have symbols that stand for our freedom. For example, the eagle is a symbol of our freedom. Our flag is another symbol of our freedom. Then tell your student that we have mottos (sayings) that tell what we believe about freedom. For example, *E pluribus unum* means "Out of many, one" in Latin. This means that many different people come to live in the United States, but they come together to form one country. Provide your student with a quarter and a penny. Together with your student find the motto *E pluribus unum* on the coins.

6   **SING AND RESEARCH** Tell your student that we also have songs that express our freedom. Explain that "The Star-Spangled Banner" is our country's national anthem. Tell your student that when Americans sing this song, they often place their right hand over their heart and look at the flag. Invite your student to sing the national anthem with you. Then find another song that represents freedom in our country and sing it together.

7   **DISTRIBUTE** Direct your student to Student Learning Page 7.A and show him or her photos of the White House and U.S. Capitol. You can go to http://www.picturesofplaces.com for a look at photos.

FOR FURTHER READING

Capital! Washington, D.C., from A to Z, by Laura Krauss Melmed (HarperCollins Children's Books, 2002).

Voting and Elections, by Patricia J. Murphy (Compass Point Books, 2002).

Branching Out

TEACHING TIP

When watching the news on television or reading the newspaper with your student, point out the president. Discuss with your student what the president is doing and what the president's job is.

CHECKING IN

To assess your student's understanding of the lesson, ask your student to tell you a symbol, a motto, and a song that celebrate our freedom.

Visit the White House and the U.S. Capitol

Look at the photos of the White House and the U.S. Capitol.
Write the descriptions in the correct box.

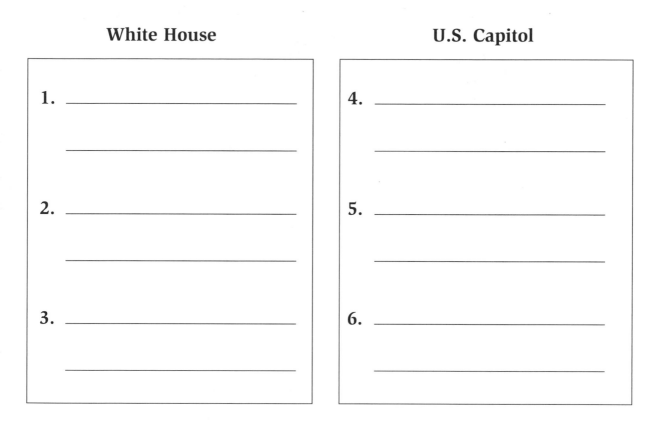

White House

1. _____

_____

2. _____

_____

3. _____

_____

U.S. Capitol

4. _____

_____

5. _____

_____

6. _____

_____

Descriptions

❑ The president lives and works here.

❑ Laws are made here.

❑ Members of Congress work here.

❑ Leaders of other countries sometimes have dinner here.

❑ It's also called the Executive Mansion.

❑ People elected from all states meet here.

What's Next? You Decide!

Now it's your turn to choose what to do next in the lesson. Read the activities and decide which one you want to do—you may want to try them both!

Make a Freedom Poster

MATERIALS

- ❑ 1 posterboard
- ❑ markers, crayons, or colored pencils

STEPS

Make a freedom poster to show what you've learned!

- ❑ Write "Freedom" in the middle of your posterboard.
- ❑ Draw pictures on your posterboard that tell about freedom. You may also draw pictures of the eagle or the American flag.
- ❑ Write some mottos about freedom on your poster such as *E pluribus unum,* or "Out of many, one."
- ❑ Make up some new symbols and mottos that say something about freedom. Add them to your poster.

Make Voting Buttons

MATERIALS

- ❑ 1 sheet construction paper
- ❑ 1 pair scissors
- ❑ markers, crayons, or colored pencils
- ❑ tape

STEPS

In an election, some people wear buttons to remind others to vote.

- ❑ Cut out three circles from the construction paper.
- ❑ Write "Vote!" on the circles.
- ❑ Then add the name of someone whom people should vote for as a leader. You can write your name if you wish!
- ❑ Decorate your buttons with pictures or symbols.
- ❑ Tape a button on your shirt.
- ❑ Give the other buttons to your friends or family members. Let them tape their buttons on their shirts, too!

Meeting the Native Americans

Who were the first Americans? The Native Americans!

OBJECTIVE	BACKGROUND	MATERIALS
To help your student understand how different Native American groups lived and how they influenced the history of our country	Not only have Native Americans lived in America for thousands of years, they have contributed much to our country's history. In this lesson, your student will learn about the traditions and cultures of various Native American groups. He or she will also learn about how these groups live today.	■ Student Learning Pages 8.A–8.B

VOCABULARY
TRIBES groups of people who live and work together
TEEPEES cone-shaped shelters made of poles and covered with buffalo hides
POTTERY clay bowls and pots
TRADITIONS ways of doing things that are passed down from one generation or age group to another
RESERVATION an area of land that the government set aside for Native Americans

Let's Begin

1 **INTRODUCE** Tell your student that there are groups of people who have lived on the land that is now the United States for thousands of years. They were here before the colonists settled along the Atlantic coast. They were here even before explorers came to the Americas from Europe. Say to your student, *Take a guess. Who do you think were the first Americans?* [Native Americans] Correct your student as needed.

2 **LOCATE** Inform your student that many different Native American **tribes,** or groups, lived throughout the land. Define a tribe as a group of people who live and work together. Then tell your student that three important Native American tribes were the Pueblo, the Sioux, and the Powhatan. Say, *The map of the United States on the next page shows where the Pueblo, Sioux, and Powhatan tribes lived.* Together discuss the map. Help your student pronounce the names of the Native American tribes as you ask questions. Ask, *Which tribe lived near the*

northern part of the United States? [the Sioux] *Which tribe lived near the southern part of the United States?* [the Pueblo] *Which tribe lived near the eastern part of the United States?* [the Powhatan]

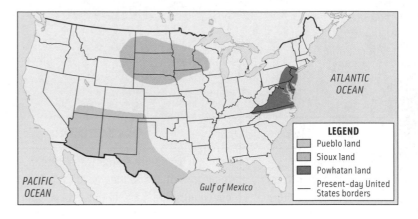

ATLANTIC OCEAN

PACIFIC OCEAN

Gulf of Mexico

LEGEND
Pueblo land
Sioux land
Powhatan land
Present-day United States borders

Teach your student a Powhatan children's game. Drop a small handful of toothpicks on a table. Without touching the toothpicks, have a contest where you and your student silently count the toothpicks mentally. The player who calls out the correct number first wins!

The Sioux used buffaloes for food, clothing, and shelter covering.

3 **RELATE** Inform your student that Native Americans used the natural resources in their area to live. Tell your student that natural resources are things from Earth that people use. Point out that water is an example of a natural resource. Tell your student that years ago the Native Americans depended completely on nature for water. Ask, *Where do you think many Native Americans lived so they could get water easily?* [near rivers or lakes] If your student answers oceans, explain that people can't drink saltwater without getting sick.

4 **EXPAND** Tell your student that the Powhatan tribe lived near the Atlantic coast, along rivers and near forests. They built canoes, or wooden boats, out of trees so they could travel by water. Many animals lived in the forests. The Powhatans hunted these animals for their meat and fur. Ask, *What do you think the Native Americans made out of the animals' fur?* [clothing and blankets]

5 **REVEAL** Explain that the Sioux lived on flat, grassy plains. Many buffalo also lived on the plains. Tell your student that a buffalo is a large four-legged animal. Then point out the picture of the buffalo below. Explain that since there were a large number of buffalo, the Sioux were able to use them to meet many of their needs. For example, the Sioux used the buffalo's fur to make clothing, blankets, ropes, and coverings for their shelters. They used the meat from the buffalo for food. They used the bones from the buffalo to make needles, spoons, and arrows. They even used the buffalo's tail to swat flies! Ask your student to use the information in this lesson and the photo to describe the buffalo in three words.

6 **ELABORATE** Tell your student that the Sioux lived in **teepees.** Explain that teepees were cone-shaped shelters made of poles and covered with buffalo hides, or skins. Explain further that the buffalo liked to wander from place to place. Because the teepees were small and lightweight, the Sioux could easily pack up their homes and follow the animals when they began to roam. Ask, *If you were a Native American child, do you think you would like to pack up and move every time the buffalo began to roam?* Encourage your student to share both the positive and negative points of frequently moving from place to place.

SOCIAL STUDIES
LESSON 4.8

7 **EXPLAIN** Point out again on the map where the Pueblo tribe lived. Tell your student that because this area of the country was very hot and dry, not many plants and animals lived there. Therefore, the Pueblo had to grow much of the food they ate. Explain that the Pueblo learned to grow corn, squash, and other vegetables. They made clothes from cotton plants they grew. These Native Americans also made clay called adobe by baking mud in the hot sun. The Pueblo used this clay to make homes and **pottery,** or clay bowls and pots. Ask your student, *How did the hot weather help the Pueblo?* [they were able to make clay by baking mud]

8 **DISCUSS** Tell your student that many groups of people have special **traditions.** Define a tradition as a way of doing something that's passed down from one generation or age group to another. To provide further context for the vocabulary word, help your student identify family or national traditions, such as holidays. Explain that Native Americans have their own special traditions. One tradition that has been practiced in the Sioux tribe is the art of storytelling. Tell your student that for many years Sioux stories were not written down. Instead, people learned and remembered the stories from hearing them told out loud. Invite your student to tell you a story he or she likes. Be sure your student tells the story from his or her memory rather than reading it to you.

?
DID YOU KNOW?

The word *pueblo* is a Spanish word that means "village." Explorers from Spain called the Native Americans of the Southwest the Pueblo because they lived in small villages made up of adobe shelters.

9 **RESPOND** Retell the story your student just told you. Then point out that although many of the Sioux stories weren't exactly the same, they had the same message or taught the same lesson. Tell your student that the Sioux retold stories to teach and guide younger people. Explain further that the storytelling tradition also helped different generations of relatives and tribe members feel close to one another. Ask your student to share a lesson that he or she has learned by hearing someone tell a story. Then invite your student to share a tradition that brings his or her family or friends closer together.

10 **INFORM** Tell your student that we have learned much about the Sioux from a woman who decided to pass down their stories to the rest of the world. Reveal that this woman was a Sioux named Ella Cara Deloria. She was born on a **reservation** in South Dakota. Explain that a reservation is an area of land that the government set aside for Native Americans. Tell your student that Deloria wrote books about the Sioux and their way of life. Ask, *If you could speak to Deloria today, what question would you ask her about the Sioux?*

11 **CONNECT** Be sure your student understands that Native Americans still live in the United States today. Explain that many members of different tribes live on reservations. Some Native Americans still practice the traditions of their people. For example, some still speak Native American languages, tell traditional stories, and make traditional crafts, such as jewelry, clothing, and pottery. Many Native Americans work and live in the city, but they still remember and enjoy their culture. Challenge your student to name one thing that Native Americans probably don't do today. [they don't hunt buffalo anymore]

12 **EXPAND** As your student shows interest, together find out information about the Native Americans that first inhabited your area. Head to your local historical society or museum for more information and artifacts. You can also ask your librarian for books about your area's history. Try to find out what children your student's age did, such as what games they played and what chores they did. Have your student tell you how his or her life would be different and the same if he or she was one of the area's first inhabitants.

13 **APPLY** Distribute Student Learning Page 8.A. Be sure your student understands the activity. Then allow time for him or her to complete the page.

Branching Out

FOR FURTHER READING

Eastern Woodland Indians (Native Americans), by Mir Tamim Ansary (Heinemann Library, 2001).

Grandma Maxine Remembers: A Native American Family Story, by Ann Morris (Millbrook Press, 2002).

Secret Worlds: Native Americans, by Laura Buller (DK Publishing, 2001).

TEACHING TIP

To provide a deeper appreciation of the Native Americans' influence, point out that many words we use today are Native American in origin. For example, the words *canoe, pecan, raccoon,* and *moccasin* all come from Native American languages.

CHECKING IN

To assess your student's understanding of the lesson, invite your student to compare and contrast the Native American tribes. Ask your student to name one way the Sioux, Pueblo, and Powhatan are similar and one way they are different.

Fill in the Native American Chart

Read the sentences. Write them in the correct column of the chart.
Put a check in the box when you have used the sentence.

❏ They lived in teepees.

❏ They built canoes.

❏ They grew corn and squash.

❏ They lived near the Atlantic coast.

❏ They made adobe from mud.

❏ They followed the buffalo.

Pueblo	Sioux	Powhatan

What's Next? You Decide!

Now it's your turn to choose what to do next in the lesson. Read the activities and decide which one you want to do— you may want to try them both!

Make Clay Artwork

MATERIALS

❏ 1 package modeling clay

❏ paints

❏ several pictures of Sioux pottery

STEPS

❏ Take some modeling clay. Shape the clay into a bowl or a cup (or whatever you would like to make).

❏ Let the clay dry.

❏ Ask an adult to help you find some pictures of Sioux pottery. Look at the pictures to get an idea of a design you would like to make.

❏ Then paint the clay so it looks like Sioux pottery.

Tell a Story

MATERIALS

❏ 1 audiocassette recorder (optional)

❏ 1 audiocassette tape (optional)

STEPS

Tell a story to teach a lesson, just like the Sioux.

❏ Think of a story you've heard that taught you a lesson.

❏ Practice telling the story to yourself.

❏ Think about what the lesson of the story is.

❏ Tell the story to an adult. Then explain how the story teaches an important lesson.

❏ If you'd like, record the story.

Exploring the Early History of the United States

Family and friends are the most valuable gifts.

OBJECTIVE	BACKGROUND	MATERIALS
To help your student learn more about the early history of our country	It's important for your student to understand the challenges and struggles the United States faced as a young country. In understanding these struggles, your student will gain a better appreciation of his or her freedom. In this lesson, your student will learn about the explorers, the first colonies, and the colonists' fight to win independence from England.	■ Student Learning Pages 9.A–9.B ■ 1 world map or globe

VOCABULARY

EXPLORERS people who travel to discover new lands

COLONIES places in a new land where people from another country come to live

COLONISTS the people who live in a colony

PILGRIMS people from England who moved to North America and started a colony in Plymouth, Massachusetts

WAMPANOAG a Native American group who lived in the East

NATIONAL HOLIDAY a special time of celebration for a country

CROPS plants that are grown in large quantities for food

TAXES money that people must pay to support the government

INDEPENDENCE freedom from the control of others or of other countries

Let's Begin

1 **USE A MAP** Show your student a map of the world or a globe and point out the continents of Europe and North America. Explain that many **explorers** from Europe traveled by ship to North America. Tell your student that an explorer is a person who travels to discover new lands. Christopher Columbus was an explorer who sailed across the ocean to reach North America. Look at the map or globe with your student. Ask, *Which ocean did explorers such as Christopher Columbus have to cross to get to North America?* [the Atlantic Ocean] Help him or her find a biography of Columbus to find out more about him.

2 **EXPLAIN** Tell your student that after the explorers arrived, more and more people from their countries came to live in North

America. The places where these people settled are called **colonies.** A colony is a place in a new land where people from another country come to live. The people who lived there are called **colonists.** Tell your student that St. Augustine is the oldest colony in the United States. St. Augustine was settled in Florida by people from Spain. Another colony, called Jamestown, was settled by people from England. Life for the colonists was not easy. They were very hungry and many colonists became very sick. They had to learn how to farm the new land. Ask, *What do you call a place in a new land where people from another country go to live?* [a colony]

3 **INFORM** Tell your student that a group of people called **Pilgrims** traveled from England to settle in North America. The Pilgrims weren't allowed to practice their religion in England, so they decided to start a new life in North America. In 1620, the Pilgrims began sailing across the Atlantic Ocean on a ship called the *Mayflower.* They arrived at Plymouth, Massachusetts, where they started a settlement. Many Pilgrims died during their first winter at Plymouth because the weather was so cold and there wasn't enough food to eat. Then the Pilgrims met the **Wampanoag,** Native Americans who showed them where to fish and hunt and how to grow foods such as corn, pumpkin, and squash. Ask, *How did the Wampanoag help the Pilgrims?* [they showed them where to fish and hunt and how to grow food]

4 **DRAW AND WRITE** Tell your student that the Pilgrims wanted to have a celebration to give thanks for their food. Their celebration lasted for three days. They invited the Wampanoag to their celebration. They probably ate wild ducks, deer, turkey, fish, carrots, beans, berries, dried fruit, and cornbread. They also sang songs, danced, and played games. This celebration is often called the First Thanksgiving. Provide your student with Student Learning Page 9.A. Invite him or her to draw a picture of the First Thanksgiving in the box and answer the questions in complete sentences on the lines.

5 **RELATE** Explain to your student that today Thanksgiving is a **national holiday.** A national holiday is a special time of celebration for a country. Thanksgiving is celebrated on the fourth Thursday in November. Families and friends usually get together to share a meal and to give thanks for the important people and things in their lives. The meal often includes turkey, gravy, stuffing, sweet potatoes, cranberry sauce, and pumpkin pie. Many big cities in the United States also have Thanksgiving parades. Ask, *How does your family celebrate Thanksgiving?*

6 **DISCUSS** Remind your student that Native Americans taught the Pilgrims how to plant and harvest corn. The Pilgrims had never seen or eaten corn in England, so it was a new food to them. Corn became an important **crop** for the Pilgrims. A crop is plants that are grown in large quantities for food or for some other use. The Pilgrims were able to dry the corn to make cornmeal, which could be used for cornbread and cornmush. Today on Thanksgiving many people still eat corn as a part of

their special dinner. Invite your student to name some other
crops the Pilgrims grew. [pumpkin, squash, and sweet potatoes]

7   **ASK** Tell your student that more and more people began to come
to North America from England, Spain, and other countries. There
were thirteen separate colonies in North America. These colonies
were ruled by England. The colonists had to pay **taxes** to the
English government. They also had to follow other laws set by
the English government. The colonists didn't want to be governed
by England so they decided to work together to gain their
independence. This means that the colonists wanted to be free from
England's rule. Ask, *What country ruled the 13 colonies?* [England]

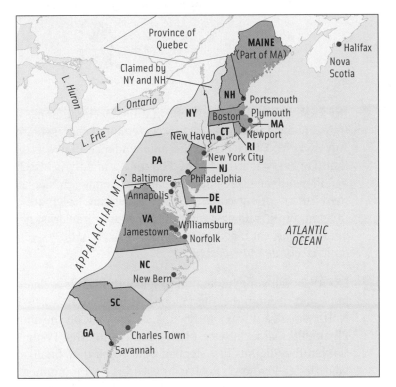

8   **LOCATE** Tell your student that after the colonies decided to
work together to gain their independence from England, Thomas
Jefferson wrote the Declaration of Independence. The Declaration
of Independence united the separate colonies. It stated that all
people are equal and have the right to freedom. Representatives
from all 13 colonies met in Philadelphia, Pennsylvania. On
July 4, 1776, the representatives approved the Declaration of
Independence. John Hancock was the first to sign the document.
Help your student find Philadelphia, Pennsylvania, on the map
of the colonies above. Remind your student that this is where
the representatives of the 13 colonies signed the Declaration of
Independence. Now suggest that your student read a biography
about Jefferson, Hancock, or another person from this time
period that he or she finds interesting.

ENRICH THE EXPERIENCE

Take your student to a
museum or your local
historical society to learn
more about the early his-
tory of the United States.

9   **EXPAND** Tell your student that England did not want the colonies
to be independent, so the colonists had to fight for their freedom.
The colonists' fight for independence from England is called the
American Revolution. The colonists were helped by France and

Exploring the Early History of the United States

Spain. George Washington was the leader of the colonial army. He also became the first president of the United States. The American Revolution was fought from 1775 to 1783. At the end of the long war, the Americans gained their independence from England. Ask, *Which countries helped the colonists win their independence from England?* [France and Spain]

10 **INFORM** Remind your student that the Declaration of Independence was approved by the colonial representatives on July 4, 1776. We celebrate the independence that was expressed that day every fourth of July. The fourth of July is also known as Independence Day and is a national holiday. It's considered the birthday of our country. Many Americans celebrate their freedom on this day by gathering to watch fireworks, go to parades, and eat together at picnics. Ask, *What does your family do to celebrate our freedom?*

11 **EXPAND** Tell your student that Plymouth Rock is a sign of the hope and freedom the Pilgrims had as they began a new life in North America. Plymouth Rock is a large rock on the shore of Plymouth, Massachusetts. Many people think that Plymouth Rock is what the Pilgrims first stepped onto when they finally reached land. Today Plymouth Rock is housed inside a monument where visitors can see it. Ask your student to imagine that he or she is a Pilgrim and write a short paragraph about what he or she thinks it would've felt like to step onto Plymouth Rock for the first time.

Branching Out

TEACHING TIP

Enrich your student's understanding of the lesson by taking him or her to the library. Find books dealing with topics such as the Pilgrims and Thanksgiving, or the events leading up to the Declaration of Independence. Have him or her write about a topic from one of these books.

CHECKING IN

To assess your student's understanding of the lesson, ask your student to tell you why we celebrate Thanksgiving and Independence Day.

FOR FURTHER READING

Christopher Columbus, by Peter Roop (Scholastic, Inc., 2001).

Independence Day (National Holidays), by Helen Frost and Gail Saunders-Smith (Pebble Books, 2000).

Thanksgiving: A Time to Remember, by Barbara Rainey (Crossway Books, 2002).

The Wampanoags (True Books, American Indians), by Alice K. Flanagan and Brendan January, ed. (Children's Press, 1998).

Draw and Write About the First Thanksgiving

Draw a picture of the First Thanksgiving in the picture frame. Write your answers to the questions on the lines in complete sentences.

1. Who was at the First Thanksgiving?

_____

_____

2. Why were they thankful?

_____

_____

3. What did they eat?

_____

_____

What's Next? You Decide!

Now it's your turn to choose what to do next in the lesson. Read the activities and decide which one you want to do—you may want to try them both!

Give Thanks

MATERIALS

- ❏ 1 posterboard
- ❏ 3 sheets different colored construction paper
- ❏ 1 pair scissors
- ❏ markers, crayons, or colored pencils
- ❏ glue

STEPS

Thanksgiving is a time to give thanks. What are you thankful for?

- ❏ Write "Thanks" in the middle of the posterboard.
- ❏ Cut the three sheets of different colored construction paper into 10 to 12 strips.
- ❏ Write a thing, a person, or a place you are thankful for on each of the strips of paper.
- ❏ Glue the strips of paper onto the posterboard.
- ❏ Hang the poster in a place where your family can see it.

Make Your Own Fireworks

MATERIALS

- ❏ fuzzy rubber balls
- ❏ 3–4 sheets white paper
- ❏ paint
- ❏ glitter

STEPS

Make your own fireworks on paper!

- ❏ Take your materials outside. Put the paper on the ground.
- ❏ Dip your fuzzy rubber balls into the paint.
- ❏ Throw the fuzzy rubber balls onto the paper.
- ❏ Add glitter to the paper while the paint is still wet.
- ❏ Let the paint dry. You've made your own fireworks!

Learning About Our Growing Country

Exploration opens the door to new experiences and opportunities for the future.

OBJECTIVE	BACKGROUND	MATERIALS
To teach your student about the growth of the United States	Brave explorers paved the way for U.S. expansion. In this lesson, your student will learn about the contributions of Lewis and Clark and the subsequent pioneers who settled the West.	■ Student Learning Pages 10.A–10.B

VOCABULARY
EXPLORERS people who travel to discover new lands
EXPEDITION a trip that's taken to gather information
PIONEERS people who settle new lands

Let's Begin

1 **INTRODUCE** Tell your student that he or she is going to learn about two important American **explorers,** Meriwether Lewis and William Clark. Explain that an explorer is a person who travels to discover new lands and to learn about them. Thomas Jefferson, the third president of the United States, asked Lewis and Clark to go on an **expedition.** Say that an expedition is a trip that's taken to gather information. Point out that Jefferson bought a large amount of land from France through the Louisiana Purchase. This land extended from the Mississippi River to the Rocky Mountains. Jefferson wanted the explorers to travel to the unknown land and learn about the people, plants, and animals there. Ask your student to explain why Jefferson wanted to learn about the land he had bought.

Thomas Jefferson's Louisiana Purchase doubled the size of the United States.

2 **EXPAND** Inform your student that in May 1804 Lewis and Clark started their trip by boat from the Missouri River in St. Louis, Missouri. Their goal was to find a way across the Louisiana Territory to the Pacific Ocean. Invite your student to trace their route on the map on the next page.

Louisiana Purchase

ENRICH THE EXPERIENCE

Take your student on a historic tour or to a museum to learn about the pioneers that first settled in your area, and how they relate to the pioneers discussed in the lesson.

? DID YOU KNOW?

If you look up the word *pioneer* in a dictionary, you'll learn that it comes from the Latin word for foot. This is because the pioneers did not travel the way many modern people do. They had to walk a lot!

FOR FURTHER READING

The Lewis and Clark Expedition, by Patricia Ryon Quiri (Compass Point Books, 2001).

The Opening of the West, by Rebecca Stefoff (Benchmark Books, 2002).

Sacajawea, by Joyce Milton and Shelly Hehenberger, ill. (Penguin Putnam Books for Young Readers, 2001).

3 **EXPAND** Tell your student that a Native American woman named Sacajawea helped Lewis and Clark find their way. She was a member of the Shoshone tribe. She translated the Native American language for the explorers. She also helped them get horses and travel across the Rocky Mountains. Invite your student to list some qualities that a guide like Sacajawea should have. Help your student find a biography of Sacajawea as he or she shows interest.

4 **EXPLAIN** Lewis and Clark traveled more than 7,000 miles as they explored the Louisiana Territory for the United States. Their expedition encouraged people called **pioneers** to settle new lands in the West. Tell your student that the early pioneers came from different places. They traveled by horseback or covered wagon. They often had to leave behind their belongings to travel west. Invite your student to share his or her ideas about how the life of a pioneer might be both exciting and difficult.

5 **READ** Have your student read a biography about Lewis and Clark and write a short paragraph about how they paved the way for pioneers to settle in the West. Ask, *What difficulties did Lewis and Clark experience?*

6 **APPLY** Distribute Student Learning page 10.A. Have your student use the information he or she learned in the lesson to complete the news story about Lewis and Clark.

Branching Out

TEACHING TIP

For a better understanding of pioneer life, take your student to the library. Help him or her find books that discuss the hardships and rewards pioneers experienced as they settled in the West.

CHECKING IN

To assess your student's understanding of the lesson, encourage him or her to tell you the story of Lewis and Clark in his or her own words.

Complete a News Story

Complete this news story about Lewis and Clark. Use the words from the word box. Draw a picture of the explorers to go with the news story.

| maps | Louisiana | Rocky | Sacajawea |
| animals | Pacific | France | pioneers |

Lewis and Clark Explore New Lands

Explorers Lewis and Clark have come back from the _____ Territory. They found a way across this territory and the _____ Mountains to reach the _____ Ocean. President Thomas Jefferson asked them to explore the land that he bought from _____. A Shoshone woman named _____ helped them on their expedition. Lewis and Clark learned a lot about different plants and _____ on this important trip. They made new _____ of the West. Now _____ will be able to settle these new lands.

What's Next? You Decide!

Now it's your turn to choose what to do next in the lesson. Read the activities and decide which one you want to do—you may want to try them both!

Create a Shoebox Diorama

MATERIALS

- ❑ books about Lewis and Clark
- ❑ 1 shoebox
- ❑ glue
- ❑ construction paper
- ❑ markers, crayons, or colored pencils

STEPS

Plan a scene from Lewis and Clark's expedition.

- ❑ Cover the inside of a shoebox with construction paper.
- ❑ Make figures of Lewis, Clark, and Sacajawea. Glue them in your shoebox so they look three dimensional.
- ❑ Make a scene from the Lewis and Clark trip. Draw pictures on the inside of the shoebox of trees, canoes, or whatever you'd like.

Make Biography Trading Cards

MATERIALS

- ❑ 5–10 large index cards
- ❑ books about pioneers or Lewis and Clark
- ❑ markers, crayons, or colored pencils

STEPS

- ❑ Ask an adult to help you research the lives of famous pioneers, such as Davy Crockett. Or find out more about the lives of important people involved with the Lewis and Clark expedition.
- ❑ Make biography trading cards to show what you have learned.
- ❑ On one side of each index card, draw a picture of one of the people you researched.
- ❑ On the other side, write a few facts about this person's life.
- ❑ Have a friend make trading cards and trade them with each other.

Recognizing America's Diversity

The diversity of people makes our country rich with customs and traditions.

OBJECTIVE	BACKGROUND	MATERIALS
To help your student learn more about the diversity of the United States	It's important for your student to understand the influence of immigration on the identity of the United States. Your student can appreciate this diversity by learning about the customs and holidays unique to different groups while also appreciating the unity of the United States in the ways we celebrate national holidays. In this lesson, your student will learn about immigration, customs, and holidays.	▪ Student Learning Pages 11.A–11.B ▪ 1 world map ▪ 1 calendar

VOCABULARY

IMMIGRANT a person who was born in one country and moves to a different country to live and work

DIVERSITY difference

CUSTOM the usual way that a group of people does something

Let's Begin

1 **INTRODUCE** Explain to your student that an **immigrant** is a person who was born in one country and moves to a different country to live and work. Immigrants who move to the United States often hope they can improve their lives and enjoy many freedoms. Immigrants are important to the past and present of the United States. Ask, *What is an immigrant?* [a person who was born in one country and moves to a different country to live and work] Invite your student to name some countries from which many immigrants in the United States come.

2 **TELL** Explain that the United States is a unique country because of the **diversity** of people who live and work here. Tell your student that diversity means difference. People in the United States come from different cultures, which have their own foods, languages, art, and beliefs. Ask, *What makes the United States a special country?* [diversity]

3 **DISCUSS** Explain to your student that a **custom** is the usual way that a group of people does something. For example, on

ENRICH THE EXPERIENCE

When talking about immigration with your student, tell him or her about his or her family history. When did his or her relatives come to the United States? What country or countries did they come from?

Thanksgiving Day it's a custom for American families to get together and eat a special meal that usually includes turkey, stuffing, and pumpkin pie. Many Mexican Americans celebrate Cinco de Mayo by having parties where they eat food such as tamales and tortillas and play a game with piñatas. Kwanzaa is a special holiday celebrated by many African Americans to remember their history. One special custom for Kwanzaa is lighting seven candles. Each candle stands for something important in African culture. Discuss some of the customs in your family with your student.

4   **EXTEND** Tell your student that Americans celebrate many different holidays throughout the year. Some of our national holidays include Martin Luther King Jr. Day, Memorial Day, Veterans Day, Flag Day, Presidents' Day, Independence Day, Labor Day, Columbus Day, and Thanksgiving. Help your student use a calendar to find the days on which we celebrate these holidays. Then find a biography of a person that we honor with a holiday for your student to read, and have him or her write a paragraph explaining why that person's contribution was important to the country.

5   **WRITE AND DRAW** Discuss with your student some of the holidays that are important to his or her family. Then guide your student through Student Learning Page 11.A. Tell your student to pick a favorite holiday and draw a picture in the box of his or her family celebrating that day.

FOR FURTHER READING

Dreaming of America: An Ellis Island Story, by Eve Bunting (Troll Association, 1999).

My First Kwanzaa Book, by Deborah M. Newton (Cartwheel Books, 1999).

Our National Holidays (Let's See Library, Our Nation), by Patricia J. Murphy (Compass Point Books, 2002).

Branching Out

TEACHING TIP

To strengthen your student's understanding of immigration, take him or her to the library to find books about this topic. Then have a discussion about what he or she learned from the readings. Encourage him or her to write down his or her opinions or feelings about what he or she just read.

CHECKING IN

To assess your student's understanding of the lesson, ask your student to tell what the words *immigrant, holiday,* and *custom* mean. Then have your student give an example of cultural diversity.

Draw and Write About Your Family

Draw a picture in the box showing your family at a holiday or celebration. Finish the sentences about your family.

1. On birthdays, my family likes to

_____

_____

2. On Independence Day, my family likes to

_____

_____

3. On Thanksgiving, my family likes to

_____

_____

What's Next? You Decide!

Now it's your turn to choose what to do next in the lesson. Read the activities and decide which one you want to do—you may want to try them both!

Be a Reporter

MATERIALS

❑ 1 audiocassette recorder

❑ 1 audiocassette tape

STEPS

❑ Ask a grandparent or other adult in your family questions about family customs and holidays.

❑ Write five to ten questions about family customs and holidays on a sheet of paper. What country did they come from? When did they come? Did they speak a different language? You can also ask about how the family came to the United States.

❑ Then record what the person says.

❑ If you don't have a recorder, write the answers down on paper.

❑ Play the recording for your family and friends, or tell them what you learned.

Make a Welcome Sign

MATERIALS

❑ 1 posterboard

❑ markers, crayons, or colored pencils

STEPS

❑ Think about what it's like to be an immigrant moving to the United States. How would you feel?

❑ Suppose there is a new family moving to your neighborhood. They are moving to the United States from a different country.

❑ Create a colorful sign on the posterboard welcoming the family to the United States.

❑ If a new family does move to your neighborhood from a different country, then use the sign!

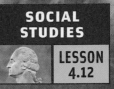

Investigating Landmarks

Around the world, landmarks commemorate special historical events and values.

OBJECTIVE	BACKGROUND	MATERIALS
To help your student identify and learn about state, national, and world landmarks	Landmarks are buildings, monuments, or places that symbolize an important historical event or a cultural value. In this lesson, your student will have the opportunity to learn about landmarks from all over the world. He or she will also learn why the landmarks are significant today.	■ Student Learning Pages 12.A–12.B ■ crayons or markers

VOCABULARY
LANDMARKS special or important places, monuments, or buildings

Let's Begin

1 **SHOW AND DISCUSS** Have your student look at the monument and building in the pictures. Ask, *Do you recognize these places?* [the Statue of Liberty and the White House] Tell your student that the Statue of Liberty and the White House are important **landmarks** in the United States. Tell him or her that a landmark is an important place, monument, or building. Explain that a landmark may symbolize an important event in history or a value that is important, such as freedom. Ask your student to share anything he or she knows about the Statue of Liberty and the White House.

2 **EXPAND** Invite your student to talk about other important national landmarks. For example, you might want to discuss Mount Rushmore. Tell your student that Mount Rushmore is a sculpture of four great U.S. presidents: George Washington, Thomas Jefferson, Theodore Roosevelt, and Abraham Lincoln. This sculpture was created in the Black Hills of South Dakota. Show your student a picture of Mount Rushmore from an encyclopedia or the Internet. Then explain that the U.S. Capitol is another national landmark. Tell your student that the people who meet in the U.S. Capitol make laws for our country. Ask your student to tell you one important fact about a U.S. landmark.

3 **READ** Help your student find and read a biography of a person to whom a sculpture or landmark has been dedicated. Then have him or her write about how he or she feels about this person.

The Statue of Liberty is located in New York Harbor.

In 1800, John Adams became the first president to live in the White House.

Investigating Landmarks **289**

Thousands of people visit South Dakota's Mount Rushmore every year.

The Egyptians built the pyramids for the pharaohs, or ancient kings.

FOR FURTHER READING

Historic Landmarks, by Lynn M. Stone and Jason Cooper (Rourke Book Company, 2001).

Landmarks, by Emma Nathan (Blackbirch Publishing, 2003).

4   **EXPLAIN AND RESEARCH**   Inform your student that some landmarks are important to a city or state. For example, in Chicago, Illinois, Wrigley Field is a baseball stadium that was built in the early 1900s. Therefore, it's older than almost every other baseball stadium in the United States. An important city and state landmark in New York City is the Brooklyn Bridge, which was built over the East River to connect Brooklyn to Manhattan. Ask, *Can you think of any landmarks in your town, city, or state?*

5   **DISCUSS AND COMPLETE**   Discuss why certain buildings, monuments, and places become important landmarks. Tell your student that some landmarks, such as the Lincoln Memorial in Washington, D.C., and Mount Rushmore, honor people who did great things. Other landmarks represent a special event or time in the past. For example, the Alamo in San Antonio, Texas, is a landmark where an important battle was fought to win Texas's independence from Mexico. The Gateway Arch in St. Louis, Missouri, was built to celebrate the settling of western land in the United States. Show your student pictures of these landmarks from an encyclopedia or the Internet. Then instruct your student to review his or her learning by completing Student Learning Page 12.A.

6   **EXPLAIN**   Inform your student that there are landmarks all around the world. Ask, *Can you think of tall structures built by the Egyptians in Africa thousands of years ago? Here's a clue: They have four triangular sides.* [pyramids] Tell your student that although the Egyptians didn't have all the machines we have today, some of the pyramids they made are bigger than many soccer fields and are hundreds of feet high! Ask, *Can you think of a landmark that will still be standing in thousands of years?* Together with your student, research a landmark from around the world and have him or her write a paragraph explaining what it is and why it is important.

7   **CONNECT**   Together with your student locate local landmarks. Take a field trip to the landmark, and help your student find out information about it. Then have him or her write a paragraph about what he or she has learned.

Branching Out

TEACHING TIP

Go on an Internet field trip with your student to find out more about other famous landmarks. Some international landmarks to learn about include the Eiffel Tower, the Colosseum, and the Acropolis.

CHECKING IN

To assess your student's understanding of the lesson, ask him or her to tell what a landmark is in his or her own words. Then ask your student to name two landmarks.

Locate Landmarks

Look at the map. Answer the questions about landmarks.
Then color the map.

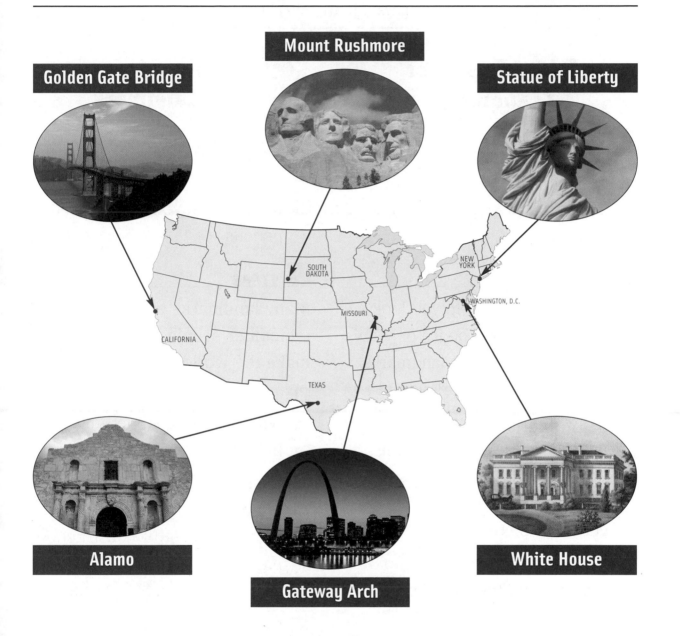

Golden Gate Bridge

Mount Rushmore

Statue of Liberty

Alamo

Gateway Arch

White House

1. What landmark can be found in Texas? _____

2. In what state can you find Mount Rushmore? _____

3. The Gateway Arch can be found on the border of _____

   and _____.

4. What landmark could you visit in New York? _____

What's Next? You Decide!

Now it's your turn to choose what to do next in the lesson. Read the activities and decide which one you want to do—you may want to try them both!

Make a Poster of a Landmark

MATERIALS

❑ 1 posterboard

❑ markers, crayons, or colored pencils

STEPS

❑ Ask an adult to help you look through resource books or Web sites about different landmarks. Then pick a landmark you like.

❑ Draw a picture of the landmark you picked on the posterboard. Use markers, crayons, or colored pencils to color the picture.

❑ Write the name of the landmark at the top of the posterboard.

❑ Write some facts about the landmark on the posterboard.

❑ Show your poster to family and friends. Tell them why the landmark is special.

Design Your Own Landmark

MATERIALS

❑ 1 sheet construction paper

❑ markers, crayons, or colored pencils

STEPS

Many landmarks were built to remember people who helped make the world a better place.

❑ Think of someone you know who has done something to help other people.

❑ Design a landmark to remember this person. Draw it on the sheet of construction paper.

❑ Write a paragraph. Tell what the landmark says about this special person you know.

Connecting Our World

Communication and transportation join people from around the world.

OBJECTIVE	BACKGROUND	MATERIALS
To help your student understand how means of communicating and traveling have changed over time	Today there are many ways to communicate and travel, so people can choose the methods that suit their needs and abilities. We can communicate and travel more efficiently than people in the past because of technological inventions. In this lesson, your student will learn about forms of communication and transportation and how they have changed over time.	■ Student Learning Pages 13.A–13.B

VOCABULARY
COMMUNICATE to express ideas and thoughts to others

Let's Begin

1 **BRAINSTORM AND LIST** Explain to your student that today there are many ways to **communicate** with others. Tell your student that to communicate means to express ideas and thoughts to others. Long ago, people wrote messages and drew symbols on walls to communicate. Today, people often use machines to communicate. For example, most people regularly communicate by using a telephone. Ask your student to brainstorm some other ways people may have communicated a long time ago and how they communicate today. Then have him or her write a paragraph explaining how communication has changed over time.

2 **EXPAND** Explain to your student that some people who are physically challenged communicate in special ways. For example, many people who can't hear use sign language to communicate. In sign language, people use hand movements to communicate words, phrases, and sentences. Tell your student that many people who are blind use Braille to read. Braille is a way of writing in which letters are shown with patterns of raised dots. Blind people read these dots by touching them. Have your student tell you what senses people who can't see or hear can use to communicate. [the hearing impaired can use their sense of sight and the visually impaired can use their sense of touch]

ENRICH THE EXPERIENCE

Show your student that people can communicate by using body movements and gestures. Play a game of charades with your student. Show him or her how to communicate an idea to another person without even saying one word!

The invention of the automobile changed transportation in America.

Cars today offer little resemblance to those of yesteryear.

3 **BRAINSTORM** Explain that years ago many people had to walk or ride a horse to get from one place to another. The railroad wasn't invented in this country until the 1800s. Ask, *What are some ways that people can travel today?* [airplanes, helicopters, subways, cars, buses, motorcycles, boats, bicycles]

4 **REVEAL** Inform your student that the first car was invented in 1893 by Henry Ford. He called the car a "horseless carriage" because it ran using gasoline, not a horse. Ford started the Ford Motor Company, which still sells cars today. Look at the photos. Invite your student to share how cars have changed. Ask if he or she thinks the cars of today are safer, faster, more comfortable, and so on.

5 **EXPAND AND COMPLETE** Tell your student that the first airplane was invented in 1903 by two brothers, Orville Wright and Wilbur Wright. Soon after, a few brave pilots ventured to set world records for flying certain distances or to certain places. For example, Amelia Earhart was the first woman to fly over the Atlantic Ocean by herself, and she made many successful trips. However, in 1937 her plane disappeared as she flew on a route that would have taken her around the world. Ask, *How do you think traveling in an airplane has changed?* If your student has ever traveled in an airplane, invite him or her to describe the experience. Then direct your student to Student Learning Page 12.A. Review the directions and allow time for your student to complete the page.

6 **READ** Encourage your student to find biographies of the people he or she has learned about in this lesson. After he or she is done reading one, have him or her write a few paragraphs about what he or she has learned, and how it would feel to be the person your student has just read about.

FOR FURTHER READING

The Big Book of Airplanes, by Caroline Bingham (DK Publishing, 2001).

The Courage of Helen Keller, by Francene Sabin (Troll Associates, 1998).

Richard Scarry's Cars and Trucks and Things That Go, by Richard Scarry (Golden Books Publishing Company, 1998).

Branching Out

TEACHING TIP

Be sure your student understands that means of communication and travel are still changing and advancing. Ask your student to explain how he or she thinks transportation and communication may be different in 100 years.

CHECKING IN

To assess your student's understanding of the lesson, ask him or her to name a means of communication and travel from the past or present. Then ask your student to briefly tell how communication and travel have changed.

Draw How You Communicate and Travel

Draw a picture of yourself doing each of the activities. On the line below each drawing, label the activity "communication" or "transportation."

1. Riding your bike

_____

3. Writing a letter to a relative

_____

2. Riding in your parent's car

_____

4. Whispering to a friend

_____

Student Learning Page 13.A: Draw How You Communicate and Travel   **295**

What's Next? You Decide!

Now it's your turn to choose what to do next in the lesson. Read the activities and decide which one you want to do—you may want to try them both!

Draw Faces

MATERIALS

- ❏ several paper plates
- ❏ markers, crayons, or colored pencils
- ❏ craft sticks

STEPS

People communicate through facial expressions as well as words. A smile shows that you're happy. Tears show that you're sad.

- ❏ On each paper plate, draw a face that shows a different feeling. You can show a face that's happy, sad, scared, angry, excited, or any other feeling you can think of.

- ❏ Tape a craft stick (or branch) to the back of each plate.

- ❏ Have fun with your new mood masks.

Make a Traveling Machine

MATERIALS

- ❏ markers, crayons, or colored pencils

STEPS

How will people travel in the future? Will cars fly above the land? How fast will planes fly? Make up a new traveling machine for the future!

- ❏ Draw a picture or build a model of your traveling machine.

- ❏ Give your traveling machine a name.

- ❏ Write a paragraph that tells about the special things your traveling machine does.

- ❏ Show your traveling machine to family and friends.

Researching a Social Studies Topic

Knowing how to research is a valuable skill that will serve a person for a lifetime.

OBJECTIVE	BACKGROUND	MATERIALS
To give your student the tools needed to research a social studies topic	Researching a topic can help your student learn important facts and provide a springboard for more learning. In this lesson, your student will learn how to research, develop ideas, and evaluate information from different sources.	■ Student Learning Pages 14.A–14.B ■ several index cards

VOCABULARY

RESEARCH to collect information about a chosen topic
REFERENCE SOURCES books and other media that provide information

Let's Begin

1 **BRAINSTORM** Explain that a way to learn more about social studies or any other subject is to **research.** Tell your student that to research is to collect information about a topic and that a research report tells what a person learned about a topic. Research reports should be written in the researcher's own words. Have your student brainstorm a list of five topics he or she would like to learn more about. Guide him or her in thinking of common topics that are easy to research. Ask your student to choose the topic he or she is most curious about.

2 **DEVELOP THE IDEA** Tell your student that a research topic should be focused. For example, if your student wants to research U.S. presidents, suggest that he or she focus on one president. Explain that many people also focus their research by writing a topic sentence. By writing "Thomas Jefferson was a good inventor," he or she will look for information about Jefferson's inventions. Help your student write a topic sentence for the area he or she chose in Step 1.

3 **CONNECT** Tell your student that many people use **reference sources** to research. Point out examples of reference sources, such as encyclopedias, nonfiction books, atlases, dictionaries, almanacs, and videos. Have your student name reference

---

+

ENRICH THE EXPERIENCE

Select materials that are at a reading level with which your student is comfortable. Help your student select books with colorful pictures and visuals that convey meaning in a child-friendly way.

sources he or she has used. Explain further that many people use the Internet for research. Educational Web sites are often helpful for finding out information. Tell your student that a person can even visit a place or talk to someone who knows a lot about a topic to do research. Then use reference sources at home, at your local library, or on the Internet to help your student research information about his or her topic. If you wish, you may also visit relevant and accessible places or talk to experts you know to help your student research.

4 **EVALUATE** Tell your student that after a researcher looks through reference sources, he or she should decide if the information is useful. Help your student determine if the information he or she found tells more about the topic sentence. Tell him or her that useful information also answers questions a researcher has about a topic. Make sure your student understands that it's best to check facts in two or more places. Explain further that it's also better to use newer reference sources. Help your student use index cards to take brief and simple notes of the information he or she found. Tell your student to write notes in his or her own words. Have him or her also write the title and author of all the sources he or she used and the page numbers on which the information was found.

5 **WRITE** Have your student use the notes on his or her index cards to write a first draft. Tell him or her to write a title for the report. Encourage your student to begin the report in a way that would get a reader's attention. For example, he or she can begin with a question, a joke, or an unexpected statement. Then tell your student to organize his or her report in a way that makes sense. Guide your student as necessary.

6 **EDIT AND PROOFREAD** Tell your student that after writing a report, it's important to read it to make sure there are no mistakes and the sentences make sense. Show him or her how to look for errors. Then help your student make changes to his or her report. Invite your student to read the final research report out loud. Then distribute Student Learning Page 14.A.

FOR FURTHER READING

Get Ready! For Social Studies: Essays, Book Reports, and Research Papers, by Nancy White and Francine Weinberg (McGraw-Hill 2002).

The New York Public Library Kid's Guide to Research, by Deborah Heiligman (Scholastic Trade, 1998).

Branching Out

TEACHING TIP

Tell your student that many research reports include pictures. Invite your student to draw a picture and write a caption to go with his or her research report.

CHECKING IN

To assess your student's understanding of the lesson, ask him or her to name three important steps in researching a topic.

Run the Research Report Race

Write the steps for a research report to get to the finish line! Be sure to put the steps in the correct order. Put a check in the box when you have used the step.

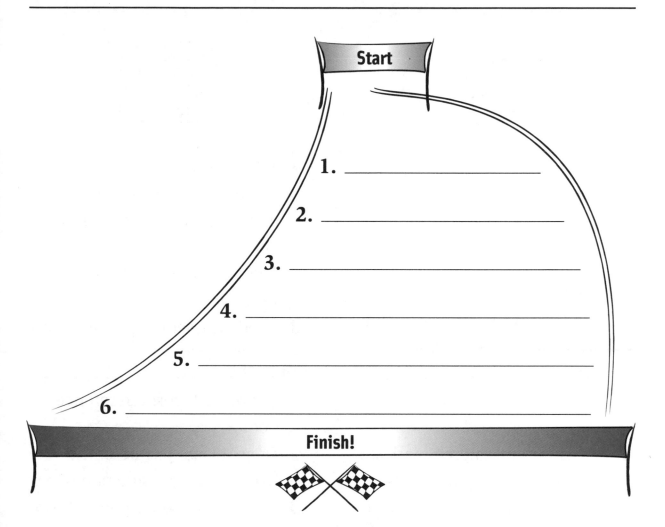

Start

1. _____

2. _____

3. _____

4. _____

5. _____

6. _____

Finish!

Steps

☐ Correct mistakes in your first draft.

☐ Share your final report with others.

☐ Choose a topic.

☐ Take notes on your topic.

☐ Look for information.

☐ Write a first draft.

What's Next? You Decide!

Now it's your turn to choose what to do next in the lesson. Read the activities and decide which one you want to do—you may want to try them both!

Make Your Own Web Page

MATERIALS

- ❏ 1 sheet construction paper
- ❏ markers, crayons, or colored pencils

STEPS

Make a Web page about a person you know a lot about—you!

- ❏ Draw pictures on your Web site that tell something about you.
- ❏ Use different colored markers, crayons, or colored pencils to write links on your Web page. The links show where people can go on the Web site to learn more information.
- ❏ The links can be about your hobbies, pets, family, friends—anything about you!
- ❏ Write a title for your Web page.
- ❏ Share your Web page with your friends and family members.

Write a Commercial

MATERIALS

- ❏ 1 sheet construction paper
- ❏ markers, crayons, or colored pencils
- ❏ 1 videocassette camera (optional)
- ❏ 1 videocassette tape (optional)

STEPS

- ❏ Choose a favorite reference book.
- ❏ Draw a large picture of the book on the construction paper.
- ❏ Write down what you will say in your commercial.
- ❏ Give reasons why you like the book and tell what the book is about.
- ❏ Act out the commercial for your family. Use your picture of the book.
- ❏ If possible ask an adult to videotape your commercial.

In Your Community

To reinforce the skills and concepts taught in this section,
try one or more of these activities!

Map Skills in Everyday Life

Tell your student that people often use maps to obtain directions to places and things they are not familiar with. Find a map of your town and locate your home and a few locations or landmarks that your student is familiar with. Then have him or her use the map to write clear directions to each place from your home. Make sure your student includes all the necessary information, such as directions, street names, and distances. When the directions are complete, take your student on a trip to each of the locations by following the directions he or she wrote to test their accuracy.

Visit Contrasting Communities

Your student has learned to compare urban, rural, and suburban communities. Now give your student an opportunity to see firsthand the similarities and differences between communities. If you live in a rural community, take a trip with your student to an urban community. If you live in an urban community, take your student to a rural community. As you explore, discuss with your student the similarities and differences of the community you're viewing to your own.

Research Customs and Celebrations

The United States is a diverse country. Illustrate this to your student by exploring the different customs and celebrations of people. Have your student think and write about the customs and celebrations of your family. Then research some of the varying ethnic backgrounds of people in your community with your student. Discover what celebrations and customs they may have. Check your community calendar for upcoming events that celebrate a heritage other than your own. For example, there are often festivals that showcase specific ethnic foods, music, and dance. Then discuss with your student the similarities and differences of other cultures to your own.

Caring for Our Resources

Your student has learned that we must conserve and replenish our resources. Discuss with your student the many ways you can reuse or recycle things. Find items around the house that can be recycled or reused and collect and distribute them appropriately. For example, you can take aluminum cans and plastic bottles to a recycling center or unwanted clothes and household items to a secondhand store for reuse. If possible arrange a tour of a local recycling facility so your student can view the steps of recycling beyond collection. In addition, there are many stores that feature goods made from recycled materials. Take your student to view these concrete examples of recycling's end result.

Explore Symbols, Mottoes, and Songs in Your Community

Your student has learned some of the symbols, mottoes, and songs connected to the United States. Now explore the symbols, mottoes, and songs native to your community. Visit your local library and research with your student to find out what symbolic artifacts or rhetoric are attributed to your community. You can expand this activity to include symbolism from the various cultures that your community consists of. For example, if your community has a strong Irish background, you could explore some of the Irish symbolism that has made its way into your community.

We Have Learned

Use this checklist to summarize what you and your student
have accomplished in the Social Studies section.

❑ **Social Studies Skills**
❑ reading time lines, tables, graphs, and diagrams
❑ reading and identifying features of a map and globe

❑ **Where We Live**
❑ understanding and comparing neighborhoods and communities
❑ urban, suburban, and rural communities

❑ **Communities in the World**
❑ communities, states, and countries in the world
❑ Earth, continents

❑ **Our Earth**
❑ Earth's resources: meeting needs through the environment and its resources
❑ conservation, replenishment

❑ **Working Together**
❑ choosing goods and services
❑ services in our community and government
❑ producing and consuming, development of products
❑ trading versus bartering, why countries are linked through trade

❑ **Our Country Today**
❑ local government: mayor, citizens, functions
❑ state government: governor, capitals
❑ federal government: president, Congress
❑ voting, symbols, mottoes, songs for freedom

❑ **History of Our Country**
❑ Native American groups, their contributions, and their regions
❑ colonies, explorers, Thanksgiving
❑ Independence Day, the Declaration of Independence
❑ our growing country: pioneers and Lewis and Clark

❑ **People and Places in History**
❑ customs and holidays, the diversity of the United States
❑ state, country, landmarks, symbols
❑ communication, transportation

❑ **Social Studies Research**
❑ conducting research and developing an idea
❑ assessing and evaluating information from a variety of sources

We have also learned:

_____

_____

Read each question and the answer choices that follow. Circle the letter of the correct answer.

1. Which type of writing often has rhyming words?

   A science fiction

   B nonfiction

   C fiction

   D poetry

2. Which word is a noun?

   A bear

   B red

   C the

   D happy

3. Which word is a compound word?

   A football

   B sleeping

   C distaste

   D rolling

4. Which sentence is correct?

   A She are going to the fair.

   B She is going to the fair.

   C She am going to the fair.

   D She as going to the fair.

5. Which sentence is correct?

   A They have a new car.

   B They has a new car.

   C They have a new cars.

   D They have as new car.

6. Which sentence is correct?

   A I saw the game next Friday.

   B I saw the game tomorrow.

   C I saw the game next week.

   D I saw the game today.

7. Which sentence is correct?

   A She said she would come.

   B They says they will come.

   C She say she will come.

   D They says they will come.

8. Which sentence is correct?

   A Please have a apple.

   B Please have an apple.

   C Please have a apples.

   D Please have an apples.

9. Which sentence is correct?

   A They will have an new house.

   B They will have and new house.

   C They will have a new house.

   D They will had a new house.

10. Which word is a synonym of **silly**?

   A slow

   B goofy

   C angry

   D serious

11. Which word is an antonym of **full**?

   A over

   B filled

   C empty

   D loaded

12. Which word is a homophone of **hear**?

   A clear

   B deaf

   C see

   D here

13. Which word is a conjunction?

   A the

   B his

   C and

   D it

14. Which word best completes the sentence?

| We went to the park _____ the zoo. |

A and

B or

C but

D always

15. Which type of writing tells the story of a person's life?

A folktale

B science fiction

C fiction

D biography

16. Which word best completes the sentence?

| We will go to the store _____ not the park. |

A and

B or

C but

D nor

Read each sentence in the box. Choose the correct meaning of the underlined word. Circle the letter of the correct answer.

17.

| He ran to the store very quickly. |

A very fast

B very slow

C very tired

D very happy

18.

| The dog had a pretty coat of hair. |

A beautiful

B ugly

C shiny

D short

Read each sentence in the box. Choose the opposite meaning of the underlined word. Circle the letter of the correct answer.

Read each selection. Read the questions and the answer choices that go with each selection. Circle the letter of the correct answer.

19.

The building was <u>tall</u>.

A high

B slow

C short

D flat

20.

The sink was <u>clean</u>.

A shiny

B ugly

C smooth

D dirty

Use for 21–24.

When very young bear cubs first start to explore the world outside the den, they are still completely dependent on their mother for food and protection. They follow her about wherever she goes. By watching their mother, the cubs learn how to find food. At first they catch ants and caterpillars, but soon they learn to catch mice and voles and other small animals to vary their mostly vegetarian diet.

21. Which type of writing is this?

A fiction

B poetry

C nonfiction

D science fiction

22. From this passage you can conclude that—

  A bear cubs can live alone.

  B bear cubs learn from their mother.

  C bear cubs help each other.

  D bear cubs eat meat.

23. Which is NOT a meaning of the underlined word in the sentence below?

  > By watching their mother, the cubs learn how to find food.

  A studying

  B observing

  C seeing

  D sitting

24. A good title for this passage would be—

  A "Learning from Mother Bear."

  B "Dangerous Bear Cubs."

  C "Animals in the Forest."

  D "What Bear Cubs Eat."

Use for 25–29.

The Lion and the Fly

Once there was a lion who traveled through the jungle yelling so that everyone would know he was the king. The animals could never sleep because of this yelling, but they were afraid to ask him to stop. One day a fly said to the lion, "Why do you yell all the time and wake up the other animals?" The lion became angry and said, "I am the king, and I can do whatever I want." The fly decided to teach the lion a lesson and flew up the lion's nose. The lion tried to get the fly out of his nose, but no matter what he did he could not get rid of the fly. The fly asked the king, "Do you now believe that you are not really a king and cannot do everything you want?" The lion said, "Yes, yes, I believe I am not the king." Then the fly flew out of his nose and left the lion alone.

25. This passage is an example of—

A fiction.

B poetry.

C nonfiction.

D a fable.

26. From this passage you can conclude that—

A the lion did not make as much noise anymore.

B the lion kept waking up the other animals.

C the fly went back into the lion's nose.

D the lion and the fly became friends.

27. Who learned an important lesson in this story?

A the lion

B the other animals

C the fly

D the king

28. What is the setting of the story?

A the zoo

B the lion's den

C the jungle

D the fly's nest

29. What is the theme of the story?

A You should only worry about yourself.

B It's good to think about other people.

C Don't anger a lion.

D Lions are afraid of flies.

Read each selection. Decide what type of writing it is. Write "poetry," "science fiction," "nonfiction," or "fiction."

30. Before the tea party, Ella the Ant invited all her friends. She wore her favorite party dress and shoes. She wondered if the cupcakes and leaves would be ready in time. She had a lot of work to do before her guests arrived.

_____

31. The spaceship landed. The captain couldn't believe he had just left Earth two days ago. He wanted to explore the planet to see if there was any life.

_____

32. It's important to have proper table manners. You need to know how to use a fork, spoon, and knife the correct way. Always remember to put a napkin on your lap.

_____

Use the words in the box to complete the sentences for 33–37.

in	from	by
on		to

33. Debbie shopped _____ the store.

34. Jake was _____ the roof.

35. Elena put her towel _____ the pool.

36. Jorge sent a letter _____ his friend.

37. Shakira got a card _____ the store.

Use the words in the box to complete the sentences for 38–40.

with	at	of

38. Samantha left her scarf

_____ the party.

39. Jonathan did his work

_____ Robin.

40. That's the end _____

the story.

Write the base word of each word.

41. helpful _____

42. softly _____

43. unhappy _____

44. unhook _____

Add *–ly* to each base word.

45. kind _____

46. careful _____

Add *–able* to each base word.

47. wash _____

48. drink _____

Add *–ful* to each base word.

49. fruit _____

50. mind _____

Add *un–* to each base word.

51. wind _____

52. lock _____

Add *re–* to each base word.

53. gain _____

54. play _____

Add *–ness* to each base word.

55. strange _____

56. bright _____

Circle the correct homophone in each sentence.

57. Tim didn't **know / no** how to paint.

58. Mary **red / read** the book.

59. He asked **to / too / two** go home early.

60. Did you **buy / by** a hat?

61. The **for / four** birds flew away.

62. We have **to / too / two** dogs.

63. The shirt is **red / read.**

64. **No / know,** I already have one.

65. The water is **to / too / two** cold.

66. She is over **their / there.**

67. My pen is **buy / by** my desk.

68. **Their / there** car is green.

69. Can you **write / right** your name?

70. It is **for / four** my sister.

Read each question. Write the answers in complete sentences.

71. Today is your birthday. Write a journal entry describing the day.

_____

_____

_____

_____

_____

_____

_____

_____

_____

_____

72. Write a poem about your favorite season. Make sure you include rhyming words at the ends of some lines.

_____

_____

_____

_____

_____

_____

_____

_____

_____

_____

_____

_____

73. Write a paragraph describing someone you know or have learned about who is a hero. Write a topic sentence and supporting details.

_____

_____

_____

_____

_____

_____

_____

_____

_____

_____

_____

_____

_____

_____

_____

_____

_____

74. Write a paragraph describing your favorite book. Make sure you include the main characters and the plot.

_____

_____

_____

_____

_____

_____

_____

_____

_____

_____

_____

_____

_____

_____

_____

_____

Read each question and the answer choices that follow. Circle the letter of the correct answer.

1. Which number comes next?

98, 99, _____

A 97

B 100

C 101

D 102

2. How much money is here?

A $2.18

B $1.18

C $1.08

D $1.05

3. 2 tens + 3 ones =

A 1

B 5

C 23

D 231

4. Which number is even?

A 23

B 10

C 5

D 1

5. Which number is odd?

A 9

B 18

C 20

D 88

6. How long is the paper clip?

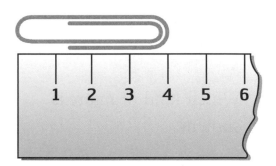

A 6 cm

B 4 cm

C 3 cm

D 2.5 cm

7. Pablo had $1.00. He found 2 quarters and 3 dimes. How much money does Pablo have now?

   A $1.23

   B $1.53

   C $1.75

   D $1.80

8. Which number comes next?

   15, 11, _____

   A 7

   B 9

   C 13

   D 17

9. Which kind of figure is shown?

   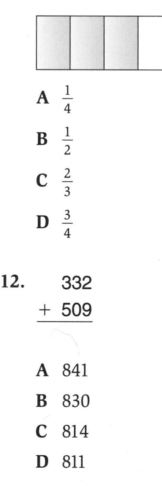

   A octagon

   B pentagon

   C hexagon

   D triangle

10.　　56
    + 53
    ─────

    A 119

    B 109

    C 103

    D 3

11. How much is shaded?

    A $\frac{1}{4}$

    B $\frac{1}{2}$

    C $\frac{2}{3}$

    D $\frac{3}{4}$

12.　　332
    + 509
    ─────

    A 841

    B 830

    C 814

    D 811

13. Which is the name of the figure?

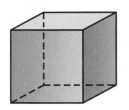

   A triangle

   B cube

   C circle

   D pyramid

14. $56 - 48 =$

   A 104

   B 12

   C 8

   D 6

15. Which unit would you use to measure the weight of a desk?

   A pounds

   B ounces

   C feet

   D meters

16. 1 pint = 2 cups.

   2 pints = _____ cups

   A 2

   B 4

   C 8

   D 12

17.
$$\begin{array}{r} 227 \\ -\ 111 \\ \hline \end{array}$$

   A 338

   B 118

   C 116

   D 112

18. Which fraction of men have hats?

   A $\frac{2}{6}$

   B $\frac{2}{3}$

   C $\frac{4}{6}$

   D $\frac{6}{6}$

19. Erin began to read at 8:15. She read for 30 minutes. At what time did she stop?

A 8:30

B 8:45

C 9:00

D 9:15

20. If $\frac{1}{2}$ of the apples are eaten, how many will be left?

A 16

B 4

C 2

D 0

21. $8 \times 2 =$

A 6

B 10

C 16

D 19

22. What time is it?

A 7:12

B 7:10

C 3:35

D 2:35

23. $3 \times 4 =$

A 1

B 7

C 8

D 12

24. Jen bought a cupcake for $1.25. She paid $2.00. How much change did she get?

A $3.25

B $1.00

C $0.75

D $0.50

Read each question.
Write the answers.

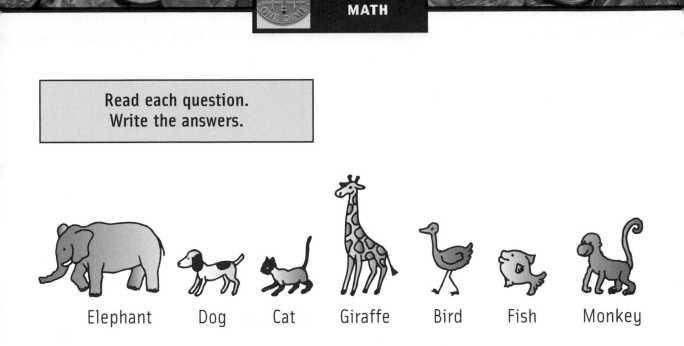

Elephant   Dog   Cat   Giraffe   Bird   Fish   Monkey

25. Which animal is fourth?

_____

26. Which animal is seventh?

_____

27. Which animal is second?

_____

28. If the bird goes to the front
of the line, which animal
becomes fifth?

_____

Write the missing number.

29. 400, _____, 398

30. 117, _____, 113

31. 858, _____, 838

32. Circle the set with the most money.

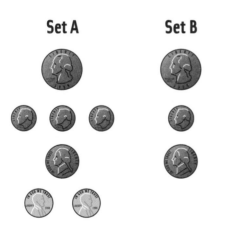

Set A   Set B

Circle the larger number.

33. 156   165

34. 892   891

35. 597   575

Circle the number sentence that is true.

36. 5 + 0 = 50   5 + 0 = 5

37. 0 + 23 = 23   23 + 0 = 203

Use for 38–40.

September						
S	M	T	W	T	F	S
		1	2	3	4	5
6	7	8	9	10	11	12
13	14	15	16	17	18	19
20	21	22	23	24	25	26
27	28	29	30			

38. How many days are in September? _____

39. How many Tuesdays are in September? _____

40. What day of the week is September 13? _____

41. Draw a line of symmetry for the figure.

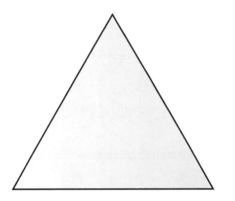

> **What is the place value of each underlined number? Write "hundreds," "tens," or "ones."**

42. 724 _____

43. 248 _____

44. 927 _____

45. Shade $\frac{1}{3}$ of the circle.

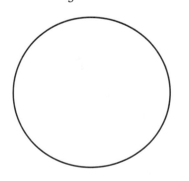

46. Write a division sentence for the picture. Then solve.

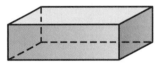

_____

Use for 47–48.

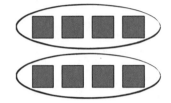

47. How many corners are there?

_____

48. How many sides are there?

_____

> **Which unit would you use to measure each object? Write "grams" or "kilograms."**

49. Horse _____

50. Apple _____

51. Computer _____

Joe collected data on cars he saw. He recorded the data in a tally chart. Use it to answer the questions.

Car Colors

Color	Tally
Red	𝍤 |||
White	|||
Black	𝍤 𝍤 ||

52. How many red cars did Joe see? _____

53. Which color car did Joe see the most of? _____

54. How many white cars did Joe see? _____

55. How many cars in total did Joe see? _____

56. There are six different ways to make $0.17 using dimes, nickels, and pennies. One way is shown. Write the other five ways.

1 dime, 1 nickel, 2 pennies

_____

_____

_____

_____

_____

_____

_____

_____

_____

_____

_____

1. Which of the following is the first stage in the life cycle of a frog?

   A egg

   B pupa

   C larva

   D tadpole

2. Which of the following does the rose use to protect itself?

   A petals

   B stem

   C thorns

   D color

3. A hole in a tooth is called a—

   A gum.

   B cavity.

   C floss.

   D filling.

4. Which plant parts make new plants?

   A flowers, seeds, and fruit

   B seeds, leaves, and flowers

   C beans, leaves, and seeds

   D sunlight, seeds, and flowers

5. Which plant parts make food?

   A pollen

   B spores

   C fruit

   D leaves

6. Which of the following is made by plants that grow flowers?

   A pollen

   B mosses

   C spores

   D ferns

7. Which of the following do animals NOT need to survive?

A sunlight

B air

C shade

D water

8. Fish breathe through their—

A fins.

B noses.

C gills.

D mouths.

9. High and low sounds are called—

A volume.

B waves.

C pitch.

D booms.

10. Which animals do NOT live in groups?

A fish

B snakes

C wolves

D bees

11. Shown is—

A a rock.

B a mineral.

C a fossil.

D sand.

12. Which of the following does NOT help make rocks smaller?

A wind

B water

C plants

D waves

13. Soil gets washed away by—

A silt.

B sand.

C erosion.

D weathering.

14. Which of the following is NOT something that makes up soil?

    A fertilizer

    B minerals

    C rocks

    D plants

15. Which of the following moves an object?

    A force

    B speed

    C position

    D energy

16. Fossil fuels are used for—

    A watering plants.

    B heating homes.

    C studying animals.

    D building cars.

17. Shown is the foot of—

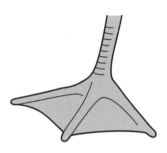

    A a cat.

    B a duck.

    C an eagle.

    D a rabbit.

18. Which of the following is NOT a natural resource?

    A tree

    B factory

    C water

    D wind

19. Most of Earth's surface is covered with—

    A land.

    B mountains.

    C water.

    D air.

20. Humans can help take care of Earth by—

   A using natural resources.

   B using fossil fuels.

   C recycling resources.

   D burning coal.

21. How fast an object moves is its—

   A motion.

   B speed.

   C force.

   D direction.

22. Earth revolves around—

   A the sun.

   B the moon.

   C other planets.

   D the stars.

23. Which of the following makes an object fall to the ground?

   A gravity

   B motion

   C speed

   D direction

24. How do messages go from the sense organs to the brain?

   A blood

   B nerves

   C veins

   D arteries

25. Your body loses water when you—

   A sleep.

   B sweat.

   C eat.

   D speak.

26. Teeth are needed to eat and—

   A sleep.

   B breathe.

   C hear.

   D speak.

27. Your back teeth are used for—

   A grinding.

   B biting.

   C pulling.

   D tearing.

28. Which of the following senses is the boy using?

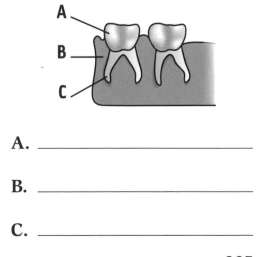

A sight

B sound

C touch

D taste

29. Day and night are caused by Earth rotating around—

A the sun.

B its axis.

C the moon.

D other planets.

30. How long does it take the moon to revolve around Earth?

A a day

B a week

C 29 days

D a year

31. Which of the following is NOT a fuel used to make heat?

A wood

B friction

C natural gas

D oil

32. Joe is writing a research report about zebras. Which step would he do last?

A publish

B find information

C choose a topic

D proofread

Read each question.
Write the answers.

---

33. Label the diagram. Write "gum," "root," and "crown."

A. _____

B. _____

C. _____

34. Name two ways this parent takes care of its young.

_____

_____

_____

_____

_____

_____

_____

_____

_____

_____

_____

35. Name two variations used to identify the girls.

_____

_____

_____

_____

_____

_____

_____

_____

_____

_____

_____

_____

_____

36. Label each moon phase. Write "full moon," "half moon," and "quarter moon."

37. Write 1, 2, or 3 under each picture to show the correct order.

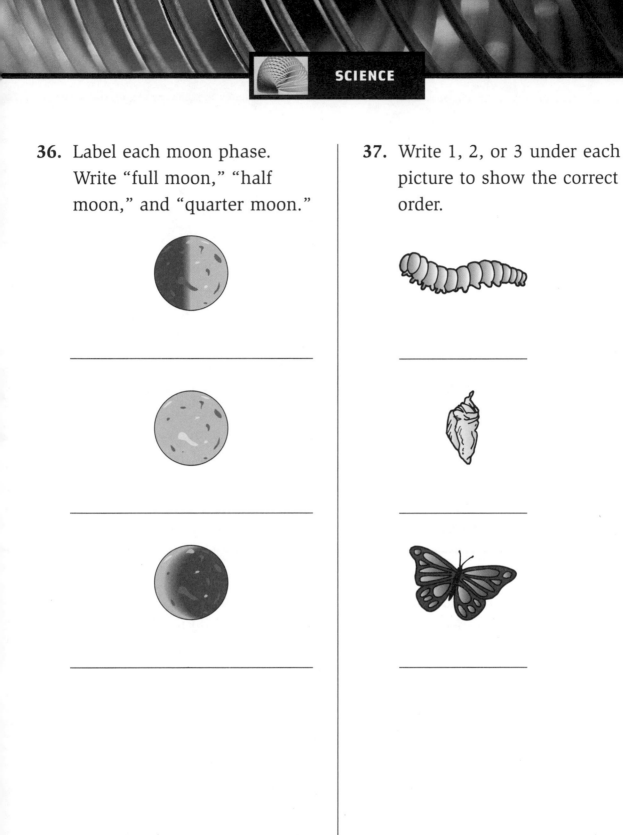

_____   _____

_____   _____

_____   _____

Use for 38–40.

Food Guide Pyramid

Fats, oils, and sweets: Use sparingly

Milk, yogurt, and cheese group: 2–3 servings

Meat, poultry, fish, dry beans, eggs, and nuts group: 2–3 servings

Vegetable group: 3–5 servings

Fruit group: 2–4 servings

Bread, cereal, rice, and pasta group: 6–11 servings

38. Which type of food should you eat the most of each day?

_____

39. Which type of food should you eat the least of each day?

_____

40. About how many servings of fruit should you eat each day?

_____

Use the words in the box to complete the sentences for 41–42.

volume	noise

41. Unpleasant sounds are called

_____.

42. The loudness or softness of a sound is called _____.

Answer each question.

43. Name the five senses.

_____

_____

_____

_____

_____

44. Name two ways that your

body uses water. _____

_____

_____

_____

_____

_____

_____

45. Name two types of fossil

fuels. _____

_____

46. Name two ways that plants

help animals. _____

_____

_____

_____

_____

_____

Use the words in the box to complete the sentences for 47–50.

light	absorb
reflect	shadow

47. If light hits a material that

it can't pass through, a

_____ can form.

48. _____ helps us see.

49. Dark-colored surfaces

_____ light.

50. Light-colored surfaces

_____ light.

Answer each question.

51. Draw three objects that are made from natural resources.

52. Describe different ways that plants and animals protect themselves.

_____

_____

_____

_____

_____

_____

_____

_____

_____

_____

_____

_____

_____

> **Read each question and the answer choices that follow. Circle the letter of the correct answer.**

1. A community is made up of several—

   A neighborhoods.

   B states.

   C people.

   D nations.

2. Which type of community is crowded and includes people who get around by subway, buses, and taxis?

   A rural

   B urban

   C international

   D suburban

3. The care and protection of land, water, plants, and animals is called—

   A a natural resource.

   B a landform.

   C conservation.

   D recycling.

4. Something found in nature that people use is called a—

   A producer.

   B natural consumer.

   C service.

   D natural resource.

5. Corn, wheat, and cotton are examples of—

   A vegetables.

   B crops.

   C minerals.

   D organisms.

6. Someone who is the leader of a town is called the—

   A governor.

   B president.

   C senator.

   D mayor.

7. Money people earn is called—

   A goods.

   B income.

   C bank.

   D trade.

8. Why do most people work?

   A They need something
      to do.

   B They want to invent new
      things.

   C They need to earn money.

   D They need to exercise.

9. Which group of Native
Americans lived along the
Atlantic coast and had
homes built by women?

   A Dakota

   B Powhatan

   C Sioux

   D Pueblo

10. Which group of Native
Americans lived in the
Southwest desert?

   A Dakota

   B Powhatan

   C Sioux

   D Pueblo

11. Congress, the president, and
the Supreme Court are all
part of the—

   A local government.

   B federal government.

   C international government.

   D state government.

12. Who helped the colonists
learn how to become better
workers?

   A Columbus

   B John Smith

   C James Town

   D Squanto

13. Which of the following listed
the reasons why the colonies
wanted to be free?

   A the Constitution

   B the Magna Carta

   C the Bill of Rights

   D the Declaration of
      Independence

14. Which ocean did Columbus cross to reach North America?

  A Indian Ocean

  B Pacific Ocean

  C Arctic Ocean

  D Atlantic Ocean

15. Why did Thomas Jefferson send Lewis and Clark on an expedition?

  A to set up a government

  B to find a way to the Pacific Ocean

  C to plant crops

  D to meet Native Americans

16. Pioneers moved West to—

  A own land and build homes.

  B live with Native Americans.

  C leave the country.

  D find freedom.

17. A person who comes from one country to live in another is called—

  A a tourist.

  B an immigrant.

  C a citizen.

  D an explorer.

18. Who invented the horseless carriage?

  A Benjamin Franklin

  B Henry Ford

  C Orville Wright

  D Amelia Earhart

19. Which of the following is a landmark?

  A the Rocky Mountains

  B the Pacific Ocean

  C New York Art Museum

  D Mount Rushmore

20. Writing and speaking are examples of—

  A transportation.

  B communication.

  C government.

  D trade.

21. India is located on the continent of—

A Africa.

B Australia.

C Asia.

D South America.

22. Bartering is when—

A goods are sold for money.

B goods are traded for other goods.

C good are sold in another country.

D goods are traded for money.

23. People who make goods are called—

A shoppers.

B traders.

C consumers.

D producers.

24. Who invented the airplane?

A the Wright brothers

B Amelia Earhart

C John Smith

D Charles Lindbergh

Answer each question. Use complete sentences.

25. How are urban and rural communities different?

_____

_____

_____

_____

_____

_____

_____

_____

_____

_____

_____

_____

_____

_____

_____

Use for 26–30. Use coordinates, such as A3, to answer the questions.

City Park

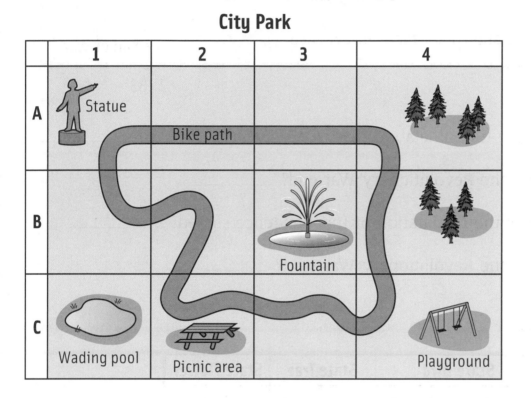

26. Where is the fountain? _____

27. Where is the picnic area? _____

28. Where is the statue? _____

29. Where is the playground? _____

30. Which two squares do NOT have the bike path going

through them? _____

Use for 31–34.

Revolutionary War Time Line

• Start of War
   • Declaration of Independence Signed
                                          • End of War

1775   1776   1783

31. What is the time line about? _____

32. When did the Revolutionary War end? _____

33. When was the Declaration of Independence signed? _____

34. When did the Revolutionary War start? _____

Use for 35–40.

	State Bird	State Tree	State Flower
Kansas	Western meadowlark	Cottonwood	Sunflower
Utah	Seagull	Blue spruce	Sego lily
Wisconsin	Robin	Sugar maple	Wood violet

35. What is the state bird of Utah? _____

36. What is the state flower of Wisconsin? _____

37. What is the state tree of Kansas? _____

38. Which state's state bird is the robin? _____

39. Which state's state tree is the sugar maple? _____

40. Which state's state flower is the sunflower? _____

> Read each selection in Part A and answer the questions. Then read the directions in Part B and write your paragraph.

Part A: Short Answer

Use for 41.

Water is very important. Our planet, Earth, is covered mostly by water. For every square mile of dry land there are about three square miles of water. All forms of life—animals, plants, and people—need water to live.

41. What living things need water to live? _____

_____

_____

Use for 42–44.

There are three ways to get water to people. The first way is from a lake. A lake that supplies water to a town is called a reservoir. A reservoir is where water is stored until it is needed.

The second way is from an aquifer. To get water from an aquifer, people must drill a deep hole called a well. When the well is finished, powerful pumps are used to draw the water out of the ground.

The third way to get water is through an aqueduct. An aqueduct can be a big ditch or canal that is paved with stones, bricks, or concrete. It can be a tunnel deep under the ground. Or it can be pipes on top of the ground.

42. How many ways are there to get water to people?

_____

43. If a city isn't near a lake or river, where does the water come from?

_____

44. What is an aqueduct?

_____

_____

Part B: Paragraph

Write a paragraph. Use the information from the documents. You may also use your knowledge of social studies.

45. In your paragraph, include what living things need water and how people get water.

_____

_____

_____

_____

_____

_____

_____

_____

_____

_____

_____

_____

_____

Assessment Answers

ing PROMOTING LITERACY

1. D	**25.** D	**49.** fruitful
2. A	**26.** A	**50.** mindful
3. A	**27.** A	**51.** unwind
4. B	**28.** C	**52.** unlock
5. A	**29.** B	**53.** regain
6. D	**30.** fiction	**54.** replay
7. A	**31.** science fiction	**55.** strangeness
8. B	**32.** nonfiction	**56.** brightness
9. C	**33.** in	**57.** know
10. B	**34.** on	**58.** read
11. C	**35.** by	**59.** to
12. D	**36.** to	**60.** buy
13. C	**37.** from	**61.** four
14. A	**38.** at	**62.** two
15. D	**39.** with	**63.** red
16. C	**40.** of	**64.** no
17. A	**41.** help	**65.** too
18. A	**42.** soft	**66.** there
19. C	**43.** happy	**67.** by
20. D	**44.** hook	**68.** their
21. C	**45.** kindly	**69.** write
22. B	**46.** carefully	**70.** for
23. D	**47.** washable	
24. A	**48.** drinkable	

Scoring Rubric for Question 71:

4 POINTS

The journal entry is dated and uses a proper opening and closing. It describes the day in detail. It is well organized and there are few, if any, grammar, spelling, punctuation, or capitalization errors.

3 POINTS

The journal entry is dated and uses a proper opening and closing. It describes the day in detail. It is organized and there are minor grammar, spelling, punctuation, or capitalization errors.

2 POINTS

The journal entry is dated but does not use a proper opening or closing. The day is described in only partial detail. There are many grammar, spelling, punctuation, or capitalization errors.

1 POINT

The journal entry is not dated and does not use a proper opening and closing. Rather than describing the day it veers off into other topics.

0 POINTS

The writing is not dated and does not resemble a journal entry. There are a wide variety of grammar, spelling, punctuation, and capitalization errors.

Scoring Rubric for Question 72:

4 POINTS

The poem vividly describes a season. A wide variety of rhyming words are used skillfully and creatively.

3 POINTS

The poem successfully describes a season. It uses a variety of different rhyming words.

2 POINTS

The poem describes a season. It uses several rhyming words.

1 POINT

The poem is only somewhat descriptive. It uses only a few rhyming words.

0 POINTS

The poem is not descriptive. It does not use rhyming words.

Scoring Rubric for Question 73:

4 POINTS

The paragraph vividly describes a person. It includes a topic sentence and supporting details. It is well organized and there are few, if any, grammar, spelling, punctuation, or capitalization errors.

3 POINTS

The paragraph describes a person. It includes a topic sentence and supporting details. It is organized and there are minor grammar, spelling, punctuation, or capitalization errors.

2 POINTS

The paragraph somewhat describes a person. The topic sentence and the supporting details are vague. There is little organizational structure. There are a variety of grammar, spelling, punctuation, or capitalization errors.

1 POINT

The paragraph is only partially descriptive. It lacks a topic sentence and has an insufficient number of supporting details. There are many grammar, spelling, punctuation, or capitalization errors.

0 POINTS

The paragraph is not descriptive. It lacks a topic sentence and supporting details. It is not organized and there are a wide variety of grammar, spelling, punctuation, or capitalization errors.

Assessment Answers

Scoring Rubric for Question 74:

4 POINTS
The paragraph thoroughly describes a book. It includes a detailed description of the main characters and the plot. It is well organized and there are few, if any, grammar, spelling, punctuation, or capitalization errors.

3 POINTS
The paragraph successfully describes a book. It includes a description of the main characters and the plot. It is organized and there are minor grammar, spelling, punctuation, or capitalization errors.

2 POINTS
The paragraph partially describes a book. The main characters and the plot are not described in appropriate detail. There is little organizational structure. There are a variety of grammar, spelling, punctuation, and capitalization errors.

1 POINT
The paragraph is difficult to understand. It mentions the book but does not successfully describe characters or the plot.

0 POINTS
The paragraph does not describe a book, characters, or plot.

MATH

1. B	23. D
2. B	24. C
3. C	25. giraffe
4. B	26. monkey
5. A	27. dog
6. B	28. giraffe
7. D	29. 399
8. A	30. 115
9. B	31. 848
10. B	32. Set B
11. D	33. 165
12. A	34. 892
13. B	35. 597
14. C	36. $5 + 0 = 5$
15. A	37. $0 + 23 = 23$
16. B	38. 30
17. C	39. 5
18. A	40. Sunday
19. B	
20. B	
21. C	
22. D	

41. Possible answer:

42. tens
43. hundreds
44. ones
45. Possible answer:

46. $8 \div 4 = 2$
47. 8
48. 6
49. kilograms
50. grams
51. kilograms
52. 8
53. black
54. 3
55. 23

Scoring Rubric for Question 56:

4 POINTS
The student correctly shows all five of the other solutions: 1 dime, 7 pennies; 3 nickels, 2 pennies; 2 nickels, 7 pennies; 1 nickel, 12 pennies; and 17 pennies.

3 POINTS
The student correctly shows four of the above solutions.

2 POINTS
The student correctly shows three of the above solutions.

1 POINT
The student correctly shows one or two of the above solutions.

0 POINTS
The student does not show any of the above solutions.

Assessment Answers

SCIENCE

1. A	9. C	17. B	25. B
2. C	10. B	18. B	26. D
3. B	11. C	19. C	27. A
4. A	12. C	20. C	28. D
5. D	13. D	21. B	29. B
6. A	14. A	22. A	30. C
7. C	15. A	23. A	31. B
8. C	16. B	24. B	32. A

33. A. crown, B. gum, C. root

34. Answers will vary. Possible answers: feeding them, providing shelter, and providing protection

35. hair type and height

36. Moons should be labeled (from top to bottom): half moon, full moon, and quarter moon.

37. Pictures should be labeled (from top to bottom): 2, 1, and 3.

38. bread, cereal, rice, and pasta

39. fats, oils, and sweets

40. 2 to 4

41. noise

42. volume

43. sight, hearing, smell, taste, and touch

44. Water carries nutrition and cools you off when you are hot.

45. coal and oil

46. Plants provide animals with shelter and food.

47. shadow

48. light

49. absorb

50. reflect

Scoring Rubric for Question 51:

4 POINTS
There are three drawings and all of them correctly show products made from natural resources, such as a wooden chair, a steel beam, a window, and a tire.

3 POINTS
There are three drawings and two of them correctly show products made from natural resources.

2 POINTS
There are two drawings and one of them correctly shows a product made from a natural resource.

1 POINT
There is one drawing and it correctly shows a product made from a natural resource.

0 POINTS
There are no drawings or the drawings do not show any products made from natural resources.

Scoring Rubric for Question 52:

4 POINTS
The response indicates a solid understanding of plant and animal protection. There are three or four examples cited. Example: Some animals make themselves look like dangerous animals. Some animals make themselves look larger to frighten other animals away. Some plants have poison so that they will not be eaten.

3 POINTS
The response indicates an understanding of plant and animal protection. There are one or two examples cited.

2 POINTS
The response indicates a partial understanding of plant and animal protection. There are one or two examples cited, but they are only partly correct.

1 POINT
The response indicates a poor understanding of plant and animal protection. The examples cited are incorrect.

0 POINTS
The response indicates no understanding of plant and animal protection. There are no examples cited.

SOCIAL STUDIES

1. A		17. B	
2. B		18. B	
3. C		19. D	
4. D		20. B	
5. B		21. C	
6. D		22. B	
7. B		23. D	
8. C		24. A	
9. B			
10. D			
11. B			
12. B			
13. D			
14. D			
15. B			
16. A			

Assessment Answers

Scoring Rubric for Question 25:

4 POINTS

The response indicates an excellent understanding of the difference between urban and rural communities. There is a clear distinction made between both communities. Example: Urban communities are more crowded, have more streets, roads, and vehicles, and are noisier than rural areas.

3 POINTS

The response indicates a good understanding of the difference between urban and rural communities. It makes a distinction between both communities.

2 POINTS

The response indicates an adequate understanding of the difference between urban and rural communities. There may be one or two descriptions that do not make a distinction between both communities.

1 POINT

The response indicates only partial understanding of the difference between urban and rural communities. There are several descriptions that confuse the two communities.

0 POINTS

The response indicates little understanding of the difference between urban and rural communities. There are no distinctions made.

26. B3
27. C2
28. A1
29. C4
30. B3, C1
31. Revolutionary War
32. 1783
33. 1776
34. 1775
35. seagull
36. wood violet
37. cottonwood
38. Wisconsin
39. Wisconsin
40. Kansas
41. all living things
42. three ways
43. from an aquifer
44. a big ditch or canal

Scoring Rubric for Question 45

4 POINTS

The paragraph states that all living things need water and correctly describes the three main ways that people get water to their homes.

3 POINTS

The paragraph states that most or all living things need water and correctly describes two of the three main ways that people get water to their homes.

2 POINTS

The paragraph states that some living things need water and correctly describes one way that people get water to their homes.

1 POINT

The paragraph states that most, but not all, living things need water. The description of how people get water to their homes is undeveloped or only partially correct.

0 POINTS

The paragraph explains that some, but not all, living things need water. It does not describe how people get water to their homes.

Answers

Lesson 1.1

Student Learning Page 1.B

who: Dan, Mother, Father, Timmy
where: Dan's family's home
when: during a winter storm

beginning: A power line is broken and the house loses power.
middle: Dan's family has to do special things to stay warm, eat, and keep the pipes from freezing.
end: A worker from the power company comes in a truck and fixes the power line.

Lesson 1.2

Student Learning Page 2.A

Answers will vary. The story should begin with the sentence made.

Lesson 1.3

Student Learning Page 3.B

The pictures should show the beginning, middle, and end of the story, with a caption for each picture.

beginning: Ella wants to play in the honeysuckle tub but her brothers think she is too scared, too small, and can't climb.
middle: Ella goes away to play on her own. She makes up stories about an elephant and a dragon. She tells her brothers her make-believe stories.
end: Ella's brothers think her stories are real. At bedtime, they invite her to play in the honeysuckle tub the next day.

Lesson 1.4

Student Learning Page 4.A

present: I am, you are, he/she/it is, we are, you are, they are
past: I was, you were, he/she/it was, we were, you were, they were

Student Learning Page 4.B

Answers will vary. Possible answers:

1. This woman is an astronaut. She saw craters on the moon.
2. The football player has a football in his hand. He will go to the Super Bowl.
3. The police officer is wearing a uniform. Her job is to keep us safe.

Lesson 1.5

Student Learning Page 5.A

1. a
2. an
3. a
4. A
5. an
6. an
7. An
8. a

9. An elephant has a long trunk.
10. The cat liked to chase the mouse.
11. We had a sandwich and an apple.

Lesson 1.6

Student Learning Page 6.A

1. brother, sister, zoo
2. boy, lions
3. girl, seals
4. elephants
5. people, park

A favorite zoo animal should be drawn with its name written below the drawing.

Lesson 1.7

Student Learning Page 7.A

2. snowman = snow + man
3. mailbox = mail + box
4. C
5. A
6. E
7. B
8. D

Lesson 1.8

Student Learning Page 8.B

Answers will vary. Possible answers:

2. Picture should show coins.
3. Picture should show the bearded man counting money; words: The king makes the bearded man treasurer.
4. Picture should show the chief counselor talking to the king.
5. words: When they opened the bearded man's secret room, it was empty.
6. Picture should show the bearded man dressed as chief counselor.

Lesson 1.10

Student Learning Page 10.B

Biographies will vary. The topic should be about a hero who has done something great or whom your student looks up to. The events of the person's life should be described in the order in which they happened.

Answers

Lesson 1.11

Student Learning Page 11.B

Book reports will vary. The report should describe the most important ideas of the selection. It may include your student's opinion of the selection. A picture should be included in the box at the bottom.

Lesson 1.12

Student Learning Page 12.A

Answers will vary. Possible answers:
1. My brother and sister play outside.
2. My dad asked us if we want juice or milk.
3. I read or watch television before I go to bed.
4. Joey put on his shoes and socks.

Lesson 1.13

Student Learning Page 13.A

The little bird sat <u>in</u> the old oak tree, she spread her wings and flew <u>to</u> me.

She flapped and landed <u>on</u> my arm, and said she moved <u>from</u> a northern farm.

When winter came <u>with</u> air that chills, she flew to a tree <u>by</u> the southern hills.

Lesson 1.14

Student Learning Page 14.A
1. cleaner, cleanest
2. colder, coldest
3. quicker, quickest
4. longer, longest
5. deeper, deepest
6. softer, softest

Student Learning Page 14.B
1. word: sad, kind, or quiet; new word: sadly, kindly, or quietly
2. word: treat or chew; new word: treatable or chewable
3. word: care, help, or hope; new word: careful, helpful, or hopeful
4. word: care, help, or hope; new word: careless, helpless, or hopeless
5. word: sad, kind, or quiet; new word: sadness, kindness, or quietness
6. word: sad, kind, or quiet; new word: sadly, kindly, or quietly
7. word: care, help, or hope; new word: careful, helpful, or hopeful
8. word: treat or chew; new word: treatable or chewable

Student Learning Page 14.C
1. untrue
2. replace
3. untie
4. repay
5. unhappy
6. retest
7. unlock
8. revisit

Lesson 1.15

Student Learning Page 15.A
1. short
2. good
3. quiet
4. weak
5. smooth
6. hard
7. fast
8. happy

Student Learning Page 15.B

The synonyms from the bottom of the mountain to the top should be: quick, laugh, small, yell, hot, high.

The antonyms from the bottom of the mountain to the top should be: slow, cry, big, whisper, cold, short.

Student Learning Page 15.C
1. Carla's room is always <u>clean</u>.
2. The room was large and <u>bright</u>.
3. Jason had a <u>loud</u> party last week.
4. Our bus driver has a <u>nice</u> voice.
5. Carla's room is always <u>messy</u>.
6. The room was large and <u>dark</u>.
7. Jason had a <u>quiet</u> party last week.
8. Our bus driver has an <u>unpleasant</u> voice.

Lesson 1.16

Student Learning Page 16.A

The words in the paragraph should be (in order): Aunt, sea, ant, bee, be, see.

Pictures will vary. Check that the pictures have to do with the sun and a male child.

MATH

Lesson 2.1

Student Learning Page 1.A
1. B and D
2. B
3. C

Student Learning Page 1.B

Sets 2, 3, and 4 should be circled.

Student Learning Page 1.C
1. 80
2. Answers may vary. Possible answer: Count the number of people on one bus (20) then count by 20s or add four 20s together to get 80.

Answers

Lesson 2.2

Student Learning Page 2.A

1. 3
2. 9, 7, 97
3. 70
4. 62
5. 1, 4
6. 6, 1
7. 13, 14, 16
8. 25, 40, 50
9. 8, 10, 12, 14, 16, 18, 20, 22, 24
10. <
11. <
12. 66, 61, 43

Lesson 2.3

Student Learning Page 3.A

1. 60
2. 60
3. 22
4. 67
5. 90; addition fact: 8 + 1 = 9
6. 50; addition fact: 2 + 3 = 5
7. B

Lesson 2.4

Student Learning Page 4.A

1. 70
2. 40
3. 45
4. 6
5. 22
6. 48
7. 63
8. 21
9. 17
10. 33; 33 + 29 = 62
11. 9; 9 + 36 = 45

Lesson 2.5

Student Learning Page 5.A

1. 4 hundreds, 2 tens, 7 ones
2. 400 + 20 + 7
3. 427
4. Drawing should represent 335 and 282; 335 should be circled.
5. Drawing should represent 114 and 479; 479 should be circled.
6. 4
7. 3
8. 5

Lesson 2.6

Student Learning Page 6.A

1. 359
2. 711
3. 894
4. 589
5. 437
6. 359
7. 359

Student Learning Page 6.B

1. 312; 1 hundred, 4 tens, 9 ones; 1 hundred, 6 tens, 3 ones; 3 hundreds, 1 ten, 2 ones
2. 895; 6 hundreds, 8 tens, 2 ones; 2 hundreds, 1 ten, 3 ones; 8 hundreds, 9 tens, 5 ones
3. 553
4. 940

5. 830
6. 159; 6 hundreds, 7 tens, 4 ones; 5 hundreds, 1 ten, 5 ones; 1 hundred, 5 tens, 9 ones
7. 324; 5 hundreds, 8 tens, 7 ones; 2 hundreds, 6 tens, 3 ones; 3 hundreds, 2 tens, 4 ones
8. 27
9. 665
10. 190

Lesson 2.7

Student Learning Page 7.A

1. 67 cents
2. 67¢
3. $0.67
4. 80 cents
5. 80¢
6. $0.80
7. Student should circle the $0.41 set.
8. $0.18

Lesson 2.8

Student Learning Page 8.A

1. C
2. A
3. B

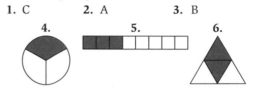

4. 5. 6.

7. 8 pieces; $\frac{1}{8}$
8. Monica

Student Learning Page 8.B

1. $\frac{3}{5}$
2. $\frac{3}{5}$
3. $\frac{1}{5}$
4. $\frac{2}{5}$
5. green faces
6. smiling faces
7. 2
8. 3

Lesson 2.9

Student Learning Page 9.A

1. first arc: 21 (red); second arc: 0 (orange); third arc: 25 (yellow); fourth arc: 12 (green); fifth arc: 16 (blue); sixth arc: 22 (dark blue); seventh arc: 18 (violet)
2. 8 ÷ 4 = 2
3. 10 ÷ 5 = 2
4. 15 ÷ 5 = 3
5. 9 jelly beans

Answers

Student Learning Page 9.B

Number of Equal Sets	Number of Counters in Each Set	Remainder: Yes or No? If yes, how many?	
1	20	No	
2	10	No	
3	6	Yes	2
5	4	No	
8	2	Yes	4
10	2	No	

Lesson 2.10

Student Learning Page 10.A

1. 2
2. 7
3. 3
4. 5
5. 1
6. 3
7. 8
8. 5
9. 4
10. 5
11. 4 holes

Lesson 2.11

Student Learning Page 11.A

1. A circle should be drawn.
2. A square should be drawn.
3. A triangle should be drawn.
4. A rectangle should be drawn.
5. The pyramid should be circled.
6. The sphere should have an X.
7. The cone should be colored blue.
8. The cube should be colored red.
9. The butterfly should be circled.

Lesson 2.12

Student Learning Page 12.A

1–3. Chart should be filled in accurately.
4. 100
5. 12
6. meters
7. centimeter

Student Learning Page 12.B

The feather, coin, pencil, and tennis ball should be circled in red. The whale, large dictionary, barbell, and truck should be circled in blue.

1. 1
2. liter
3. 2
4. quart

Lesson 2.13

Student Learning Page 13.A

1. 7:15
2. 15 minutes after seven
3. Quarter after seven
4. 9:40
5. 40 minutes after nine
6. 20 minutes to ten
7–11. Calendar should be filled in accurately.

Lesson 2.14

Student Learning Page 14.A

1. 17
2. 29
3. 16
4. 6
5. 45
6. 51
7. 68
8. cars
9. bikes
10. Question 10 should relate to the chart.

Student Learning Page 14.B

1. 1 in 6
2. Predictions will vary. Ten is the most likely.
3–6. Answers will vary. The tally chart should be filled in accurately.

SCIENCE

Lesson 3.1

Student Learning Page 1.A

The order of the pictures should be egg, tadpole, frog.

Lesson 3.2

Student Learning Page 2.A

1. Picture of flowers should be drawn and labeled correctly on a separate sheet of paper.
2. Answers will vary. The number of male and female flower parts may vary. Shape or color may vary. Some flowers are made up of clusters of small flowers.
3. Answers will vary. All flowers help the plant make seeds. Most have petals and pollen and male and/or female parts.

Lesson 3.3

Student Learning Page 3.A

1. long neck
2. helps giraffe reach treetops to eat leaves
3. claws
4. helps hawk catch small animals
5. long tongue
6. helps frog catch insects for food

Lesson 3.4

Student Learning Page 4.A

Answers may vary. Most people have more sweet taste buds on the tips of their tongues, bitter near the back, salty on the sides toward the back, and sour on the sides closer to the front of the tongue. Sometimes the tip of the tongue can also taste salt.

Answers

Lesson 3.5

Student Learning Page 5.A

1–3. Student's favorite foods should be listed in the correct group. Food guide pyramid should be drawn on separate sheet of paper.

Lesson 3.6

Student Learning Page 6.A

Baby, adult, biting, tearing, and chewing teeth should be labeled correctly.

1–5. Answers will vary.

Lesson 3.7

Student Learning Page 7.A

Answers will vary. Possible answers:

1. Turning off a light when I leave a room helps conserve fossil fuels.
2. There will be less garbage in landfills if we recycle glass, cans, and paper.
3. Water is an important natural resource and shouldn't be wasted.

Lesson 3.8

Student Learning Page 8.A

1. erosion   2. weathering

Fossil formation drawing should show steps similar to those in the fish fossil diagram.

Lesson 3.9

Student Learning Page 9.A

Moon phases should be shaded accurately.

1. No, the moon is always the same shape. It's round like a ball. What changes is the amount of the light side of the moon that we can see from Earth.
2. 29 days

Lesson 3.10

Student Learning Page 10.A

1. pull; a line drawn to the hand
2. pull; a line drawn to the hand
3. both; a line drawn to the foot
4. pull; a line drawn to the hand
5. both; a line drawn to the hand
6. push; a line drawn to the hand

Lesson 3.11

Student Learning Page 11.A

1. low pitch, low volume
2. high pitch, high volume
3. low pitch, low volume
4. low pitch, high volume
5. high pitch, high or low volume

6. low pitch, high volume
7. Sound is energy that we can hear.
8. Sound is caused by vibrations that produce sound waves.
9. Answers will vary.

Lesson 3.12

Student Learning Page 12.A

A line should connect each object with the correct shadow.

Lesson 3.13

Student Learning Page 13.A

1. *Weather Facts*
2. *Whales of the World*
3. *What Do Gorillas Do?*
4. *Everything You've Always Wanted to Know About the Sun*

Lesson 4.1

Student Learning Page 1.A

1. Answers will vary. Events should be listed in chronological order.
2. most popular: cat; least popular: fish
3. the school
4. B1

Lesson 4.2

Student Learning Page 2.A

1. rural area   3. suburban area
2. urban area

Pictures will vary.

Lesson 4.3

Student Learning Page 3.A

All seven continents should be labeled: Antarctica, Asia, Australia, North America, South America, Europe, and Africa.

All four oceans should be labeled: Atlantic, Pacific, Indian, and Arctic.

Lesson 4.4

Student Learning Page 4.A

1. popcorn   5. bread
2. cornmeal   6. pancakes
3. french fries 7. apple pie
4. soup   8. apple juice

Student Learning Page 4.B

Designs will vary.

Answers

Student Learning Page 4.C

glass: jam jar, juice bottle

paper: pizza box, newspaper, milk carton

aluminum: soup can, soda can

Lesson 4.5

Student Learning Page 5.A

Answers will vary. Each picture should be of a person doing a different job; the sentences should match the pictures.

Lesson 4.6

Student Learning Page 6.A

1. governor
2. mayor
3. state capitol
4. citizens

Lesson 4.7

Student Learning Page 7.A

1. The president lives and works here.
2. Leaders of other countries sometimes have dinner here.
3. It's also called the Executive Mansion.
4. Laws are made here.
5. Members of Congress work here.
6. People elected from all states meet here.

Lesson 4.8

Student Learning Page 8.A

Pueblo: They grew corn and squash. They made adobe from mud.

Sioux: They lived in tepees. They followed the buffalo.

Powhatan: They built canoes. They lived near the Atlantic coast.

Lesson 4.9

Student Learning Page 9.A

Pictures will vary.

1. The Pilgrims and the Wampanoag were at the First Thanksgiving.
2. They were thankful because they had food to eat.
3. They ate food such as wild ducks, deer, fish, turkey, corn, beans, cornbread, carrots, dried fruit, and berries.

Lesson 4.10

Student Learning Page 10.A

The words in the news story should be (in order): Louisiana, Rocky, Pacific, France, Sacajawea, animals, maps, pioneers.

Lesson 4.11

Student Learning Page 11.A

Answers will vary. Information should be included about what the student's family likes to do on birthdays, the Fourth of July, and Thanksgiving. A picture should be drawn that shows something the student's family does on the chosen holiday.

Lesson 4.12

Student Learning Page 12.A

1. Alamo
2. South Dakota
3. Illinois and Missouri
4. Statue of Liberty

Lesson 4.13

Student Learning Page 13.A

1. transportation
2. transportation
3. communication
4. communication

Drawings will vary.

Lesson 4.14

Student Learning Page 14.A

1. Choose a topic.
2. Look for information.
3. Take notes on your topic.
4. Write a first draft.
5. Correct mistakes in your first draft.
6. Share your final report with others.

GLOSSARY

Like any other specialty area, teaching and homeschooling have their own unique vocabulary. We've included some terms we thought might be helpful.

accelerated learning

when a student completes a certain set of lessons faster than most students; this can happen due to a student's natural motivation or in a more structured manner, such as continuing lessons throughout the year versus taking the summer off

assessment

a review of a student's learning progress and comprehension; traditionally done through tests or grades; assessments in progressive learning environments such as homeschooling take on many different forms, including summary discussions, demonstrative projects, and oral questions and answers; formalized assessment is included in this book, beginning on page 303

auditory learner

an individual who absorbs new information most effectively by listening; an auditory learner will remember information that is spoken or related through sound such as musical lyrics, reading aloud, or audiocassettes

child-centered learning

a type of learning in which the teaching style places the child at the center of his or her learning, meaning that a child begins and proceeds with new subjects, such as reading, as he or she is ready; this style of teaching requires intimate awareness of the student by the teacher

correlated to state standards

a phrase that means that something meets or exceeds a particular state's mandatory educational requirements for the intended grade level

critical thinking skill

the ability to assess information, make independent judgments, and draw conclusions; this skill is independent of and goes beyond the memorized information that a student has learned

curriculum

an ordered list of specific topics of study that is used as a teaching map

distance learning

a type of instruction in which classes are completed at a different physical location than at the school that offers them; formerly known as correspondence classes, this term now includes video and Internet classes

graphic organizer

a way to visually organize information for the purpose of learning enhancement; usually referring to charts and graphs, these can be useful for visual learners; several graphic organizers are included in this book: Venn Diagram, Comparison Chart, Web, and Sequence Chain

inclusive

a homeschool group that is inclusive and welcomes anyone who homeschools regardless of religious or educational beliefs or practices; as homeschooling becomes more popular, more inclusive groups have been formed; in the traditional classroom setting, an inclusive school is focused on reaching out to the increasingly diverse student populations to provide a supportive and quality education to all students regardless of economic status, gender, race, or disability

kinesthetic learner

an individual who absorbs new information most effectively through experience; a kinesthetic learner will understand information by completing hands-on exercises, doing, and moving

learning style

the singular manner and rate that each child naturally pursues his or her education; educators have identified three primary ways of describing learning styles: auditory, kinesthetic, and visual

lesson plan

a detailed description of the part of the curriculum one is planning to teach on a certain day

multicultural

adapted to relate to diverse cultures; many teachers incorporate multicultural learning materials into their lessons to encourage exposure to different traditions

real books

books you get at the library or the bookstore that aren't textbooks; some homeschoolers work almost exclusively from real books and don't use textbooks at all; this book provides a curriculum that's based on reading and research with real books

scoring rubric

a measurement tool used to assess student work that includes a system of scoring levels of performance; scoring rubrics are used with some lessons in this book and with the formalized assessment section in the back of this book

self-directed learner

an individual who is free to pursue education by his or her own means and guidance versus through traditional classes or schools; a term often used in homeschool literature

self-teaching

when an individual naturally learns about a topic of particular interest on his or her own, without formal instruction and usually as a result of natural attraction to or talent in the subject matter

standardized test

a test is considered standardized when it is given in the same manner, with the same directions to children of the same grade level across a school district, state, or country; the test shows how your student is doing compared to other students; the assessment section beginning on page 303 offers examples of standardized test questions

teaching strategy

a creative way to motivate and inspire students, such as using a visual aid, entertaining or humorous delivery, interactive activity, or theme-based lessons; if your student is bored, he or she might benefit from a change in teaching strategies

unschooling

a teaching philosophy first identified by educator John Holt that's based on the idea that the child directs his or her own learning based on his or her own interests; works under the assertion that textbook-type teaching can dull a child's natural zest for learning and the belief that a student will learn more when he or she is engaged, uninterrupted, and enjoying

visual learner

an individual who absorbs new information most effectively through the sense of sight; a visual learner will comprehend information by reading, watching a video, using a visual computer program, and looking at pictures in books

Waldorf

a method of education that was developed by Rudolph Steiner and attempts to teach the whole child: physical, emotional, and academic; Waldorf schools are located throughout the country, and there is also a network of Waldorf homeschoolers

Venn Diagram

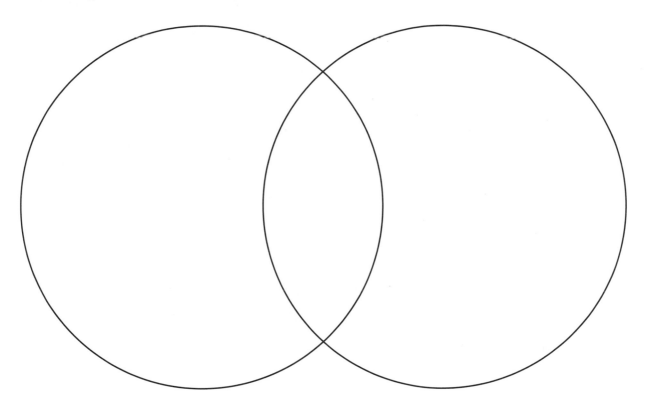

Comparison Chart

Issue:_____	A: _____	B: _____
I.	1.	2.
II.	3.	4.
III.	5.	6.

Web

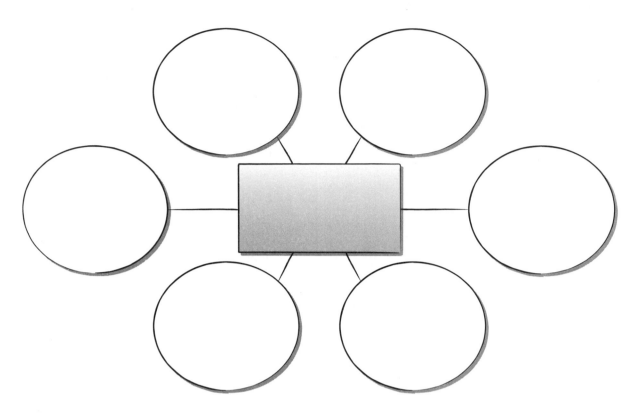

Sequence Chain

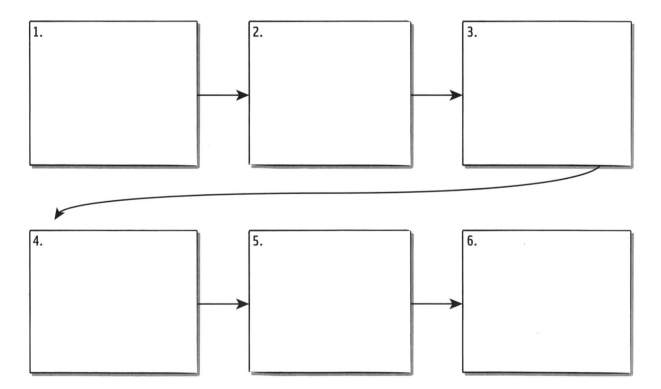

Index

Note: Page numbers in bold indicate the definition of a term.

A

a, 31–34
-able suffix, 74, 76
Absorb, **221**
Absorption of light, 221–222
Acrostic poem activity, 52
Act It Out activities
  folktale, 48
  life cycle, 172
  verbs, 29
Addition
  facts, patterns and, 141–144
  monetary concepts, 104
  optional activities, 104, 108, 112
  practice problems, 103, 107, 123–124
  of three-digit numbers, 119–120, 123–124
  of two-digit numbers, 105–108
Adjectives, **80**–84
Adult teeth, 193–194, 195
Airplanes, 294
Alamo, 290, 291
Algebraic methods
  concepts and analysis, 141–142
  optional activities, 144
  practice problems, 143
American Revolution, 277–278
an, 31–34
and, 65–67
Animals
  classifying sounds of, 219
  connect the dots exercise, 181
  defensive/protective qualities, 178–179
  diversity, 245
  feeding adaptations, 179
  group living, 179–180
  habitats, 177–178
  life cycles, 169–172
  natural resources and, 250
  optional activities, 182
  plant reproduction and, 179
Animals, life cycles of
  concepts and analysis, 169–170
  frog exercise, 171
  optional activities, 172
Antonyms and synonyms, **79**
  concepts and analysis, 79–80
  exercises, 81–83
  optional activities, 84
Ants, 179
Ants on a log snack activity, 192
Arrays (mathematical), **135,** 136
Art activities. *See also* Drawing activities; Picture activities; Poster activities
  neighborhood model, 242
  paper dragon, 24
  set of teeth, 196
  Sioux pottery, 274

Articles (parts of speech), **31**
  concepts and analysis, 31–32
  optional activities, 34
  writing exercise, 33
Assessment
  literacy, 303–314, 341–342
  math, 315–322, 342
  science, 323–332, 343
  social studies, 333–340, 343–344
Automobiles, 294
Axis, **207**
  Earth's rotation around, 208
  Earth's seasons and, 209–210

B

Babies and parents poster activity, 172
Baby teeth, **193,** 195
Balance activity, 188
Banks/banking, **257**
  concepts, 257
  optional activities, 260
Bar graph, 233–234
Bartering, **258**
Base words, **73**–78
be, 26, 27
Beginning of story, 9, 23
Bingo activity, 144
Biography, **53**
  concepts and analysis, 53–54
  optional activities, 58, 284
  reading selection, 55–56
  writing exercise, 57
Bird feeder activity, 182
Bitter substances, tasting, 185, 187
Body parts
  motion exercise, 215
  plant and animal, 179, 181
  sense organs, **183**
Book report, writing, 63
Book-making activities
  future activities book, 29
  homophone book, 88
  picture book, 10
  preposition book, 72
Borders, geographic, **245**
Bouillon cube dissolution activity, 192
Braille, 293
Brain
  hole in your hand activity, 188
  sensory signals to, 184, 185
Brooklyn Bridge, 290
but, 66
Butterflies, 179
Button-making activities
  conservation button, 252
  voting buttons, 268

C

Calendar concepts, 158, 159–160

Capacity units of measure, 154, 156
Capitalization of sentences, 48
Capitol building (U.S.), 266, 267, 289
Car race activity, 216
Cars, 294
Cause and effect (literary), 4, 16
Cavity, **193,** 194
Centimeters, **151,** 152–153
Characters (literary), **15**
  fictional, 4, 15, 43
  folktales, 43
  story map exercise, 9
Charting information
  as addition strategy, 105–106
  concepts and analysis, 233–234
  division activity, 140
  graphs. *See* Graphs
  hundreds place chart activity, 104
  Native American exercise, 273
  practice exercise, 235
  soil chart, 206
  tally chart, 161
  time lines, 233, 235
Circle, 145, 149
Cities. *See also* Communities
  geographic concepts, 243–244
  government leaders, **261**–262, 264
  landmarks, 290
Citizens, **261**–262
City council, **261**–262, 264
Clark, William. *See* Lewis and Clark expedition
Clay pottery activity, 274
Climb the Mountain exercise, 82
Clock concepts, 157–160
Clues, context, 60
Coins. *See* Money
Collage activity, emergency supplies, 10
Colonies, **276**
  growth and independence, 277–278
  settlement, Native Americans and, 276
Colonists, **276**
Color, as plant/animal defense mechanism, 178
Commercial, writing activity, 300
Communicate, **293**
Communication
  drawing exercise, 295
  methods, 293
  parent–school, xvii–xviii
Communities
  diversity, 238
  globe/geographic concepts, 243–248
  Guess Where You Are exercise, 241
  history, 238
  laws governing, 237–238, 239

  optional activities, 242
  resources, 240
  similarities across, 239
  types and locations, 239
Community outreach activities
  literary, 89
  mathematics, 165
  science, 229
  social studies, 301
Comparing
  communities, 237–242
  comparison sentences, 75–76
  three-digit numbers, 115–116
  two-digit numbers, 102
Comparison Chart graphic organizer, 353
Compass rose activity, 236
Complete sentences, 12
Compound words, **39**
  concepts and analysis, 39–40
  optional activities, 42
  practice exercise, 41
Cone (geometric), 146, 147, 149
Congress (U.S.), **265**–266
Congruent shapes, **146**
Conjunctions, **65**
  concepts and analysis, 65–66
  optional activities, 68
  writing exercise, 67
Connect the dots animal exercise, 181
Conservation, **197, 250**
  button-making exercise, 252
  optional activities, 202, 254
  strategies, 198–199, 201, 246, 250
Consonants, using *a* before words beginning with, 31–34
Consume, **256**
Consumption of goods, 256–257
Context clues, 60
Continents, **244**–245, 247
Contractions, grammatical, **26,** 28
Correspondence. *See* Letter-writing
Counting. *See also* Mathematics
  addition strategies, 100, 106
  community sign count, 242
  by hundreds and tens, 116
  money. *See* Money
  optional activities, 98, 108
  subtraction strategies, 109
  by tens, 99
Countries, geographic/map concepts, 243–245
Crater (lunar) activity, 212
Creative writing
  concepts and analysis, 11–12
  optional activities, 14
  writing exercise, 13

Index

Note: Page numbers in bold indicate the definition of a term.

Crops, **249**
    concepts and analysis,
      249–250
    food product exercise, 251
    of Native Americans and
      colonists, 276
    planting activity, 254
Cube
    bouillon cube dissolution
      activity, 192
    geometric, 146, 147, 149
Cups, **151**, 154, 156
Custom(s), **285**
    optional activity, 288
    U.S. diversity, 285–286
Cylinder, 146, 147, 149

D

Data, **161**
    concepts and analysis,
      161–162
    practice problems, 163–164
Declaration of Independence,
    277, 278
Defenses, plant/animal,
    178–179
Deloria, Ella Cara, 271
Dentition, 193–196
Deposit, 257, 260
Design your own landmark
    activity, 292
Details. *See* Supporting details
Dictionary, 44
Diet, **189**
    concepts and analysis,
      189–190
    food guide pyramid
      exercise, 191
    optional activities, 192
Diorama activity, 284
Direction of movement, **213**,
    214
Dissolution activity, 192
Diversity, **238, 285**
    community, 238
    global, 244
    plant and animal, 245
    U.S. population, 285–286
Division
    of compound words, 41
    concepts and analysis,
      137–138
    optional activities, 140
    practice problems, 139
Dollar concepts, 126. *See also*
    Money
Dragon activity, 24
Drama. *See* Act It Out activities
Drawing activities. *See also*
    Picture activities
    communication and travel
      means, 295, 296
    facial expressions, 296
    family, 287
    First Thanksgiving, 279
    flower diagram, 175
    folktale illustration, 48
    jobs, 259
    mathematical sets, 98
    Web page, 300

E

Ear
    balance activity, 188
    diagram, 184
    hearing and, 183, 184, 185
Eardrum, **185**
Earhart, Amelia, 294
Earth
    caring for, 249–254
    land *versus* water surfaces,
      245
    moon and, 208–209, 211
    natural resources,
      197–202, 249–251
    optional activities, 202,
      206, 212
    orbit, 208
    rotation, 207–208
    seasons, 209–210
    surface changes, 203–206
Eating. *See* Food
Editing research report, 299
Effect, cause and (literary), 4,
    16
Egg shell activity, 196
Egyptian pyramids, 290
Elected, **265**–266
Emergency-related activities,
    4, 10
End of story, 9, 23
End punctuation, 48
Energy, **189**
    diet and, 189–190
    heat, 221, 222, 224
    light, 221–224
    sound. *See* Sound
    waves, sensory responses
      to, 184–185
England, American colonies
    and, 276, 277–278
Environment(s), **198**
    conservation measures.
      See Conservation
    plant and animal,
      177–178, 179–180
    pollution effects, 198, 246
    recycling and. *See*
      Recycling
    sensory responses to, 186
Equal parts of shapes, 148
Equator, **244**
-er suffix, 73–75, 78
Erosion, **203**, 204–205
-est suffix, 73–75, 78
Estimating
    length, 152
    number of items in a set,
      94–98
    optional activities, 98
Evaluate, **225**, 226, 298
Even number rules, 101–102
Even sets, 137–138
Events, **53**. *See also* Sequence
    of events
Expedition
    definition of, **281**
    of Lewis and Clark, 281–283
Explorers, **275, 281**
    colonial era, 275–276
    Lewis and Clark, 281–283
Eyes, sight and, 183, 184

F

Faces of shapes, 146–147
Facial expressions activity, 296
Fact, **60, 225**
Fact families, **141**, 142, 144
Fact *versus* opinion, **60**
Families
    diversity and customs,
      285–286
    holiday/celebration
      exercise, 287
    interview activity, 288
    math fact, **141**, 142, 144
    military, homeschooling,
      xiii
Family tree math activity, 144
Fantasy stories, **15**
    concepts and analysis,
      15–16
    optional activities, 24
    reading selection, 17–22
    summarizing, 16, 23
Federal government, **265**
    concepts, 265–266
    optional activities, 268
    U.S. Capitol/White House
      exercise, 267
Feet (units of measure), 152,
    155
Fiction
    concepts and analysis, 3–4,
      15–16
    folktales, 43–48
    optional activities, 10
    reading selection, 5–8
    story map exercise, 9
Figurative *versus* literal
    language, 44
Filling, dental, **194**
Fireworks activity, 280
Floss, **194**
Flowers, **173**
    drawing exercise, 175
    plant life cycles and,
      173–174
Flowing honey activity, 216
Folktales, **43**
    optional activities, 48
    reading selection, 45–46
    story map, 47
Follow the shadow activity, 212
Food
    animal feeding adaptations,
      179
    bird feeding activity, 182
    crops, 249–251, 254, 276
    diet concepts, 189–192
    dissolution activity, 192
    food guide pyramid,
      189–191
    fraction treat activity, 133
    Thanksgiving menu,
      276–277
Food guide pyramid, **189**–191
Foot (unit of measure), 152, 155
Force, **213**
    body part exercise, 215
    concepts and analysis,
      213–214
    optional activities, 216

Ford, Henry, 294
Forest habitats, **177**–178
Fossil fuels, **198**
Fossils, **204**
Fractions
    concepts and analysis,
      129–130
    optional activities, 133–134
    practice problems, 131–132
Freedoms, U.S., 266
    July 4th celebration, 278
    poster activity, 268
Friction, **214**
Frog life cycle, 170, 171
Fuels, fossil, **198**
-ful suffix, 74, 76
Future-related activities
    book-making project, 29
    traveling machine project,
      296

G

Game(s)
    acting out verbs, 29
    noun-verb matching, 30
    subtraction, 112
    using articles of speech, 34
    using compound words, 42
    using conjunctions, 66
    using nouns, 38
    using prefixes and
      suffixes, 78
    using prepositions, 72
Garden activity, 206
Gateway Arch, 290, 291
Geoboard activity, 150
Geography
    globe concepts, 243–245,
      247–248
    solar system concepts, 246
Geology
    concepts and analysis,
      203–204
    erosion and weathering
      exercise, 205
    optional activities, 206
Geometry
    equal parts, 148
    exercises, 149
    optional activities, 150
    plane shapes, 145–146
    space shapes, 146–147
    symmetry, line of,
      147–148, 149
Gifted students, xvii–xviii
Globe (map), **243**
    concepts, 244–245
    map exercise, 247
    optional activity, 248
Glossary, 351–352
Go Fish with nouns game, 38
Golden Gate Bridge, 291
Goods, **255**
    food products, 250, 251
    production and
      consumption, 256–257
    trade and transport,
      257–258

Index

Note: Page numbers in bold indicate the definition of a term.

Government, **261**
 employees, tax revenues and, 256
 federal, 265–266
 laws, 237–238, 239
 local and state, 261–262
 optional activities, 264, 268
 U.S. Capitol/White House, 266, 267, 289
 word-matching exercise, 263
Governor, **261**, 262
Grab bag activity, 14
Grams, **151**, 153–154
Graphs, 233–234. *See also* Charting information
Gravity, **213**–214
Greater than/less than, 102, 103
Grid map, 234, 235
Group living among animals, 179–180
Guess Where You Are exercise, 241

H

Habitats
 plant and animal, 177–178
 sensory responses to, 186
Hand, hole in your hand activity, 188
Handout on conservation activity, 202
have, 26
Health, diet and, 189–192
Hearing, 183, 184–185
Hearing impaired, communication by, 293
Heat, **221**, 222, 224
Height units of measure, **151**–153, 155
Heroes, 54, 57
History, **237**
 of communities, 238
 local resources, 272
 18th century America, 275–278
Hole in your hand activity, 188
Holidays. *See* National holidays
Homeschooling, xi
 military families, xiii
 regulations, xi–xiii
 resources, xiv–xvi
Homonyms, 16
Homophones, **85**
 concepts and analysis, 85–86
 exercise, 87
 optional activities, 88
Honey flow activity, 216
Honeybees, 179–180
Humans
 five senses, 183–188
 health, diet and, 189–192
 tooth care, 193–194
Humorous story activity, 84
Hundreds
 adding, 120, 123–124
 place chart activity, 104
 subtracting, 121, 123–124

I

Immigrants, **285**
 diversity of customs, 285–286
 optional activities, 288
In the Box preposition game, 72
Inches, 152, 155
Income, **257**
Income taxes, 257
Independence, **277**–278
Industry, community resources, 240
Instrument (musical) activity, 220
Interest, savings account, **257**
Internet research, 298
Interview activities
 family customs, 288
 personal life, 58
Irregular verbs, **25**–26

J

Jefferson, Thomas, 281
Jobs. *See* Work
Jungle sounds activity, 220

K

Kilograms, **151**, 153–154, 156
Kwanzaa, 286

L

Labeling noun objects activity, 38
Land *versus* water on Earth's surface, 245
Landfill, **197**, 199
Landmarks, **289**–290
 map exercise, 291
 optional activities, 292
Language
 figurative *versus* literal, 44
 global diversity, 244, 245
 sign language, 293
Larva, **170**
Laws, **237**–238, 239
Length units of measure, **151**–153, 155
-less suffix, 74, 76
Less than/greater than, 102, 103
Letter-writing activities
 letter to mayor, 264
 North America description, 248
Lewis, Meriwether. *See* Lewis and Clark expedition
Lewis and Clark expedition, 281–282
 news story exercise, 283
 optional activities, 284
Life cycle, **169**. *See also* Animals, life cycles; Plants, life cycles

Light, **221**
 concepts and analysis, 221–222
 moonlight, 208–209, 211
 optional activities, 212, 224
 shadow exercise, 223
 sunlight. *See* Sunlight
Lincoln Memorial, 290
Line of symmetry, **147**–148, 149
Lines. *See* Number line; Time line
Literacy skills
 antonyms and synonyms, 79–84
 articles (*a, an, the*), 31–34
 assessment, 303–314
 assessment answers, 341–342
 compound words, 39–42
 conjunctions, 65–68
 contractions, 26, 28
 creative writing, 11–14
 homophones, 85–88
 nouns, 35–38
 prefixes and suffixes, 73–78
 prepositions, 69–72
 verbs, 25–30
Literal *versus* figurative language, 44
Literature
 biography, 53–58
 fantasy, 15–24
 fiction, 3–10, 15–24
 folktales, 43–48
 nonfiction, 59–64
 poetry, 49–52
Liters, **151**, 154, 156
Local government. *See* Government
Louisiana Purchase, 281, 282
-ly suffix, 74, 76

M

Main idea
 biography, 54
 creative writing, 12
 fiction, 4
Maps
 concepts and analysis, 233–234
 globe concepts, 243–245, 247–248
 grid map, 234, 235
 landmarks exercise, 291
 Louisiana Purchase, 282
 Native American regions, 270
 optional activities, 236, 248
 reading exercise, 235
 state and country concepts, 243–244
 tongue taste map exercise, 187
Marshmallow count exercise, 98
Matching activities/exercises
 addition/subtraction game, 112

compound words, developing, 41
 nouns with verbs, 30
Mathematics
 adding three-digit numbers, 119–120, 123–124
 adding two-digit numbers, 105–108
 algebraic methods, 141–144
 assessment, 315–322
 assessment answers, 342
 calendar concepts, 158, 159–160
 data collection and use, 161–164
 dividing, 137–140
 fractions, 129–134
 geometry, 145–150
 measuring, 151–156
 money, 125–128
 multiplying, 135–137, 139–140
 number patterns, three-digit, 113–114, 117
 number patterns, two-digit, 101–104
 number sense, 93–98
 subtracting three-digit numbers, 120–124
 subtracting two-digit numbers, 109–112
 telling time, 157–160
 three-digit numbers, 113–124
 two-digit numbers, 99–112
Mayor, **261**–262, 264
Measurement
 capacity units, 154, 156
 length and height units, 151–153, 155
 metric units, **151**, 152–153
 temperature activity, 182
 weight units, 153–154, 156
Meters, **151**, 152–153
Metric units of measure, **151**, 152–153
Middle of story, 9, 23
Military families, homeschooling, xiii
Mimicry, **178**–179
Minerals, **203**
Mining, 198
Mobile activity with conjunctions, 68
Modeling of neighborhood activity, 242
Money
 banking concepts, 257
 coin concepts, 104, 125–126
 dollar concepts, 126
 income, 257
 optional activities, 104, 128, 260
 pattern modeling with, 104, 113–114
 practice problems, 127
 tax revenues, 256

Index

Note: Page numbers in bold indicate the definition of a term.

Moon
crater activity, 212
moonlight, 208–209
rotation and phases, 209, 211
Moral of the story, 43
Motion, **213**
body parts exercise, 215
concepts and analysis, 213–214
optional activities, 216
Mount Rushmore, 289, 290, 291
Movement
direction of, **213**, 214
Westward Movement, 282
Multiplication
array strategy, 136
concepts and analysis, 135–137
optional activities, 140
practice problems, 139
Musical instrument activity, 220

N

National holidays, **276**
diversity, 286
Independence Day, 278
optional activities, 280, 288
Thanksgiving, 276–277
Native Americans
American colonists and, 276
classifying exercise, 273
concepts, 269–270
map, 270
optional activities, 274
Powhatan, 270, 273
Pueblo, 270, 271, 273
reservations, 271–272
Sioux, 270–271
Wampanoag, **276**
Natural resources, **197, 249**
communities and, 240
conservation of. *See* Conservation
crops as, 249–251
fossil fuels, 198
Native Americans and, 270
optional activities, 202, 254
replenishing, 250
reusing/recycling, 199–200, 250, 253
Neighborhood modeling activity, 242
-*ness* suffix, 74, 76
News story exercise, 283
Nonfiction, **59**
book report exercise, 63
concepts and analysis, 59–60
optional activities, 64
reading selection, 61–62
North America
letter-writing activity, 248
map concepts, 243–245
Nose
smell and, 183, 184
taste and, 185–186

Nouns, **35**
articles and, 31–34
concepts and analysis, 35–36
conjunctions and, 65–67
identification exercise, 37
noun-verb matching game, 30
optional activities, 38
plural, 31–32, 37
singular, 31–32
Number line
addition strategies, 105, 108
subtraction strategies, 109
Number patterns
three-digit, 113–114, 117
two-digit, 101–104
Number sense
concepts and analysis, 93–94
optional activities, 98
practice problems, 95–97
Numbers. *See* Mathematics; *specific number form*
Nutrients, **189,** 190

O

Object of the preposition, **70**
Oceans, **245**
map concepts, 245, 247
protecting, 245–246
Odd number rules, 101–102
Opinion *versus* fact, **60**
Opposites, antonyms as. *See* Antonyms and synonyms
or, 66–67
Orbit of Earth, **208**
Ordering
three-digit numbers, 116
two-digit numbers, 102, 103
Organs, sensory, **183**

P

Paint an illustration activity, 14
Parents and babies poster activity, 172
Parts of speech. *See* Literacy skills; *specific form*
Patterns
addition and subtraction facts, 141–144
number, to one hundred, 101–104
number, to one thousand, 113–114, 117
Pen pal activity, 248
Pencils, production, 257
People. *See* Humans; *See also specific people*
Phases of moon, **209,** 211
Photographic activities
research project, 228
sign search and display, 242
Physically challenged people, communication methods, 293

Picture activities
compound words, 41
drawings. *See* Drawing activities
fraction-related, 133, 134
photo research, 228
picture book, making, 10
posters. *See* Poster activities
sequence of events, 30
shapes, 150
signs display, 242
Pilgrims, **276,** 278
Pints, **151,** 154, 156
Pioneers, **281,** 282
Pitch (audio), **218,** 219
Pizza fractions activity, 133
Place value
addition strategies, 106–107, 119–120
hundreds chart activity, 104
subtraction strategies, 109–110, 121–122
three-digit numbers, 114–115, 117
two-digit numbers, 99–100
Plane shapes, **145–146**
Planets, **246.** *See also* Earth
Plants
animal interactions, 179
crops, 249–251
defensive/protective qualities, 178–179
diversity, 245
habitats, 177–178
life cycles, 173–176
optional activities, 182, 254
reproduction, 173–174, 179
Plants, life cycles of
concepts and analysis, 173–174
flower exercise, 175
optional activities, 176
Play, shadow drama activity, 224
Plot, **15**
fiction, 4, 16–17, 43
folktale, 43
story map exercise, 9
Plural nouns, **31, 36**
identification exercise, 37
using *the* with, 31–32
Plymouth Colony, 276, 278
Plymouth Rock, 278
Pocahontas poster activity, 58
Poetry, **49**
acrostic, 52
compound words in, writing, 42
concepts and analysis, 49–50
optional activities, 52
reading selection, 51
Pollen, **173,** 174, 179
Pollution, **198, 246**
Poster activities. *See also* Picture activities
babies and parents, 172
freedom concepts, 268
landmark, 292
money concepts, 128
photo research, 228

Pocahontas, 58
Thanksgiving, 279
using antonyms and synonyms, 84
using -*er* and -*est* words, 78
welcome sign, 288
zoo-related, 64
Pottery, **271,** 274
Pound (unit of measure), 153, 156
Powhatan, 270, 273
Prairie dogs, 179
Prefixes and suffixes, **73**
concepts and analysis, 73–74
writing exercises, 75–76
Prepositions, **69**
concepts and analysis, 69–70
optional activities, 72
selection exercise, 71
Prism, rectangular, 146, 147, 149
Probability, **162,** 164
Produce (*verb form*), **256**
Product, mathematical, **135**
Production of goods, 256–257
Products, food, 250, 251. *See also* Goods
Proofreading, 298
Protective mechanisms
plant/animal, 178–179
sensory, 186
Public schools, communicating with, xvii–xviii
Pueblo, 270, 271, 273
Punctuation
poetry and, 49–50
of sentences, 48
Pupa, **170**
Puzzle activity using sentences, 68
Pyramids
Egyptian landmarks, 290
food guide pyramid, 189–191
geometric shape, 146, 147, 149

Q

Quarts, **151,** 154, 156

R

Race car activity, 216
Rain forest, tropical, **177**
re- prefix, 74, 77
Read-aloud activity, 24
Reading selections. *See* Literature
Realistic fiction, 3
Recording activities
family interview, 288
fantasy story, 24
jungle sounds, 220
research tape, 228
Rectangle, 145–146, 149
Rectangular prism, 146, 147, 149

Index

Note: Page numbers in bold indicate the definition of a term.

Recycling, **199, 250**
  handout activity, 202
  matching exercise, 253
  purpose and process, 199–200, 246, 250
Reduce, **199**, 202
Reference sources, **297**–298. *See also* Sources of information
Reflects, **208, 221**. *See also* Light; Sunlight
Regrouping, 100
  addition strategies, 119
  subtraction strategies, 110, 121
Replenishing, **250**
Reporter activity, 288
Reports. *See also* Research
  book reports, 63
  writing, 298, 299
Reproduction, plant, 173–174, 179
Research, **225, 297**
  concepts and methods, 225–226, 297–298
  identifying sources exercise, 227
  optional activities, 228
  science topic, 225–228
  sequence of events exercise, 299
  social studies topic, 297–300
Research report, 298, 299
Reservations, Native American, **271**–272
Resources. *See* Natural resources; Sources of information
Reuse, **199**, 202, 250
Revolutionary War, 277–278
Revolves (with Earth, moon, sun), **208**
Rhyming, 49, 50
Riddle activity using multiplication, 140
Rock(s), **203**
  composition, 203, 204
  garden activity, 206
  weathering, 203–205
Roots, plant growth and, 174
Rotate, **207**
Rotation of Earth, 207–208
Rural communities, **237, 239**

S

Sacajawea, 282
Salty substances, tasting, 185, 187
Savings accounts, **257**, 260
Schedule-making activity, 160
Schools, communicating with, xvii–xviii
Science
  animals, 169–172, 177–182
  assessment, 323–332
  assessment answers, 343
  diet, 189–192
  Earth's surface changes, 203–206

life cycles, 169–176
light and heat, 221–224
motion, 213–216
natural resources, 197–202
plants, 173–182
research project, 225–228
senses, 183–188
sound, 217–220
sun, moon, and Earth, 207–212
teeth, 193–196
Seasons, **207**, 209–210
Second graders, xix–xxii
Seeds, **173**
  optional activity, 176
  plant life cycles and, 173–174
  transport, reproduction and, 179
Senses, **183**
  concepts and analysis, 183–186
  energy waves and, 184–185
  optional activities, 188
  taste map exercise, 187
Sentences
  capitalization, 48
  complete, 12
  end punctuation, 48
  noun-verb matching game, 30
  puzzle activity, 68
  using suffixes, 75
  verb tense exercises, 27, 28
  with *a* or *an*, writing, 33
  with conjunctions, writing, 67
Sequence Chain graphic organizer, 354
Sequence of events
  before and after art activity, 30
  creative writing exercise, 12, 13
  research report, 298, 299
  story beginning, middle, and end, 9, 23
  story maps, 9, 47
Services, **255**
  bartering systems, 258
  service jobs, 255–256
Set(s) (in mathematics), **129**
  in division, 137–140
  estimating number of items in, 94–98
  even, 137–138
  fractions of, 130–134
  in multiplication, 135–136, 139–140
Setting
  fiction, 4, 43
  folktale, 43
  story map exercise, 9
Shadow(s), **207**
  formation, 208, 222
  matching exercise, 223
  optional activities, 212, 224
Shape(s)
  geometric. *See* Geometry
  plant/animal defense and, 178

Shoebox diorama activity, 284
Sight, 183, 184
Sign activities
  community sign count, 242
  welcome sign, 288
Sign language, 293
Singular nouns
  definition of, **31**
  using articles (*a, an, the*) with, 31–32
Sioux, 270–271, 273
Size, plant/animal defense and, 178
Skin, touch and, 183, 184, 186
Smell, 183, 184, 185–186
Sneak In Between activity, 118
Social studies
  assessment, 333–340
  assessment answers, 343–344
  caring for Earth, 249–254
  colonial America, 275–280
  communication and transportation, 293–296
  communities, comparing, 237–242
  communities, global relationships, 243–248
  diversity in America, 285–288
  freedom, 265–268
  government, federal, 265–268
  government, local and state, 261–264
  landmarks, 289–292
  Lewis and Clark expedition, 281–284
  maps and charts, 233–236
  Native Americans, 269–274
  natural resources, 249–254
  research project, 297–300
  working together, 255–260
Soil, **204**, 206
Solar system, **246**
Songs
  conservation writing activities, 202, 254
  of freedom, 266
  as poems, singing, 52
Sound, **217**
  animal sounds exercise, 219
  concepts and analysis, 217–218
  hearing and, 183, 184–185
  optional activities, 220
Sound waves, 185, **217**–218
Sour substances, tasting, 185, 187
Sources of information, **225, 297**–298
  dictionary, 44
  evaluating, 226, 298
  historical, 272
  homeschooling resources, xiv–xvi
  identification exercise, 227
Space shapes, **146**–147
Special days calendar activity, 160
Special needs students, xvii

Speed, **214**
Sphere, 146, 147, 149
Spores, **173**, 174, 176
Square, 145–146
  exercise/activity, 149, 150
  symmetry of, 147, 148
Stack Up Numbers activity, 118
States
  geographic and map concepts, 243–244
  government leaders, 261–262
  landmarks, 290
Statistics, **162**. *See also* Data
Statue of Liberty, 289, 291
Store activity, 128
Stories. *See* Fantasy stories; Fiction; Folktales; Storytelling
Story map exercises, 9, 47
Storytelling, 271, 274
Subject of sentence, 12
Subtraction
  facts, patterns and, 141–144
  optional activities, 112
  practice problems, 111, 123–124
  of three-digit numbers, 120–124
  of two-digit numbers, 109–112
Suburban communities, **239**
Suffixes. *See* Prefixes and suffixes
Sugar
  dissolution activity, 192
  tooth decay and, 194
Summarizing, **15**, 16, 23
Sun
  Earth's rotation around, 208
  solar system and, 246
Sunlight
  Earth's rotation and, 207–208
  moonlight and, 208–209, 211
  seasons and, 209–210
  shadow activity, 212
Supporting details
  biography, 54
  creative writing, 12
  fiction, 4
Sweet substances, tasting, 185, 187
Symbols
  greater and less than, 102, 103
  landmarks as, 289
  in maps, **266**
  national, 266
Symmetry, line of, **147**–148, 149
Synonyms. *See* Antonyms and synonyms

T

Tables. See Charting information
Tally chart, **161**
Taste
  concepts and analysis, 183, 184, 185–186
  mapping exercise, 187

Note: Page numbers in bold indicate the definition of a term.

Taste buds, **185**
Taxes, **256**
    colonial, 277
    government employees
      and, 256
    income, 257
Teepees, **270**–271
Teeth
    concepts and analysis,
      193–194
    diagrams, 195
    optional activities, 196
Telling time. *See* Time
Temperature activity with
    plants, 182
Tens
    adding/counting by, 99,
      100, 106
    subtracting by, 109
Tenses. *See* Verbs
Thanksgiving, 276–277, 279
That's Silly! game, 34
the, 31–34
Three-digit numbers
    adding, 119–120
    comparing, 115–116
    optional activities, 118
    ordering, 116
    patterns, 113–114
    place value, 114–115
    practice problems, 117,
      123–124
    subtracting, 120–122
    writing, 114–115
Time
    calendar concepts, 158,
      159–160
    clock concepts, 157–160
    optional activities, 160
Time line, 233, 235
Tomato plant activity, 254
Tongue, taste and
    concepts and analysis,
      183, 184, 185–186
    mapping exercise, 187
Tooth care, 194. *See also* Teeth
Tooth decay, **193,** 194
Topic, researching. *See* Research
Touch, sense of, 183, 184, 186
Towns, 243–244. *See also*
    Communities
Trade, **257**–258
Trading cards activity, 284
Traditions, Native American, **271**
Transportation
    drawing exercise, 295
    futuristic activity, 296
    of goods, 257–258
    modes, 294
    of plant seeds, 179
Traveling machine activity, 296
Treasure hunt activity, 236
Triangle, 145, 146, 149
Tribes, **269.** *See also* Native
    Americans
Tropical rain forest, **177**
Two-digit numbers
    adding, 105–108
    comparing and ordering,
      102
    odd and even rules,
      101–102
    optional activities, 108, 112
    patterns, 100–101
    place value, 99–100
    practice problems, 107, 111
    regrouping, 100
    subtracting, 109–112

U

un- prefix, 74, 77
United States
    Capitol and White House,
      266, 267, 289
    colonies, 276–279
    diversity, cultural and
      population, 285–288
    freedoms, symbols, and
      songs, 266
    government. *See*
      Government
    landmarks, 289–292
    Lewis and Clark expedition,
      281–283
    optional activities, 280
    Revolutionary War,
      277–278
Urban communities, **239**

V

Value, number sense, 93–98.
    See also Place value
Variations among animals, **170**
Venn Diagram graphic organizer,
    353
Verbs, **25**
    be, 26, 27
    concepts and analysis,
      12, 25–26
    conjunctions and, 65–67
    have, 26
    irregular, 25–26
    optional activities, 29–30
    sentence-writing exercises,
      27, 28
Vibrations, sound and, **185,**
    217–218
Visually impaired,
    communication by, 293
Vocabulary
    homonyms, 16
    learning, dictionaries and, 44
    parts of speech. *See*
      specific form
Volume (audio), **218,** 219
Vote, **265**
    button activity, 268
    concepts, 265–266
Vowels, using *an* before words
    beginning with, 31–34

W

Wampanoag, **276**
War of Independence, 277–278
Water, oceanic, 245–246, 247
Waves of energy, **184**–185
Weathering, **203**–205
Web graphic organizer, 354
Web page activity, 300

Weight units of measure,
    153–154, 156
Welcome sign poster activity,
    288
Westward movement, 282
White House, 266, 267, 291
Words. *See* Compound words
Work
    income and taxes, 257
    optional activities, 260
    producing goods, 256–257
    service jobs, 255–256
    trade processes, 257–258
    writing and drawing
      exercise, 259
Wrigley Field, 290
Writing activities
    acrostic poem, 52
    biography, 54
    book report, 63
    commercial, 300
    comparison sentences,
      75–76
    compound word poem, 42
    conjunction sentences, 67
    conservation song, 202,
      254
    family holiday/
      celebration, 287
    First Thanksgiving, 279
    folktale, 48
    futuristic travel, 296
    grab bag story, 14
    hero biography, 54, 57
    homophone story, 88
    humorous story, 84
    illustrated story, 14
    job descriptions, 259
    letters, 248, 264
    news story, 283
    nonfiction, 63, 64
    opposites story, 84
    poetry, 50, 52
    sensory words, 184
    summarizing, 23
    verb usage, 28
    Web site pages, 300
Writing lines, 355
Writing process
    creative, 11–14
    research reports, 298, 299

X

X rays of teeth, **193,** 194

Y

Yard (unit of measure), 152, 155

Z

Zookeeper activity, 64

Credits

Art & Photo Credits

Promoting Literacy
Background/Icon: © PhotoDisc
Opener (page 1): Creatas LLC
Page 7, 9, 13: Precision Graphics; **14, 17, 19, 20, 22:** Carol Stutz Illustration; **23, 27 (top):** Precision Graphics; **27 (bottom):** PP/FA, Inc.; **28, 33:** Carol Stutz Illustration; **37 (top):** Precision Graphics; **37 (bottom), 38, 41, 47, 51:** Carol Stutz Illustration; **52:** PP/FA, Inc.; **55, 56, 57:** Carol Stutz Illustration; **61:** Digital Stock; **63, 67, 71, 72:** Carol Stutz Illustration; **75, 76, 77, 78, 81, 82:** Precision Graphics; **84, 87 (top):** Carol Stutz Illustration; **87 (bottom):** Precision Graphics

Math
Background: © Nick Koudis/Getty Images
Icon: © Don Farrall/Getty Images
Opener (page 91): © GeoStock/Getty Images
Page 95, 96: Precision Graphics; **97:** Carol Stutz Illustration; **103, 105, 106, 107, 110, 111, 114, 115, 117, 120, 122, 123, 127, 130, 131:** Precision Graphics; **132, 137:** Carol Stutz Illustration; **139, 140, 141, 144 (left):** Precision Graphics; **144 (right):** Carol Stutz Illustration; **146 (top):** Precision Graphics; **146 (bottom), 149 (top):** PP/FA, Inc.; **149 (bottom), 153, 155:** Precision Graphics; **156:** Carol Stutz Illustration; **159, 162, 163, 164:** Precision Graphics

Science
Background: © Royalty-Free/CORBIS
Icon: © Image Source/PunchStock
Opener (page 167): © Getty Images
Page 170: © Royalty-Free/CORBIS; **171, 174, 175, 181, 184, 187, 191:** Precision Graphics; **192 (left):** Carol Stutz Illustration; **192 (right), 195, 196:** Precision Graphics; **199, 201:** Carol Stutz Illustration; **204, 205, 208, 211:** Precision Graphics; **215:** Carol Stutz Illustration; **216:** Precision Graphics; **218:** © PhotoDisc; **219:** Precision Graphics; **220, 223:** Carol Stutz Illustration; **224 (top):** Precision Graphics; **224 (bottom):** Carol Stutz Illustration; **226:** Precision Graphics; **227 (bottom right, top left):** © PhotoDisc; **227 (top right):** Digital Stock; **227 (bottom left):** National Oceanic and Atmospheric Administration/Department of Commerce

Social Studies
Background: © PhotoDisc, Library of Congress, Prints & Photographs Division, LC-USZC4-3637, Library of Congress, Prints & Photographs Division, LC-USZ62-91879
Icon: © PhotoDisc
Opener (page 231): © Getty Images
Page 235: Precision Graphics; **238 (left):** © William England/Getty Images; **283 (right):** © PictureNet/CORBIS; **241:** PP/FA, Inc.; **243:** Precision Graphics; **247:** © Map Resources; **248, 251:** Carol Stutz Illustration; **252:** PP/FA, Inc.; **253:** Carol Stutz Illustration; **257:** © PhotoDisc; **259, 263, 268:** Carol Stutz Illustration; **270 (top):** Mapping Specialists, Ltd.; **270 (bottom):** © PhotoDisc; **273:** Precision Graphics, **insets:** Carol Stutz Illustration; **277:** Mapping Specialists, Ltd.; **278:** National Archives and Records Administration; **279:** Carol Stutz Illustration; **280:** © PhotoDisc; **281:** © CORBIS; **282:** Mapping Specialists, Ltd.; **284, 286, 287:** Carol Stutz Illustration; **289 (top):** National Park Sevices; **289 (bottom):** Library of Congress, Prints & Photographs Division, LC-USZC4-3366; **290 (top):** National Park Sevices; **290 (bottom):** © PhotoDisc; **291 (center):** Mapping Specialists, Ltd.; **291 (top left, bottom middle):** © PhotoDisc; **291 (top right):** National Park Sevices; **291 (bottom right):** Library of Congress, Prints & Photographs Division, LC-USZC4-3366; **291 (top middle):** National Park Sevices; **291 (bottom left):** © Randy Faris/CORBIS; **294 (top):** © Bettmann/CORBIS; **294 (bottom):** Don Johnston/Getty Images; **295 (top):** Carol Stutz Illustration; **295 (bottom):** PP/FA, Inc.; **296:** Carol Stutz Illustration; **299:** Precision Graphics; **300:** Carol Stutz Illustration

Page 315, 316, 317 (left): Precision Graphics; **317 (right):** Carol Stutz Illustration; **318 (left):** © PhotoDisc; **318 (right):** Precision Graphics; **319:** Carol Stutz Illustration; **320, 321, 322:** Precision Graphics; **323, 324:** © PhotoDisc; **325, 327 (right):** Precision Graphics; **327 (left), 328 (right):** Carol Stutz Illustration; **328 (left):** © Royalty-Free/CORBIS; **329 (left):** Precision Graphics; **329 (right):** Carol Stutz Illustration; **330, 337, 338:** Precision Graphics; **342:** PP/FA, Inc.; **347, 348:** Precision Graphics; **353, 354:** PP/FA, Inc.

Literature Credits

5–8, Copyright © 1979 by Anne Rockwell and Harlow Rockwell. First appeared in BLACKOUT, published by Macmillan. Reprinted by permission of Curtis Brown, Ltd.

17–22, From *Ella's Games* by David Bedford and Peter Kavanagh. Text copyright © David Bedford, 2002. Illustration copyright © Peter Kavanagh, 2002. First edition for the United States and Canada published in 2002 by Barron's Educational Series, Inc.

45–46, Text from THE SECRET ROOM by Uri Shulevitz. Copyright © 1993 by Uri Shulevitz. Reprinted by permission of Farrar, Straus and Giroux, LLC.

51, © 1962 by Maxine W. Kumin

55–56, From *Pocahontas* by Lucia Raatma. Copyright © 2002 Compass Point Books. Used by permission of Compass Point Books.

61–62, From *Beautiful Bats*. Copyright © 1997 by Linda Glaser. Used by permission of the Millbrook Press, Inc. All rights reserved.

339, Adapted from WHERE DOES WATER COME FROM? by C. Vance Cast. Copyright © 1992 by Barron's Educational Series, Inc. Reprinted by arrangement with Barron's Educational Series, Hauppauge, NY.